Latinas Crossing Borders and Building Communities in Greater Washington

Latinas Crossing Borders and Building Communities in Greater Washington

Applying Anthropology in Multicultural Neighborhoods

Edited by Raúl Sánchez Molina and Lucy M. Cohen

LEXINGTON BOOKS
Lanham • Boulder • New York • London

Published by Lexington Books
An imprint of The Rowman & Littlefield Publishing Group, Inc.
4501 Forbes Boulevard, Suite 200, Lanham, Maryland 20706
www.rowman.com

Unit A, Whitacre Mews, 26-34 Stannary Street, London SE11 4AB

British Library Cataloguing in Publication Information Available

Library of Congress Cataloging-in-Publication Data

Title: Latinas crossing borders and building communities in greater Washington : applying anthropology in multicultural neighborhoods
Names: edited by Raul Sanchez Molina and Lucy M. Cohen.
Description: Lanham : Lexington Books, 2016. | Includes index.
Identifiers: LCCN 2016004375 | ISBN 9781498525329 (alkaline paper)
Subjects: LCSH: Hispanic American women--Washington (D.C.)--Social conditions. | Hispanic Americans--Washington (D.C.)--Social conditions. | Cultural pluralism--Washington (D.C.) | Community life--Washington (D.C.) | Ethnic neighborhoods Washington (D.C.) | Social adjustment--Washington (D.C.) | Applied anthropology--Washington (D.C.) | Ethnology--Washington (D.C.) | Washington (D.C.)--Ethnic relations.
Classification: LCC F205.S75 L38 2016 | DDC 305.868/0730753--dc23 LC record available at http://lccn.loc.gov/2016004375

∞™ The paper used in this publication meets the minimum requirements of American National Standard for Information Sciences Permanence of Paper for Printed Library Materials, ANSI/NISO Z39.48-1992.

Printed in the United States of America

Contents

Contents

List of Figures

List of Tables

Acknowledgments and Permissions

The edition of this book has been written thanks to the assistance of university departments, colleagues, and friends. We would like to thank the Department of Anthropology at The Catholic University of America, Washington, D.C., particularly Anita Cook and Jon Anderson for their support. We thank Angela H. Serrano, administrative officer at this Department, for her contributions in bureaucratic issues. We are also grateful to the *Departamento de Antropología Social y Cultural* and *Facultad de Filosofía* at the *Universidad de Educación a Distancia* (UNED) in Madrid, particularly Nancy A. Konvalinka, Chair at that Department, and Valentín Martínez Pérez for the resolution of administrative issues.

We express our sincere gratitude to Carole E. Hill (Georgia State University) and María Eugenia Bozzoli Vargas de Wille (Universidad de Costa Rica) for their comments and suggestions to papers based on research presented in this book at the Annual Meeting of the Society for Applied Anthropology (SfAA). We also thank María Inés Gómez, Teresita Puerta, and Peter Watkins for providing their support and collaboration during this edition. We are grateful to Joel Bergner for permission to use a picture of his mural "The Afro-Colombian Mural: Currulao y Desplazamiento," located on U Street in Washington, D.C., in the front cover selected by Ana Quintana, to whom we also express our sincere gratitude.

Introduction

Latinas Crossing Borders and Building Communities in Greater Washington

Raúl Sánchez Molina

The prominent role played by Latina immigrants, as pioneers of migratory networks in Greater Washington and Central American refugees' and migrants' widespread incorporation into the metropolitan region are major aspects to highlight in Latino communities' expansion in this U.S. metropolis.[1] Representing the most important ethnic group, Latina/o immigrants as well as refugees and migrants from around the world, particularly those coming from Asian countries, have transformed its urban and suburban areas into a multicultural society (Passel, Cohn, and Lopez, 2011; Price and Singer, 2008). Highly concentrated in the Northwestern neighborhoods of Adams Morgan, Mount Pleasant, and Columbia Heights since the late 1950s (Cadaval, 1998), Latino populations have been settling in close, outer, and even distant metropolitan suburban neighborhoods in the last decades (Singer, 2012; Friedman et al., 2005).

Since the end of the 1950s, while Washington, D.C., as the U.S. capital started to endure a postwar process of internationalization (Abbot, 1999; Kofie, 1999), women from Caribbean, Central American, and South American countries began to arrive in the city to work as domestics, live-in housekeepers, or baby-sitters initiating a gendered migratory phenomenon that would intensify with the advance of globalization and its international division of the reproductive labor force.[2]

From the 1980s, when civil wars broke out in several Central American countries, migratory networks led by Latina immigrants, largely from El Salvador and Guatemala, settled in the region resulting in major social and cultural changes in the emerging Latino communities in the Washington, D.C., metropolitan region (Repak, 1995). Since most Central American men and women who arrived in the United States during this period were excluded from refugee status (Coutin, 1993; 2000; Fagen, 1988; Gybney and Stohl, 1988; Mahler, 1995), they had to settle in the region as undocumented immigrants, which made their modes of incorporation much more difficult.[3] Once peace agreements were signed in Central American countries during the 1990s, post-civil war socio-

1

economic crises as well as natural catastrophes (hurricanes and earth-quakes) in the region continued to greatly increase the arrival of new Latino immigrants in Greater Washington (Petrozziello, 2011; Sánchez Molina, 2015). After entering the United States by land without author-ization, most of them came to the region to work in a low-paid labor market in reproductive, construction, and other service sectors (Gam-mage et al., 2005; Singer, 2003). Under these circumstances, many of them have lived separated from their children for long periods of time since their chances for regularizing their migratory status have been very scarce (Donato and Armenta, 2011). After crossing several borders in dangerous conditions, therefore, most of these immigrants, their children residing in both sending and receiving countries, and other family mem-bers have to meet many challenges in their processes of adaptation, fac-ing different kinds of social and cultural barriers that push them to main-tain more intense social and economic transnational relationships with their home societies (Hamilton and Chinchilla, 2001; Vélez-Ibañez and Sampaio, 2002).

These and other circumstances have offered opportunities for anthro-pologists and members of related disciplines and professions in Greater Washington to work together with Latina/o immigrants in activities which have contributed to both knowledge and action (Cohen, 1984). From this perspective, authors in this volume seek to address how Lati-na/o immigrants draw on a repertory of strategies in order to meet these challenges through a gender and transnational lens (Sánchez Molina, 2009; 2013; Viteri, 2014). Using ethnography and historical contextualiza-tion in a broader political and economic frame, this perspective allows researchers doing fieldwork with migrants to articulate micro and macro structures, in both sending and receiving countries, while paying atten-tion to the reproduction of gender, ethnicity, and social inequality (Kearny, 1995; Donato et al., 2006; Boehm, 2008). In doing so, transnation-al and gender studies in migration contribute to understanding how cur-rent migrants' daily experiences are affected by different linkages that make them navigate at different levels in transnational social fields (Le-vitt and Glick Schiller, 2004; Chavez, 2008).

Drawing on ethnographic research and practice, contributors to this volume highlight how Latinas/os build transnational and multicultural communities in Greater Washington, while reshaping gender, ethnic, generational, and sexual identities. In doing so, authors offer research models of collaboration and interaction in local organizations, health, labor market, education, and faith-based communities. Anthropological frameworks and methods allow them to elucidate the Latino immigrants' modes of incorporation and adaptation into the host societies in the met-ropolitan area, as well as their connections with the homes societies, as dynamic processes.

LATINAS PIONEERING MIGRATION IN WASHINGTON, D.C.

The District of Columbia emerged as a major political center during the Cold War with multilateral institutions and other national and international agencies established in the city. While Pan American multilateral institutions such as the Organization of American States (OAS) and the Pan American Health Organization (PAHO) were established in the nation's capital at the beginning of the 1900s, Washington, D.C., was chosen over New York as the city where the major organizations representing the postwar economic order arranged by the Bretton Woods agreement set up.[4] As a result, the International Monetary Fund and the World Bank were established in the city in 1944, followed by the Inter-American Development Bank in 1959 driving the region, along with embassies and other international institutions, to a process of internationalization that lured the arrival of high-skilled and low-skilled immigrants from inside and outside of the United States (Abbot, 1999).

In addition to the city's internationalization, women in the area entering the productive labor market (out of home) created a demand for household workers and domestic sectors for Caribbean, Central American, and South American women who were recruited in their countries of origin to work in the homes of Latin American civil servants and U.S. citizens (Repak, 1995). Until that time, these domestic jobs had been performed by African American immigrant women coming from rural areas in the southern states who, limited to their human capital, were not able—as Elizabeth Clark-Lewis (1996) underscores—to find higher-skilled jobs before the 1960s. With Washington, D.C., being the first city of the United States with an African American majority (Liebow, 1967; Hannerz, 1969; Williams, 1988), it was not until the 1964 Civil Rights Act took effect that it was possible for African American women to get better paid jobs as higher skilled workers outside of the home. As Carl Abbot (1999) has pointed out, processes of internationalization and desegregation, after housing covenants (1948) and school segregation (1954) came to an end in the city, led Washington, D.C., to emerge as a global city attracting an increasing number of refugees and immigrants from outside of the United States.[5] These postwar processes enabled the first Latina immigrants to find jobs in domestic, care, and service sectors, while acting as labor mediators for female and male relatives and acquaintances from their home societies (Sánchez Molina, 2008). In doing so, they started migratory chains facilitating new Latino immigrants' incorporation into the city and its metropolitan surroundings (Repak, 1995).

As these early Latina immigrants entered the United States with work or tourist visas, they often left their children at home under the care of surrogate female family members, especially grandmothers. This permitted them, as Lucy M. Cohen observed, "to engage in pioneering roles as migrants" (1979, p. xxi). This migratory pattern has intensified in successive decades. Immigrant women from developing countries who, as a result of social and political conditions, must re-shape their pre-migratory families as *transnational families* or domestic units whose members are residing in two or more nation-states (Salazar Parreña, 2001). Although the formation of transnational families is not a new pattern at all in international migration (Foner, 1997; Salazar Parreña, 2001; *see also* Thomas and Znaniecki, 1918), globalization has intensified this type of family reconfiguration since migratory policies in receiving societies have made it very difficult for low skilled foreign workers, and particularly women working in the reproductive labor market, to migrate with their children.[6]

While many Latina immigrants in Greater Washington have settled in the area without immigration papers, earlier immigrant women in the region obtained U.S. residence in a few years. They often brought their children to live with them after applying for family reunification. They availed themselves of one of the key U.S. migratory criteria introduced by the Immigration and Nationality Act of 1965. While removing the national origins quota system as a racist legacy imposed by the National Quota Act of 1924 (Massey and Pren, 2012; Foner and Alba, 2010), this legislation marked a major migratory transformation in the United States by introducing this criterion—along with qualified worker preference—as a basic principle of the U.S. migratory policy (Aleinikoff, Martin, and Motomura, 1998; Hagan, Castro, and Rodriguez, 2010). In doing so, this migratory reform contributed to the increase of Latin American and Asian immigrants in the Washington, D.C., metropolitan region (Frey, 2006; Perez, 2012; Price, 2012). This policy enabled early Latina immigrant workers to bring children and husbands to the United States (Cohen, 1979; Repak, 1995; Sánchez Molina, 2004).

The relevance of the first Latina workers as immigrant pioneers in Washington, D.C., was likewise shown, as Cohen and Fernandez (1974) have pointed out, by 1970 Census data. This was the first U.S. census introducing Latino or Hispanic heritage as an ethnic administrative category in the United States, and its data registered more women than men among the 70,904 "persons of Spanish language" residing in the metropolitan area.[7] According to this census, Latino population in the area was made up of Dominicans and Cubans from Caribbean countries (*see also* Candelario, 2010; Boone, 1981; 1989), Colombians, Peruvians, Ecuadorans, and Chileans, among other South American immigrants, and Guatemalans, Nicaraguans, and Salvadorans from Central America.[8]

Even so, 1970 U.S. Census data were considered inaccurate by Latino leaders in the District of Columbia who, as Olivia Cadaval (1998, p. 22) stated, calculated many more than the 17,561 Hispanic residents registered by the census. Given that public funds for social programs serving new immigrants depended on these official statistics, Latino spokespeople decided, according to this author, to organize the Latino Festival as a political strategy inspired by the Civil Rights Movement in Washington, D.C.[9] This public demonstration, which included a main street parade with people and floats in the Northwestern neighborhoods of Mount Pleasant and Adams Morgan, took place from 1970 until 1989, when the Latino Festival was moved downtown (*see also* Chacko, 2013). Olivia Cadaval (1998) emphasized that, by organizing these street events, Latino leaders wanted to publicly point to the diverse Latino cultures and ethnicities while demanding political recognition as a heterogeneous ethnic group with roots in the metropolitan area.

CIVIL WARS IN CENTRAL AMERICA AND CHANGING MODES OF INCORPORATION

Deepening social and political unrest in Central America in the early 1980s, when civil wars flared out in the region, made Greater Washington a major U.S. destination for refugees from Guatemala, Nicaragua, and especially El Salvador. During this late Cold War period, military conflicts in Central America caused a wide displacement of people who sought asylum in Mexico, Costa Rica, Canada, European countries, Australia, and particularly in the United States (Zolberg, Suhrke, and Aguayo, 1989; Montes and García, 1988; García, 2006). In the specific case of El Salvador, the civil war (1981-1992) displaced around a third of its population, more than one million people, to the United States (Montes, 1990; Hamilton and Chinchilla, 1991). Helped by relatives, friends, acquaintances, and also transnational civil and religious organizations, such as the U.S.-Central American Sanctuary Movement (*see* Coutin, 1993; Cunningham, 1999; Perla and Coutin, 2012), Salvadoran refugees began to concentrate in different metropolitan areas throughout the United States.[10]

As previously mentioned, although they hoped to obtain political refugee status, most Salvadorans and Guatemalans entering the United States during the civil wars in their respective countries were excluded from this status warranted by the Refugee Act of 1980. Based on principles of non-discrimination, non-penalization, and non-*refoulement* (non-expulsion) dictated by the United Nations Protocol Relating to the Status of Refugees of 1967, this legislation offers asylum to any person suffering discrimination and persecution in his or her country of origin (UNHCR, 2010; Wasem & Ester, 2006). Despite this legislation, which aimed to prevent the exclusion of people from non-communist countries seeking asylum, only a minority of Salvadorans and Guatemalans were recognized as refugees by the U.S. administrations during the 1980s (Gybney and Stohl, 1988; Coutin, 2002; Chinchilla and Hamilton, 2004). This political exclusion forced most Central Americans to settle in the country as undocumented immigrants, making them much more vulnerable during their process of incorporation and adaptation to the United States (De Genova, 2002; 2010; Coutin, 2000; Fagen, 1988; Phillips and Massey, 1999).

During the 1980s, when Central Americans began to arrive in the Washington, D.C., metropolitan area in large numbers, the region was experiencing an ongoing economic growth demanding workers for an ethnic- and gender-segmented labor market. The metropolitan area was undergoing "chronic labor shortages" (Repak, 1995: 55), as its population growth was lower than the jobs generated by an economic boom based on the expansion of the service, research/high technology and construction industries (Singer, 2003). While most Central American women continued to readily find jobs in care and domestic sectors, men typically worked in construction and related sectors, and both of them in food and cleaning services at new restaurants, hotels, and office buildings in the city and its suburban neighborhoods.

Although the Immigration Reform and Control Act (IRCA) of 1986 enacted under President Regan's administration tried to stop the flow of undocumented immigrants by penalizing employers for hiring them, undocumented Latino migration not only increased after this migratory reform took effect (Fernández-Kelly and Massey, 2007; Suarez-Orozco et al., 2011), but it also diversified to new U.S. destinations in both rural and urban areas (*see* Zúñiga and Hernández-León, 2005). Despite these political challenges, the arrival of new immigrants, particularly from Central American countries and Mexico, greatly contributed to the increase of Latino communities throughout the whole metropolis. This migratory reform also made possible for undocumented Latino immigrants entering the United States before January 1982 to regularize their migratory status by the enactment of an amnesty program that also allowed them to apply for family reunification.[11] Since then, Salvadorans have been the most numerous Latino immigrant group in Greater Washington comprising, along with their U.S. born children, more than a third of the Latino population in the region (Hoefer, Rytina, and Baker, 2008; Singer, 2012).

IMAGINING A LATINO *BARRIO* IN WASHINGTON, D.C.

In the 1950s, when most Central Americans began to arrive in the District of Columbia, Latino immigrants tended to settle in the Northwestern multi-ethnic neighborhoods of Adams Morgan, Mount Pleasant, and Columbia Heights. While there were faith-based communities that served them, stores, hair salons, travel agencies, and restaurants sought to serve Hispanic consumers were also established in these neighborhoods. The area came to be known as the Latino *barrio* of Washington, D.C., with community centers and organizations, such as health, legal consultancy, or English courses, providing services to Latinos (*see* Cadaval 1998). In addition to these Latino-oriented services, mass media in Spanish also grew with the publication of the newspaper, *El Pregonero*, in 1977, which has reported social and cultural events related to Latino communities in the metropolitan area. Other regional and local Spanish publications, radio stations, and television channels, have increased significantly in the following decades.[12]

With the settlement of Central Americans, new Latino leaders and U.S. activists called for social justice, initiating new ways of organizing and serving Latino immigrants. They sought to promote not only new immigrants' health and civil rights, but also social and political commitments with Central American countries that suffered from civil wars. As Hamilton and Chinchilla (2001) noted in the case of Los Angeles, Central American refugee leaders in Washington, D.C., also promoted transnational networks of civil organizations with Central American countries (*see also* Perla and Countin 2009). In the late Cold War context, organizations such as CARECEN (1981) and La Clínica del Pueblo (1983), among other Latino centers, were established in Columbia Heights in Washington, D.C., while the Central American Solidarity Association or CASA of Maryland (1985) in the close suburban town of Takoma Park in Montgomery County—one of the first U.S. municipal localities to be declared a *sanctuary city* in order to protect undocumented immigrants.[13]

Table 0.1.   Selected Latino Population by Countries of Origin in Greater Washington

COUNTIES & CITIES	PO	LA	ES	ME
Fairfax (VA)	1,081,725	168,482 (15.6%)	43,566 (4%)	18,823 (1.7%)
Montgomery (MD)	971.777	165,398 (17%)	52,615 (5.4%)	14,819 (1.5%)
Prince George's (MD)	863,420	128,972 (14.9%)	47,355 (5.5%)	24,247 (2.8%)
Prince William (VA)	402,002	81,460 (20.3%)	27,269 (6.8%)	14,908 (3.7%)
Washington, D.C.	601,723	54,749 (9.1%)	27,269 (6.8%)	14,908 (3.7%)
Loudoun (VA)	312,311	38,578 (12.4%)	10,473 (3.4%)	5,555 (1.8%)
Arlington (VA)	207,682	31,382 (15.1%)	7,088 (3.4%)	3,590 (1.7%)
Alexandria City (VA)	139,966	22,524 (16%)	6,436 (4.6%)	2,352 (1.7%)
Frederick (MD)	233,385	17,135 (7.3%)	3,652 (1.6%)	3,582 (1.5%)
Manassas City (VA)	37,821	11,876 (31.4%)	3,870 (10.2%)	3,754 (9.9%)
Stafford (VA)	128,961	11,875 (9.2%)	1,837 (1.4%)	3,515 (2.7%)
Spotsylvania (VA)	122,397	9,278 (7.6%)	1,783 (1.5%)	2,801 (2.3%)
Charles (MD)	146,551	6,259 (4.3%)	740 (0.5%)	1,657 (1.1%)
Manassas Park City (VA)	14,273	4,645 (32.5%)	1,724 (12.1%)	947 (6.6%)

Table 0.2.   Selected Latino Population by Countries of Origin in Greater Washington—continued

COUNTIES & CITIES	PR	GU	PE	BO	HO
Fairfax (VA)		10,463 (1.0)	12,922 (1.2%)	18,785 (1.7%)	11,418 (1.1%)
Montgomery (MD)		10,596 (1.1%)	12,005 (1.2%)		
Prince George's (MD)		13,818 (1.6%)			
Prince William (VA)	7,037 (1.8%)	4,495 (1.1%)	4,068 (1.0%)		
Washington, D.C.	7,037 (1.8%)				
Loudoun (VA)			4,188 (1.3%)		
Arlington (VA)		3,017 (1.5%)		4,225 (2.0%)	
Alexandria City (VA)	1,603 (1.1%)	1,587 (1.1%)			2,243 (1.6%)
Frederick (MD)					
Manassas City (VA)	417 (1.1%)	708 (1.9%)	369 (1.0%)		657 (1.7%)
Stafford (VA)	2,134 (1.7%)				
Spotsylvania (VA)	1,577 (1.3%)				
Charles (MD)	1,541 (1.1%)				
Manassas Park City (VA)	161 (1.1)	428 (3%)	168 (1.4%)	180 (1.3%)	198 (1.4%)

Source: U.S. Census Bureau, 2010

Legend: BO=Bolivia; ES=El Salvador; GU=Guatemala; HO= Honduras; LA= Latinas/os; ME=Mexico; PE= Peru; PO=Population; PR=Puerto Rico

After more than five decades, even though some Latino businesses and community centers are still concentrated in this Latino *barrio*, gentrification has been expelling poorer African American and Latino residents from these Northwestern inner neighborhoods, pushing most of them to look for more affordable housing in nearby and outer suburban areas. Gentrification in the capital, mainly due to the presence of federal and international institutions, as well as neoliberal urban planning policies focusing on business and services, has made Washington, D.C., one of the most expensive cities in the United States (Williams 1988; 1992; Prince, 2014; Friedman et al., 2005). In the last decade, a significant population growth has taken place with the arrival of higher income national and international professionals who have displaced African Americans and Latino immigrants from this Northwestern cluster to other inner city and suburban neighborhoods.[14]

Although Latino immigrant concentrations in the inner city, as well as nearby and outer suburbs, have followed ethnic patterns of settlement, with people residing close to family members, compatriots from their own towns, regions, countries, and other Latino immigrants (*see* Table 01-02), neither the incipient Latino *barrio* of Washington, D.C., (Cadaval, 1998), nor recent Latino concentrations in the suburbs have developed an economic ethnic enclave that facilitates newcomers' labor incorporation (Portes and Bach, 1985). According to Patricia Pessar (1995), differences based on class, ethnicity, national origin, and time of arrival have not allowed a co-ethnic social solidarity needed to develop a Latino enclave in Washington, D.C., or its metropolitan area.

LATINAS/OS IN SUBURBAN GREATER WASHINGTON

The emergence of new metropolitan corridors, with highways and public transportation connecting outer suburbs with Washington, D.C., are a result of economic expansion based on scientific and high technology industries (Knox, 1991; Singer, 2008). It has made Greater Washington one of the U.S. areas with the fastest population growth.[15] With more than six million inhabitants, the 2010 Census calculated that more than a fifth of its total population consists of foreign-born immigrants coming from Latin America (40 percent), Asia (35 percent), Africa (15 percent), and Europe (9 percent) and with Latino population, mostly constituted of immigrants from Central America and Mexico (*see* Map, Figure 0.1).

According to the 2010 Census, Latinos account for more than 70 percent of the 17,262 residents in nearby suburban neighborhoods such as Langley Park in Prince George's County, Maryland (*see* Edberg et al., 2015), and more than 40 percent in Seven Corners and Bailey's Crossroads in Fairfax County, Northern Virginia (Singer, 2012). In the cities of Manassas and Manassas Park (Northern Virginia), they make up more

Figure 0.1.   Map of Latino population in Greater Washington. Source: U.S. Census Bureau, 2010

than 30 percent, and in Prince William County (Northern Virginia), more than 20 percent. In the most populated counties in the Washington, D.C., metropolitan area, Fairfax (northern Virginia) and Montgomery (Maryland), Latino population accounts for more than 15 percent of the total.

Although Latino immigrants have expanded throughout the whole metropolitan region, as noted earlier, they tend to reside in neighborhoods where family members and compatriots have already been settled. Besides the Northwestern neighborhoods of Washington, D.C., Latino population from El Salvador is also concentrated in close suburban clusters of both Maryland and Northern Virginia, constituting major populations with neighbors who often come from the same towns in that country (Pedersen, 2013; Petrozziello, 2012). While Puerto Ricans and Mexicans have settled in close and far metropolitan suburbs, since the 1980s Bolivians have concentrated in Arlington and Fairfax, Northern Virginia (*see* Table 0.1-0.2). This is the largest immigrant population from Bolivia in the United States (Price 2012; Strunk 2013). These co-ethnic concentrations based on national, regional, and local origin have contributed to the growth of hometown associations and the maintenance of transnational relationships with home villages, towns, and countries (Basch, Glick, Schiller, and Szanton-Blanc, 1994; Levitt, 1997; Garza & Lowell, 2002). In spite of these high concentrations, however, most Latinas/os live in multicultural neighborhoods residing along with native residents and other immigrant groups, particularly from Asian and African countries.

As happened with previous census data, nevertheless, Latino immigrants in Greater Washington may be underrepresented in the 2010 Census since the number of undocumented immigrants has increased. As several studies have shown (Bean et al., 2002, Passel, 2006; Hoefer, Rytina, and Baker, 2008), later migratory reforms trying to stop undocumented migration have failed to limit the increase of undocumented immigrants in the United States. Indeed, demographers have emphasized that the Greater Washington area has one of the largest populations of undocumented immigrants, coming mostly from Mexico, El Salvador, Guatemala, and with a significant increase from Honduras (Passel, 2006; Hoefer, Rytina, and Baker, 2008). The lack of a comprehensive migratory reform has made undocumented Latinas/os in the area, as in other parts of the United States, much more vulnerable in their processes of adaptation (De Genova, 2002; 2010; Donato and Armenta, 2011; Massey and Pren, 2012). In the last decade, undocumented immigrants have not been particularly welcome in some new destinations in the outer suburbs. Nativist reactions against them led by residents, anti-immigrant organizations, and local legislation have not only made their incorporation into these suburbs much more difficult, but also displaced them to other metropolitan jurisdictions seeking more security and protection (Singer, Wilson, and DeRenzis, 2009; Price and Singer, 2008; Leitner and Strunk, 2014).

CROSSING BORDERS AND BUILDING COMMUNITIES

Facing different kinds of social and cultural obstacles in their processes of incorporation into the Washington, D.C., metropolitan area, Latinas/os have been adapting to this metropolis by building communities in multicultural neighborhoods while connecting societies and cultures. Based on ethnographic research and practice with Latinas/os in the area, contributors to this volume seek to address these processes of adaptation and transformation by highlighting how they meet these challenges at different levels. While the educational backgrounds of the authors offer diverse theoretical frameworks addressing subjects of public policy, assessment, or evaluation, they also present analyses of social and cultural changes and models of application after interacting with Latinas/os in community centers, health settings, labor environments, educational institutions, and faith-based organizations.

In "La Clínica del Pueblo: A Health Clinic for the People, by the People," (chapter 1) Marcia Bernbaum examines the important role played by Latino-oriented community centers established in Washington, D.C., since the 1960s. She focuses on La Clínica del Pueblo, established in 1983 by Salvadoran refugees and North American activists. While contextualizing its birth, evolution, and impact on its patients, she highlights its holistic approach to patients and culturally sensitive and relevant practices. Seeking to provide access to health care, this community center also advocates on behalf of the civil rights of Latinos regardless of their migratory status. She underscores its approach to health as advocacy and empowerment. In the case of a non-profit agency serving refugees and immigrants in the United States, Patricia Maloof discusses in "Hogar Immigrant Services: A Case Example of Interagency Collaboration Serving Diverse Ethnic Groups" (chapter 2) how the Catholic Legal Immigration Network, Inc. (CLINIC) helps new immigrants and refugees to incorporate and adapt to U.S. host societies. In doing so, she analyzes its core approach and programs while focusing on the Hogar Immigrant Services, a program established in Northern Virginia in 1981, that provides legal and educational services.

Lucy M. Cohen, in "Pluralistic Universe in Multicultural Medicine: Latinas Adapting Cultural Heritages in Medical Fields" (chapter 3), focuses on how Latino immigrants and their children have become incorporated into the Washington, D.C., metropolitan area. Drawing on her research and advocacy experiences, she discusses multiculturalism in health settings, cases of family separation and reunification, and implications for public policies. In "Latina Immigrants and Transnational Health Care Adaptations" (chapter 4) Marta Barkell outlines how Latina immigrants in Northern Virginia navigate the American health care system, attempting to overcome linguistic, cultural and social barriers. These circumstances frequently lead immigrants to incorporate their own health care practices and strategies brought from their home countries. She discusses how Latina immigrants need to re-shape cultural traditions and approaches to health care while trying to understand the U.S. health care system.

In "Waiting for a Job at 'New Corners': Honduran Immigrant Men Day Laboring in Greater Washington" (chapter 5), I analyze Honduran men's incorporation into a segmented labor market in the region. While many of them have to wait for jobs as day laborers, gathering at the 'new corners' (street corners or store parking lots) located in different parts of the region, they have to face different kinds of social adversities caused by employers at work, local residents, and anti-immigrant groups. Based on extensive ethnographic fieldwork with Honduran immigrants settled in the Washington, D.C., metropolitan area, I underscore how migratory policies limit new immigrants' incorporation into host societies. They have contributed not only to the growth of undocumented immigrants, but also to the development of an ethnic- and gender-segmented labor market in the region.

Tadeusz Mich in "Latin Women Organizers in Faith-Based Communities in West Virginia and Maryland" (chapter 6) emphasizes that although there are a significant number of studies of Latino immigrants in the United States, most of them have concentrated on major cities. Nevertheless, a growing number of these immigrants, especially from Mexico, are becoming incorporated into new destinations in distant suburban towns such as Charles Town (Jefferson County), Martinsburg (Berkeley County) in West Virginia, Walkersville (Frederick County), Columbia (Howard County), and Hagerstown (Washington County) in Maryland. Focusing on the implementation of a multicultural model in U.S. Catholic parishes, he underscores the key role that Latina immigrants are playing in the process of organizing Latino faith-based communities in these distant metropolitan areas.

Shaun Loria in "Educational Outcomes for Latinos in Washington, D.C.: Elementary to Higher Education," (chapter 7) asks why Latino students in Washington, D.C. are not achieving educational objectives proportionate to their demographic representation in the U.S. capital. Highlighting that Latinos have the highest dropout rate from high school in the United States, he analyzes how public and charter schools, nonprofits, and higher education address these factors among low-income students in Washington, D.C., In "Where Do We Belong?: Latinas/os in Pursuit of Their Educational DREAM" (chapter 8), Viviana Cristian analyzes how minors who have immigrated to the United States without documentation to reunite with their families have to face many obstacles in order to attain the goal of higher education. In doing so, they try to navigate state and federal laws, in order to attend public colleges and universities. Cristian addresses how these undocumented youth have become a visible group demanding their rights.

Drawing on multisited ethnographic data collected in Washington D.C. among the Lesbian, Gay, Bisexual, and Transsexual (LGBT) Latino communities, María Amelia Viteri analyzes in "At the Crossroads of Racial, Ethnic, Sexual, Gender, and National Borders," (chapter 9) how sexuality is a dimension of power re-shaping and guiding processes of migration and modes of incorporation. Using the concept of "strategic distancing," she emphasizes how Latino immigrants have to confront and re-signify experiences of heteronormativity as immigrants and Latinos.

While focusing on the feminist grassroots organization *Madre Tierra*, she addresses issues of migrant, gender, and structural inequality.

The increasing arrival of immigrants and refugees from around the world has caused new Latina/o immigrants to settle in more ethnically and culturally diverse neighborhoods, living side by side with other refugees and immigrants coming from Asian and African countries, especially with Koreans, Indians, Vietnamese, Filipinos, Ethiopians, and Eritreans.[16] While residing with Ethiopians and Eritreans in northwestern clusters of Washington, D.C., and suburban Maryland (*see* Wood, 1997; Yu and Kim, 1996; Chacko, 2008), the Latino population also lives with Koreans and Vietnamese, who have been settling in the area since the 1970s (Haines, Rutherford, and Thomas, 1981), in nearby suburban neighborhoods of northern Virginia (Arlington, Fairfax, Alexandria) and Maryland (Prince George's).

Taking into account this multi-ethnic and multicultural diversity in Greater Washington, Lucy M. Cohen examines in "Conclusions: Applying Anthropology in Multicultural Neighborhoods," the ways in which anthropologists, members of related disciplines and professions, and Latina and Latino immigrants reshape life experiences, power relations, and problem solving in these changing multicultural communities. Considering that immigrants settled in Washington, D.C., come from diverse national and cultural backgrounds, she analyzes how these contributions address questions of applied anthropology related to social and cultural change and adaptation, including Latinos' agencies in new multicultural settings.

NOTES

1. Greater Washington refers to the Washington, D.C. metropolitan area that includes, according to the Washington Primary Metropolitan Statistical Area (PMSA) (District of Columbia Government, 2011, p.36), the District of Columbia, suburban Maryland (Montgomery, Prince George's, Calvert, Charles and Frederick counties), Northern Virginia (Arlington, Fairfax, Loudoun, Prince William, Stafford, Clarke, Fauquier, Spotsylvania, and Warren counties and the cities of Alexandria, Fairfax, Falls Church, Manassas, Manassas Park, and Fredericksburg), and Jefferson County in West Virginia (*see* Map-1).

2. Reproductive labor market refers to work demands for caring or nurturing people (Salazar Parreña, 2000;2010). This kind of work has traditionally been unpaid work performed by women at home or low-paid jobs done by both women and men from ethnic minorities or the lower classes (Dill, 1988; Graham, 1991; Romero, 1992; Nakano Glenn, 1992; Hondagneu-Sotelo, 2001; Lutz, 2002; 2008).

3. Following Alejandro Portes and Robert Bach (1985), immigrants' modes of incorporation depend on national migratory policies in receiving countries, favoring or limiting some people's migration and settlement, labor market structures and opportunities, and social networks helping new immigrants' migration, settlement, and adaptation to the host society (*See also* Portes and Böröcz, 1989).

4. Although the Pan American Health Organization (PAHO) was established in Washington, D.C. in 1902 as Pan American Sanitary Bureau (1902) and the Organiza-

tion of American States (OEA) in 1910 as the Pan American Union, Washington, D.C. did not start to emerge as an international city until postwar multilateral institutions and new embassies were established in the city (*see* Cadaval, 1998). With the commercial and financial accords signed by industrial allied countries in Bretton Woods (New Hampshire) in July 1944, new world financial rules were established by regulating international exchange rates. The dollar became a world reserve currency (Harvey, 1989; Zolberg, 1992; Castles and Miller, 1993). As a result of this agreement, the major organizations running this new international capitalist order, the International Monetary Fund and World Bank, were established in Washington, D.C. (*see also* Abbot, 1996; 1999).

5. Although New York, London and Tokyo were conceptualized by Saskia Sassen (1991) as global cities where financial, communication, and migration flows take place, this internationalization process in Washington, D.C., which had not traditionally been an industrial region in the United States, has led the region to emerge as a post-industrial metropolis with an economic growth based on new high technology, scientific research, and service industries (Knox, 1991; Singer, 2003). Emerging as a new immigrant gateway in the United States (Singer, 2012), the Washington, D.C. metropolitan area also shares, as Carl Abbot has pointed out (1996), other global cities' main functions that Saskia Sassen (2002; 2005) has highlighted. As a world political center after the Second World War, likewise, not only do financial and information businesses take place in Washington, D.C., but also diplomatic decisions with important consequences at the global, regional, and international levels (Calder, 2014; Calder and Freytas, 2009).

6. The growth of transnational mothering among immigrant women working in postindustrial societies has been widely studied since the 1990s by feminist anthropologists and other social science scholars in the United States and Europe: Hondagneu-Sotelo and Avila (1997), Salazar Parreñas (2001, 2005), Bryceson and Vuorela (2002), Schmalzbauer (2005), Dreby (2010), Arnado (2010), López Pozos (2012), Parella (2007) and Åkesson, Carling, and Drotbohm (2012), among other scholars.

7. For the first time, a question referring to Hispanic heritage was included in the 1970 Census (U.S. Bureau of the Census, 1973). While beginning by asking about "persons of Spanish language, surname, and origin," this question was later replaced by "Hispanic origin" (U.S. Bureau of the Census, 1990), and currently "Hispanic or Latino" (U.S. Census Bureau, 2002). However, U.S. Latino leaders have used the term "Latina/o" over "Hispanic" since the 1970s (Padilla, 1985; Oboler, 2002; Vélez-Ibañez and Sampaio, 2002; Viteri, 2014).

8. There was, nevertheless, a higher proportion of Puerto Ricans settled in the region who, along with Mexican-Americans, started to arrive in the region during the New Deal and Second World War, according to Sprehn-Malagón, Hernández-Fujigaki, and Robinson (2014) .

9. After World War II, Civil Rights Movement in Washington, D.C. propelled the development of diverse patterns of civic participation around African American churches, community centers, associations, and social networks. With rich historical roots of civil participation in the city, leaders from these institutions were able to congregate and mobilize their members to public action to seek for political recognition and social changes (Kofie, 1999, Halfani, 1999). This African American social and political civil organization played a key role in the official recognition of Washington, D.C. as a multicultural society in the United States. This also influenced the first Latino communities' organization in the city (Cadaval, 1988; 1998; Boone, 1989).

10. Based on the Jewish and Christian traditions of a sanctuary as a place for refuge, the U.S.-Central American Sanctuary Movement became a key transnational organization for helping and protecting Salvadoran and Guatemalan refugees in the United States starting in the 1980s (Hamilton and Chinchilla, 2001). Since then, Salvadorans have become concentrated in the U.S. areas such as Los Angeles, which has the largest Salvadoran population (Hamilton and Chinchilla, 2001; Landolt, Antler and Baires, 1999; Baker-Cristales, 2004), Houston (Rodriguez, 1987), Long Island (Mahler, 1995),

San Francisco (Menjívar, 2000), New Jersey (Bailey et al., 2002), and Washington, D.C., which hosts the second largest Salvadoran population in the United States (Repak, 1995; Pedersen, 2002; 2013; Sánchez Molina, 2005; 2006; Rodríguez, 2009).

11. Although around three million undocumented immigrants benefited from IRCA amnesty (Phillips and Massey, 1999), only a small proportion of Central American refugees who entered the United States during this period were able to apply for this program (Mahler, 1995; Durand, Massey, and Capoferro, 2005).

12. After *El Pregonero* began to be published by the Archdiocese of Washington in the Spanish Catholic Center that was established in Mount Pleasant in 1967. Other local and regional newspapers have been printed in the area, among them: *La Nación USA* (1991), the only daily newspaper distributed in the metropolitan area, *El Tiempo Latino* (1991), and *Washington Hispanic* (1994). According to José Luis Benítez (2005, p. 166), around 25 weekly Spanish newspapers were published in the Washington, D.C. metropolitan area at the beginning of the 2000s, and there were more than thirteen Spanish radio stations, which started to broadcast in the 1980s, and three Spanish TV stations. Salvador Vidal-Ortiz (2004) considers that even bilingual Latino immigrants tend to use Spanish media (newspapers, radio stations, television channels, and also Internet) as a way of being connected not only with other Latinas/os in the United States, but also with their respective countries of origin. This is a cultural transnational dimension in the use of the Spanish language that has also been highlighted by Patricia Rodríguez (2005) and José Luis Benítez (2008) among Salvadoran immigrants residing in the Washington, D.C. metropolitan area.

13. In the 1980s, Los Angeles and San Francisco and other U.S. cities began to be declared sanctuaries, seeking to protect undocumented immigrants settled in their jurisdictions, by enacting municipal legislation prohibiting, among other provisions, local police to question or arrest them because of their migratory status. At present, many other U.S. cities, such as New York, Philadelphia, Miami, and Baltimore, among other urban areas, have also declared themselves sanctuary cities (*see* Rodríguez, 2008; Lippert and Rehaag, 2013). In Greater Washington, after Takoma Park (Maryland) in 1985, other jurisdictions—such as Washington, D.C., Arlington and Alexandria in northern Virginia—have enacted "sanctuary" ordinances (*see* Leitner and Strunk, 2014; Leon et al., 2009).

14. Although Washington, D.C., had been losing population since the 1970s, the city gained around 30,000 residents according to 2010 Census data. After more than five decades, however, the African American population has decreased for the first time from 60 percent of the total population in 2000 to 50 percent in 2010 (Sturtevant, 2014). Besides African Americans, who according to the 2010 U.S. Census accounted for 50.7 percent of the District of Columbia's population, and Latinos, who made up 9.1 percent, gentrification has also affected Chinese residents and businesses in the ethnic neighborhood of Chinatown, also located in northwest Washington, D.C. (*see* Lou, 2007). Although Latino population continued to concentrate in these Northwestern neighborhoods, which are part of Ward 1 (with 15,827 residents or 20.8 percent), this was, nevertheless, the only ward in the city where Latino population decreased according to 2010 Census data (*see also* District of Columbia Government, 2011).

15. Among major economic metropolitan corridors in Greater Washington, Paul L. Knox (1991, p. 203) highlighted the corridor along I-95 in Fairfax County/Prince William County in northern Virginia, mainly due to the expansion of advanced services sector, and the I-270 along Bethesda/City of Gaithersburg in Montgomery County in Maryland based on biotechnology and where major federal research institutes and agencies—the National Institutes of Health, U.S. Agricultural Center, and the Food and Drug Administration—are established. This author also pointed to another high-technology corridor in Loudon County in northern Virginia.

16. As refugees, Koreans and Vietnamese began to settle in the region after 1975 (Haines, Rutherford, and Thomas, 1981; Hackett, 1996), while Ethiopians and Eritreans after the overthrow of Haile Selassie in 1974 (Chacko, 2008; Chernela, Carattini, and Applebaum, 2009). Refugees from Somalia and Sudan as well as migrants from

18 *Raúl Sánchez Molina*

Nigeria, Ghana, Cameroon, and Sierra Leone have been also settling in the region in the last decade to such an extent that Greater Washington is the second largest metropolis, after New York, hosting African-born populations in the United States (Gambino et al., 2014; Friedman et al., 2006).

REFERENCES

Abbott, Carl. (1999). *Political Terrain. Washington, D.C., from Tidewater Town to Global Metropolis.* Chapel Hill and London: The University of North Carolina Press.
Abbott, Carl. (1996). "The Internationalization of Washington DC." *Urban Affairs Review,* 31 (5): 571–594
Åkesson, Lisa, Jørgen Carling and Heike Drotbohm. (2012). "Mobility, Moralities and Motherhood: Navigating the Contingencies of Cape Verdean Lives." *Journal of Ethnic and Migration Studies,* 38 (2): 237–260.
Aleinikoff, Thomas, David Martin and Hiroshi Motomura. (1998). *Immigration and Citizenship. Process and Policy.* St. Paul, Minn.: West Group.
Arnado, Janet M. (2010). "Performances across Time and Space: Drama in the Global Households of Filipina Transmigrant Workers." *International Migration,* 48 (6): 132–154.
Baker-Cristales, Beth. (2004). *Salvadoran Migration to Southern California: Redefining El Hermano Lejano.* Gainesville, FL: University Press of Florida.
Bailey, Adrian J., Richard A. Wright, Alison Mountz, and Ines M. Miyares. (2002). "(Re)producing Salvadoran Transnational Geographies." In *Annals of the Association of American Geographers,* 92(1): 125–144.
Basch, Linda, Nina Glick Schiller, and Cristina Szanton-Blanc. (1994). *Nations Unbound: Transnationalized Projects and the Deterritorialized Nation-State.* New York: Gordon and Breach.
Bean, Frank D, Rodolfo Corona, Rodolfo Tuiran, Karen A Woodrow-Lafield, and Jennifer Van Hook. (2002). "Circular, Invisible, and Ambiguous Migrants: Components of Difference in Estimates of the Number of Unauthorized Mexican Migrants in the United States." *Demography,* 38 (3): 411–422.
Benítez, José Luis. (2008). "Diáspora salvadoreña: identidades y mapas culturales en el ciberespacio." *Encuentro,* 40 (80): 46–56.
Benítez, José Luis. (2005). Communication and Collective Identities in the Transnational Social Space: A Media Ethnography of the Salvadoran Immigrant Community in the Washington, D.C. Metropolitan Area. PhD Dissertation: The College of Communication of Ohio University.
Boehm, Deborah A. (2008). "'For My Children': Constructing Family and Navigating the State in the U.S.-Mexico Transnation." *Anthropological Quarterly,* 81 (4): 777–802.
Boone, Margaret S. (1989). *Capital Cubans: Refugee Adaptation in Washington, D.C.* New York, NY: AMS Press.
Boone, Margaret S. (1981). "The Social Structure of a Low-Density Cultural Group: Cubans in Washington, D.C." *Anthropological Quarterly* : 103–109.
Bryceson, Deborah and Ulla Vuorela (eds). (2002). *The Transnational Family: New European Frontiers and Global Networks.* Oxford: Berg.
Cadaval, Olivia. (1998). *Creating a Latino Identity in the Nation's Capital. The Latino Festival.* New York: Garland Publishing, Inc.
Cadaval, Olivia. (1988). "New Identity for an Old." In Kathryn Schneider Smith (ed.) *Washington at Home. An Illustrated History of Neighborhoods in the Nation's Capital.* Washington, D.C.: Windsor Publications, Inc., 227–259.
Calder, Kent E. (2014). *Asia in Washington: Exploring the Penumbra of Transnational Power.* Washington, D.C.: The Brookings Institution.
Calder, Kent E. and Mariko de Freytas. (2009). "Global Political Cities as Actors in Twenty-First Century International Affairs." *SAIS Review of International Affairs,* 29 (1): 79–96.

Candelario, Ginetta E.B. (2010). "Displaying Indentity. Dominicans in the Black Mosaic of Washington, D.C." In Miriam Jiménez Román and Juan Flores eds*The Afro-Latin@ Reader. History and Culture in the United States.* Duke University Press, 326-342.

Castles, Stephen and Mark J. Miller (1993) *The Age of Migration. International Population Movement in the Modern World.* London: Mcmillan.

Chacko, Elizabeth. (2013). "La Fiesta DC: The Ethnic Festival as an Act of Belonging in the City." *Journal of Intercultural Studies,* 34 (4): 443–453.

Chacko, Elizabeth. (2008). "Washington: From Bi-Racial City to Multiethnic Gateway." In Marie Price and Lisa Benton-Short (eds) *Migrants to the Metropolis: The Rise of Immigrant Gateway Cities.* Syracuse, NY: Syracuse University Press, 203–225.

Chavez, Leo. (2008). *The Latino Threat. Constructing Immigrants, Citizens, and the Nation.* Stanford, CA: Stanford University Press.

Chernela, Janet, Amy Carattini, and Bethany Applebaum. (2009). "Ideologies of Heritage: Language, Community, and Identity among Ethiopian Immigrants in Prince George's County, Maryland." *Practicing Anthropology,* 31 (3): 15–19.

Chinchilla, Norma Stoltz and Nora Hamilton. (2004). "Central American Immigrants: Diverse Populations, Changing Communities." In David G. Gutiérrez (ed) *The Columbia History of Latinos in the United States since 1960.* New York: Columbia University Press, 187–228.

Clark-Lewis, Elizabeth. (1996). "'For a Real Better Life' Voices of African American Women Migrants, 1900-1930." In Francine Curro Cary ed *Urban Odyssey. A Multicultural History of Washington, D.C.* Washington, D.C.: Smithsonian Institution Press, 97–112.

Cohen, Lucy M. (1984). "Introduction." In Lucy M. Cohen and Timothy Ready (eds.) *Field Training in Applied Anthropology.* Washington, D.C.: The Department of Anthropology, The Catholic University of America, Vol. II, 1–10.

Cohen, Lucy M. (1979). *Culture, Disease, and Stress among Latino Immigrants.* Research Institute in Immigration and Ethnic Studies (RIIES) Washington, D.C.: Smithsonian Institution.

Cohen, Lucy M. and Carmen Fernández (1974). "Ethnic Identity and Psychocultural Adaptation of Spanish-Speaking Families." *Child Welfare,* 53: 413–422.

Coutin, Susan Bibler. (2000). *Legalizing Moves. Salvadoran Immigrants'Struggle for U.S. Residency.* Ann Arbor, MI: The University of Michigan Press.

Coutin, Susan Bibler. (1993). *The Culture of Protest. Religious Activism and the U.S. Sanctuary Movement.* Boulder, San Francisco, Oxford: Westview Press.

Cunningham, Hilary. (1999). "The Ethnography of Transnational Social Activism: Understanding the Global as Local Practice." *American Ethnologist,* 26 (3): 583–604.

De Genova, Nicholas. (2010). "The Queer Politics of Migration: Reflections on 'Illegality' and Incorrigibility." *Studies in Social Justice,* 4 (2): 101–126.

De Genova, Nicholas. (2002). "Migrant 'Illegality' and Deportability in Everyday Life." *Annual Review of Anthropology,* 31: 419–47.

Dreby, Joanna. (2010). *Divided by Borders: Mexican Migrants and their Children.* Berkeley, CA: University of California Press.

Dill, Bonnie Thornton. (1988). "Our Mothers' Grief: Racial Ethnic Women and the Maintenance of Families." *Journal of Family History,* 13 (4): 415-431.

District of Columbia Government (2011) *Indices: A Statistical Index to the District of Columbia Services.* Washington, DC: The District of Columbia Government, vol. XV.

Donato, Katharine and Amada Armenta. (2011). "What We Know About Unauthorized Migration." *Annual Review of Sociology,* 37: 529–43.

Donato, Katharine, Donna Gabaccia, Jennifer Holdaway, Martin Manalansan, and Patricia Pessar. (2006). "A Glass Half Full? Gender in Migration Studies." *International Migration Review,* 40 (1): 3–26.

Durand, Jorge, Douglas S. Massey, and Chiara Capoferro. (2005). "The New Geography of Mexican Immigration." In Victor Zúñiga and Rubén Hernández-León eds.

New Destinations: Mexican Immigration in the United States. New York, NY: Russell Sage, 1–20.

Edberg, Mark, Sean Cleary, Lauren B. Simmons, Idalina Cubilla-Batista, Elizabeth L. Andrade, and Glencora Gudger. (2015). "Defining the 'Community': Applying Ethnographic Methods for a Latino Immigrant Health Intervention." *Human Organization*, 74 (1): 27–41.

Fagen, Patricia Weiss. (1988). "Central American Refugees and U.S Policy." In Nora Hamilton, Jeffry A. Frieden, Linda Fuller, and Manuel Pastor eds. *Crisis in Central America: regional dynamics and U.S. policy in the 1980s*. Boulder, CO: Westview Press, 59–74.

Fernández-Kelly, Patricia and Douglas S. Massey. (2007). "Borders for Whom? The Role of NAFTA in Mexico-U.S. Migration." *The ANNALS of the American Academy of Political and Social Science*, 610: 98–118.

Frey, William. (2006). *Diversity Spread Out: Metropolitan Shifts in Hispanic, Asian, and Black Population since 2000*. Washington, D.C.: The Brookings Institution.

Friedman, Samantha, Audrey Singer, Marie Price, and Ivan Cheung. (2005). "Race, Immigrants, and Residence: A New Racial Geography of Washington, D.C." *Geographical Review*, 95 (2): 210–230.

Foner, Nancy. (1997). "The Immigrant Family: Cultural Legacies and Cultural Changes." *International Migration Review*, 31(4): 961–974.

Foner, Nancy and Richard Alba. (2010). "Immigration and the Legacies of the Past: The Impact of Slavery and the Holocaust on Contemporary Immigrants in the United States and Western Europe." *Comparative Studies in Society and History*, 52 (4): 798–819.

Gambino, Christine P., Edward N. Trevelyan, and John Thomas Fitzwater. (2014). The Foreign-Born Population from Africa: 2008–2012. Washington, D.C.: U.S. Census Bureau. www.census.gov/library/publications/2014/acs/acsbr12-16.html (September 8, 2015).

Gammage, Sarah, Alison Paul, Melany Machado, and Manuel Benítez. (2005). Gender, Migration, and Transnational Communities. A Draft Report Prepared for the Inter-American Foundation. Washington, D.C.

García, Mª Cristina. (2006). *Seeking Refuge. Central American Migration to Mexico, the United States, and Canada*. Berkeley: University of California Press.

Garza, Rodolfo O. and Briant Lindsay Lowell. *Sending Money Home. Hispanic Remittances and Community Development*. Lanham: Rowman and Littlefield Publishers, Inc.

Graham, Hillary. (1991). "The Concept of Caring in Feminist Research: The Case of Domestic Service." *Sociology*, 25 (1): 61–78.

Harvey, David. (1989). *The Condition of Postmodernity*. Oxford: Blackwell.

Gybney, Mark and Michael Stohl. (1988). "Human Rights and U.S. Refugee Policy." In Mark Gibney (ed.) *Open Borders? Closed Societies?:The Ethical and Political Issues*. New York, NY: Greenwood Press, 151–183.

Hackett, Beatrice N. (1996). "'We Must Become Part of the Larger American Family' Washington's Vietnamese, Cambodians, and Laotians." In Francine Curro Cary (ed) *Urban Odyssey. A Multicultural History of Washington, D.C.* Washington, D.C.: Smithsonian Institution Press, pp. 276–291.

Haines, David, Dorothy Rutherford and Patrick Thomas. (1981). "The Case for Exploratory Fieldwork: Understanding the Adjustment of Vietnamese Refugees in the Washington Area." *Anthropological Quarterly*: 94–102

Hagan, Jacqueline, Brianna Castro and Nestor Rodriguez. (2010). "The Effects of U.S. Deportation Policies on Immigrant Families and Communities: Cross-Border Perspectives." *North Carolina Law Review*, 88: 1799–1823.

Halfani, Mohamed. (1999). *Local Dynamism and the Governance of Washington, D.C.: A Study on the Scope of Civil Society-State Engagement*. Washington, D.C.: Woodrow Wilson International Center for Scholars.

Hamilton, Nora and Norma S. Chinchilla (2001). *Seeking community in a global city: Guatemalans and Salvadorans in Los Angeles*. Philadelphia, PA: Temple University Press.

Hamilton, Nora and Norma S. Chinchilla. (1991). "Central American Migration: A Framework for Analysis." *Latin American Research Review*, 26 (1):75–110.

Hoefer, Michael, Nancy Rytina and Bryan Baker. (2008). "Estimates of the Unauthorized Immigrant Population Residing in the United States: January 2008." Washington, D.C.: Homeland Security, Office of Immigration Statistics.

Hondagneu-Sotelo, Pierrette. (2001). *Doméstica. Immigrant Workers and Caring in the Shadows of Affluence*. Berkeley: University of California Press.

Hondagneu-Sotelo, Pierrette. (1994). *Gendered Transitions: Mexican Experience of Immigration*. Berkeley: University of California Press.

Hondagneu-Sotelo, Pierrette and Ernestine Avila. (1997). "I'm Here, but I'm There: The Meanings of Latino Transnational Motherhood." *Gender and Society*, 11 (5): 548–571.

Kearny, Michael. (1995). "The Local and the Global: The Anthropology of Globalization and Transnationalism." *Annual Review of Anthropology*, 24: 247–265.

Knox, Paul L. (1991). "The Restless Urban Landscape: Economic and Sociocultural Change and the Transformation of Metropolitan Washington, D.C." *Annals of the Association of American Geographers*, 81(2): 181–209.

Kofie, Nelson. (1999). *Race, Class, and the Struggle for Neighborhood in Washington, D.C.* New York and London: Garland Publishing.

Landolt, Patricia, Lilian Antler, and Sonia Baires. (1999). "From Hermano Lejano to Hermano Mayor: The Dialectics of Salvadoran Transnationalism." *Ethnic and Racial Studies*, 22 (2): 290–315.

Leitner, Helga and Christopher Strunk. (2014). "Assembling Insurgent Citizenship: Immigrant Advocacy Struggles in the Washington DC Metropolitan Area." *Urban Geography*, 35 (7): 943–964.

Leon, Edwin de, Matthew Maronick, Carol J. De Vita and Elizabeth T. Boris. (2009). Community-Based Organizations and Immigrant Integration in the Washington, D.C. Metropolitan Area. Washington, D.C.: The Urban Institute.

Levitt, Peggy. (2001). *The Transnational Villagers*. Berkeley: University of California Press.

Levitt, Peggy and Nina Glick Schiller. (2004). "Conceptualizing Simultaneity: A Transnational Social Field Perspective on Society." *International Migration Review*, 38 (3): 1002–1039.

Lippert, Randy and Sean Rehaag (eds). (2013). *Sanctuary Practices in International Perspectives: Migration, Citizenship, and Social Movements*. New York, NY: Routledge.

López Pozos. (2012). "Familias transnacionales. Migración familiar de México a Estados Unidos y del Perú a Italia." *Anuac*, 1 (1): 70–88.

Lou, Jia. (2007). "Revitalizing Chinatown Into a Heterotopia: A Geosemiotic Analysis of Shop Signs in Washington, D.C.'s Chinatown." *Space and Culture*, 10 (2): 170–194.

Lutz, Helma (ed.). (2008). *Migration and Domestic Work: A European Perspective on a Global Theme*. Burlington, VT.: Ashgate Publishing Ltd.

Lutz, Helma. (2002). "At Your Service Madam! The Globalization of Domestic Service." *Feminist Review*, 70: 89–104.

Mahler, Sarah. (1995). *Salvadorans in Suburbia. Symbiosis and Conflict*. Boston: Allyn and Bacon.

Mahler, Sarah and Patricia Pessar. (2006). "Gender Matters: Ethnographers Bring Gender from the Periphery toward the Core of Migration Studies." *International Migration Review*, 40(1): 27-63.

Massey, Douglas S. and Karen A. Pren. (2012). "Unintended Consequences of US Immigration Policy: Explaining the Post-1965 Surge from Latin America." *Population and Development Review*, 38 (1): 1–29.

Menjívar, Cecilia. (2000). *Fragmented Ties. Salvadoran Immigrant Networks in America*. Berkeley: University of California Press.

Montes, Segundo. (1990). *El Salvador 1989. Las remesas que envían los salvadoreños de Estados Unidos. Consecuencias sociales y económicas.* San Salvador: UCA Editores.

Montes, Segundo and José García. (1988). *Salvadoran Migration to the United States: An Exploratory Study.* Washington, D.C.: Hemispheric Migration Project, Center for Immigration Policy and Refugee Assistance, Georgetown University.

Nakano Glenn, Evelyn. (1992). "From Servitude to Service Work: Historical Continuities in the Racial Division of Paid Reproductive Labor."*Signs*,18: 1–4

Oboler, Suzanne. (2002). "The Politics of Labeling: Latino/a Cultural Identities of Self and Others." In Carlos G. Vélez-Ibáñez and Anna Sampaio (eds) *Transnational Latina/o communities: Politics, processes, and cultures.* Lanham, MD: Rowman & Littlefield Publishers, Inc., pp.73–89.

Padilla, Felix M. (1985). *Latino Ethnic Consciousness: The Case of Mexican Americans and Puerto Ricans in Chicago.* Notre Dame, IN: University of Notre Dame Press.

Parella, Sonia. (2007). "Los vínculos afectivos y de cuidado en las familias transnacionales migrantes ecuatorianos y peruanos en España." *Migraciones internacionales*, 4 (2):151–188.

Passel, Jeffrey. (2006). The Size and Characteristics of the Unauthorized Migrant Population in the U.S. Estimates Based on the March 2005 Current Population Survey. Washington, D.C.: Pew Hispanic Center.

Passel, Jeffrey, D'Vera Cohn and Mark Hugo Lopez. (2011). *Census 2010: 50 Million Latino Hispanics Account for More Than Half of Nation's Growth in Past Decade.* Washington, D.C.: Pew Hispanic Center.

Pedersen, David. (2013). *American Value. Migrants, Money, and Meaning in El Salvador and the United States.* Chicago: The University of Chicago Press.

Pedersen, David. (2002). "The Storm We Call Dollars: Determining Value and Belief in El Salvador and the United States." *Cultural Anthropology*, 17 (3): 431–459.

Perez, Judith. (2012). "Residential Patterns and an Overview of Segregation and Discrimination in the Greater Washington, DC, Metropolitan Region." In Enrique Pumar (ed) (2012) *Hispanic Migration and Urban Development: Studies from Washington, D.C.* Bingley, U.K.: Emerald Group Publishing Limited, pp. 111–131.

Perla, Hector and Susan Bibler Coutin. (2012). "Legacies and Origins of the 1980s US–Central American Sanctuary Movement." *Refuge*, 1(26): 7–19.

Pessar, Patricia R. (1995). "The Elusive Enclave: Ethnicity, Class, and Nationality among Latino Entrepreneurs in Greater Washington, D.C." *Human Organization*, 54 (4): 383–392.

Petrozziello, Allison J. (2011). "Feminised financial flows: how gender affects remittances in Honduran-/US transnational families." *Gender & Development*, 19 (1): 53–67.

Phillips, Julie A. and Douglas S. Massey. (1999). "The New Labor Market: Irnmigrants and Wages after IRCA." *Demography,* 36 (2): 233–246.

Portes, Alejandro and Jozsef Böröcz. (1989). "Contemporary Immigration: Theoretical Perspectives on its Determinants and Modes of Incorporation." *International Migration Review,* 23 (3): 606–631.

Portes, Alejandro and Robert L. Bach. (1985). *Latin Journey: Cuban and Mexican Immigrants in the United States.* Berkeley: University of California Press.

Price, Marie and Audrey Singer. (2008). "Immigrants, Suburbs, and the Politics of Reception in Metropolitan Washington." In Audrey Singer, Susan W. Hardwick and Caroline B. Brettell (eds.) *Twenty-First Century Gateways. Immigrant Incorporation in Suburban America.* Washington, D.C.: Brookings Institution Press, pp. 137–168.

Prince, Sabiyha. (2014). *African Americans and Gentrification in Washington, D.C. Race, Class, and Social Justice in the Nation's Capital.* Burlington, VT: Ashgate Publishing Company.

Repak, Terry A. (1995). *Waiting on Washington. Central American Workers in the Nation's Capital.* Philadelphia: Temple University Press.

Rodríguez, Cristina M. (2008). "The Significance of the Local in Immigration Regulation." *Michigan Law Review,*106: 567–642.

Rodríguez, Néstor. (1987). "Undocumented Central Americans in Houston: Diverse Populations." *International Migration Review,* 21: 4–26

Rodríguez, Ana Patricia. (2009). *Dividing the Isthmus. Central American Transnational Histories, Literature, and Cultures.* Austin: University of Texas Press.

Rodríguez, Ana Patricia. (2005). "Departamento 15": Cultural Narratives of Salvadoran Transnational Migration." *Latino Studies,* 3: 19–41.

Romero, Mary.(1992). *Maid in the U.S.A.* New York: Routledge.

Salazar Parreñas, Rhacel. (2010). "Transnational Mothering: A Source of Gender Conflicts in the Family." *North Carolina Law Review,* 88 (5):1825–1856.

Salazar Parreñas, Rhacel. (2005). *Children of Global Migration. Transnational Families and Gendered Woes.* Stanford, CA: Stanford University Press.

Salazar Parreñas, Rhacel. (2001). *Servants of Globalization. Women, Migration, and Domestic Work.* Stanford, CA: Stanford University Press.

Salazar Parreñas, Rachel. (2000). "Migrant Filipina domestic workers and the international division of reproductive labor." *Gender & Society,* 14 (4): 560–580.

Sánchez Molina, Raúl. (2015). "Caring While Missing Children's Infancy: Transnational Mothering among Honduran Women Working in Greater Washington." *Human Organization,* 74 (1): 63–73.

Sánchez Molina, Raúl. (2013). "Superando el 'carácter nacional': la antropología ante los retos de la globalización." *Revista de Antropología Experimental,* 12: 23–42.

Sánchez Molina, Raúl. (2009). "Introducción. Del colonialismo al transnacionalismo: contextos y aplicaciones de la etnografía en la antropología social y cultural' En Raúl Sánchez Molina (ed) *La Etnografía y sus aplicaciones. Lecturas desde la Antropología social y cultural.* Madrid: Editorial Universitaria Ramón Areces, pp. 13–54.

Sánchez Molina, Raúl. (2008). "Modes of Incorporation, Social Exclusion, and Transnationalism: Salvadoran's Adaptation to the Washington, D.C. Metropolitan Area." *Human Organization,* 67 (3): 269–280.

Sánchez Molina, Raúl. (2006). Proceso migratorio de una mujer salvadoreña. El viaje de María Reyes a Washington, D.C. Madrid: CIS/Siglo XXI

Sánchez Molina, Raúl. (2005). *"Mandar a traer."Antropología, migraciones y transnacionalismo. Salvadoreños en Washington.* Madrid: Editorial Universitas.

Sánchez Molina, Raúl. (2004). "Cuando los hijos se quedan en El Salvador: Familias transnacionales y reunificación familiar de inmigrantes salvadoreños en Washington, D.C."*Revista de Dialectología y Tradiciones Populares,* 59 (2): 257–276.

Sassen, Saskia. (2005). "The Global City: Introducing a Concept." the *Brown Journal of World Affairs,* 11 (2): 27–43.

Sassen, Saskia. (2002). "Locating cities on global circuits." *Environment & Urbanization,* 14 (1): 13–30.

Sassen, Saskia. (1991). *The Global City.* Princeton, NJ: Princeton University Press.

Singer, Audrey. (2012) "Metropolitan Washington: A New Immigrant Gateway." In Enrique Pumar (ed.) *Hispanic Migration and Urban Development: Studies from Washington, D.C.* Bingley, U.K.: Emerald Group Publishing Limited, pp. 1–24.

Singer, Audrey. (2008). "Twenty-First-Century Gateways: An Introduction." In Audrey Singer, Susan W. Hardwick and Caroline B. Brettell (eds.) *Twenty-First Century Gateways. Immigrant Incorporation in Suburban America.* Washington, D.C.: Brookings Institution Press, pp. 3-30.

Singer, Audrey. (2003). *At Home in the Nation's Capital: Immigrant Trends in Metropolitan Washington.* Brookings Greater Washington Research Program. Washington, D.C.: Brookings Institution.

Singer, Audrey, Jill H. Wilson, and Brooke DeRenzis. (2009). Immigrants, Politics, and Local Response in Suburban Washington. Washington, D.C.: The Brookings Institution.

Schmalzbauer, Leah. (2005). *Striving and Surviving: A Daily Life Analysis of Honduran Transnational Families*. New York: Routledge.

Sprehn-Malagón, María, Jorge Hernández-Fujigaki and Linda Robinson. (2014). *Latinos in the Washington Metro Area* . Charleston, SC: Arcadia Publishing.

Strunk, Christopher. (2013). "Circulating Practices: Migration and Translocal Development in Washington D.C. and Cochabamba, Bolivia." *Sustainability*, 5: 4106–4123.

Sturtevant, Lisa. (2014)."The New District of Columbia: What Population Growth and Demographic Change Mean for the City." *Journal of Urban Affairs*, 36 (2): 276–299.

Suárez-Orozco, Carola, Hirokazu Yoshikawa, Robert T. Teranishi and Marcelo M. Suárez-Orozco. (2011). "Growing Up in the Shadows: The Developmental Implications of Unauthorized Status." *Harvard Educational Review*, 81 (3): 438–472

Thomas, William, and Florian Znaniecki. (1918). *The Polish Peasant in Europe and America*. Boston: Gorham Press.

District of Columbia Government. (2011). *Indices*: A Statistical Index to the District of Columbia Services. Washington, DC: The District of Columbia Government, vol. XV.

UNHCR. (2010). *Convention and Protocol Relating to the Status of Refugees*. Geneva: The UN Refugee Agency. http://www.unhcr.org/3b66c2aa10.html (July 17, 2015).

U.S. Census Bureau. (2010). *United States Census 2010*. Washington, D.C.: U.S. Department of Commerce. http://www.census.gov/prod/www/decennial.html (June 6, 2015).

U.S. Census Bureau. (2002). *United States Census 2000*. Washington, D.C.: U.S. Department of Commerce. http://www.census.gov/prod/www/decennial.html (June 29, 2015)

U.S. Bureau of the Census. (1990). *1990 Census of Population*. Washington, D.C.: U.S. Department of Commerce. http://www.census.gov/prod/www/decennial.html (June 29, 2015)

U.S. Bureau of the Census. (1973). *1970 Census of Population*. Washington, D.C.: U.S. Department of Commerce. http://www.census.gov/prod/www/decennial.html (June 29, 2015)

Vélez-Ibáñez, Carlos G. and Anna Sampaio. (2002). "Introduction: Processes, New Prospects, and Approaches." In Carlos G. Vélez-Ibáñez and Anna Sampaio (eds) *Transnational Latina/o communities: Politics, processes, and cultures*. Lanham, MD: Rowman & Littlefield Publishers, Inc., pp.1–37.

Vidal-Ortiz, Salvador. (2004). "Puerto Ricans and the Politics of Speaking Spanish." *Latino Studies*, 2: 254–258.

Viteri, María Amelia. (2014). *Desbordes: Translating Racial, Ethnic, Sexual, and Gender Identities across the Americas*. New York, NY: SUNY Press.

Wasem, Ruth Ellen and Karma Ester. (2006). "Temporary Protected Status: Current Immigration Policy and Issues." *Congressional Research Service (CRS)*: 1–6.

Williams, Brett. (1992). "Poverty among African Americans in the Urban United States." In Commentary. *Human Organization*, 51 (2): 164–174.

Williams, Brett. (1988). *Upscaling Downtown: Stalled Gentrification in Washington, D.C.* Ithaca, NY: Cornell University Press.

Wood, Joseph. (1997). "Vietnamese American Place Making in Northern Virginia." *Geographical Review*, 87 (1): 58–72.

Yu, Meeja and Unyong Kim. (1996). " 'We Came Here with Dreams' Koreans in the Nations' Capital." In Francine Curro Cary (ed) *Urban Odyssey. A Multicultural History of Washington, D.C.* Washington, D.C.: Smithsonian Institution Press, pp. 292–304.

Zolberg, Aristide R. (1992). "Labour Migration and International Economic Regimes: Bretton Woods and After." In Mary M. Kritz, Lin L. Lim and Hania Zlotnik (eds.) *International Migration Systems: A Global Approaches*. Oxford: Clarendon Press, pp. 315–334.

Zolberg, Aristide R., Astri Suhrke and Sergio Aguayo. (1989). *Escape from Violence: Conflict and the Refugee Crisis in the Developing World*. New York: Oxford University Press.

Zúñiga, Victor and Rubén Hernández-León (eds.). (2005). *New Destinations: Mexican Immigration in the United States.* New York: Russell Sage.

ONE

La Clínica Del Pueblo

A Health Clinic for the People, by the People

Marcia Bernbaum

The 1980s will go down in history as a decade when the superpowers waged a Cold War that had far-reaching consequences throughout the world on relationships between countries while affecting world economies by the political fallout from this war. In Central America, in particular in El Salvador, Guatemala, and Nicaragua, the Cold War manifested itself in internal conflicts supported by the superpowers. These conflicts left hundreds of thousands of the citizens of these countries dead, thousands traumatized through the torture that they either experienced directly or observed being inflicted on others, and millions fleeing their countries in search of a safe haven where they could live in peace. Many of the latter fled to the United States, arriving without documents, to face an uncertain future. In this late Cold War context, thousands of Central Americans settled in the Washington, D.C., metropolitan area. Salvadoran and U.S. activists together with George Washington University Medical School residents founded *La Clínica del Pueblo* in 1983 in the Columbia Heights section of Northwest Washington, D.C., as a direct response to the health care and related needs of these refugees.

La Clínica began on the third floor of a former Presbyterian church on Irving St. near the corner of 15th St. in Northwest Washington, D.C., as a one-room free clinic operating one night per week in collaboration with the Central American Refugee Center (CARECEN) and Plenty International, who developed and offered services to this refugee population. The steps to climb up to the clinic were many, the room was drafty, cold in the winter and hot in the summer. By 1995, La Clínica had expanded to several rooms on the third floor of the former church/school building and incorporated as a separate non-profit 501(c) (3) entity.[1] Over the years, La Clínica del Pueblo's services have evolved to address the changing complexion and health needs of its patient and client population. Still primarily Latino immigrants from a wide variety of countries in Central and South America, patient population also includes the U.S.-born sons and daughters, even grandsons and granddaughters, of immigrants who first came to the Washington, D.C., metropolitan area in the early 1980s. The key to the clinic's success is delivering its services in Spanish, the predominant language of its patient and client population, in a way that is sensitive to their cultural backgrounds and beliefs.

Since an important underpinning of its philosophy and approach to service delivery has been to provide access to quality health care as both a human right and responsibility, patients are encouraged to take responsibility for their own health, while advocating for their own rights and those of other Latino residents living in the Washington area. In its early years La Clínica del Pueblo's voice was an important force in pushing for reform in the U.S. government's military policy in Central America. With the end of civil strife in Central American countries during the 1990s, it has increasingly focused on advocacy for equitable access to quality health care for Latinos living in the Washington area regardless of whether they are U.S. citizens or residents.

Based on fieldwork research developed by La Clínica del Pueblo between June and December of 2007, this chapter focuses on this Latino health center as a case of study describing and analyzing its evolution, within the context of international, national, and local developments with a focus on the Latino community in the District of Columbia, while highlighting its "essence" —those characteristics that give it special identity.[2] When I did this fieldwork, La Clínica del Pueblo had provided more than 55,000 services to over 7,500 individuals and had eighty-five culturally competent staff members who spoke Spanish, three quarters of them Latinos from Central and South America, and over one hundred volunteers, most from the surrounding Latino community and several of them patients. Operating six days a week, the health center offered expanded services and innovative programming in primary care focusing on family medicine [and including alternative medicine], mental health, HIV/AIDS prevention, social services, interpretation services, community health outreach and education, and advocacy.

FIELDWORK RESEARCH: OBJECTIVES AND METHODOLOGY

This case study was designed to focus on objectives that were identified as a result of intensive early discussions with key case study audiences.

First, to chart the evolution of La Clínica del Pueblo over the nearly twenty-five-year period since it was established within the context of international, national, and local developments and with a focus on the Latino community in the District of Columbia. Second, to identify what can be considered as La Clínica del Pueblo's "essence" or those characteristics that give La Clínica its special identity and how this "essence" has fared over the years. Third, to explore the impact that its approach and services have had on its patients, staff and volunteers, and on the Latino community in Greater Washington. Fourth, to identify what individuals have had a close affiliation with La Clínica over the years and to identify its strengths as well as its challenges and areas for improvement. And fifth, based on the above, to identify lessons learned for La Clínica del Pueblo itself and for primary care health clinics that serve populations with similar characteristics.

During this research, 143 individuals were interviewed including a sample of La Clínica del Pueblo's patients, current and former staff, volunteers, members of the Board of Directors, and individuals from outside of La Clínica del Pueblo who were familiar with its history and its services. These interviews followed a set of protocols developed in advance for each target group. Interviewees were asked to share something about themselves, including where they were born and, if born outside the U.S., how they got to the U.S. and what life was like when they arrived. The interview then turned to the interviewee's connection to La Clínica del Pueblo and reflections about their experiences. Patients, current and former staff, and volunteers were asked to comment on how their affiliation with the health center had impacted their lives. All interviewees were asked to reflect on what they saw as La Clínica del Pueblo's strengths along with challenges or areas for improvement.

Most interviews lasted approximately one hour. In a number of cases, individuals were interviewed multiple times. All interviews were confidential, and quotes included both in the case study document and in a previous report have been approved by the individuals quoted. In addition, a document review was conducted and the author participated in and observed a number of La Clínica del Pueblo events.

FOUNDATION AND EVOLUTION

La Clínica del Pueblo is Born (1983–1988)

La Clínica del Pueblo was founded in Washington, D.C., in 1983 by a group of Salvadoran activists (from the Central American Refugee Center, CARECEN) and North American hippies living in a group home (Plenty International) who saw the need to provide health services to refugees from El Salvador fleeing the civil war in their country. In its early years, La Clínica del Pueblo operated as a free clinic. It was run by volunteer staff and medical providers (residents from Washington area hospitals and local doctors) who came every Tuesday night to the Wilson Center, located on Irving St., N.W. near 15th St., to provide medical services free of charge to anyone who walked in the door. Latin Americans and North Americans, many of them activists, were trained as health promoters to assist the doctors with intake, interpretation, and other services. During this period, La Clínica received small donations from the Mayor's Office on Latino Affairs (OLA) and local church-related organizations.

From the time it was established, La Clínica del Pueblo gained the reputation of being a safe place where undocumented refugees—many traumatized by their experiences in Central America, coming to the U.S., and then as unwelcome newcomers in the U.S.—could come to receive compassionate assistance from people who were dedicated to helping them in any way they could. Access to quality health services as a human right was an important principle from the start. For the Salvadorans volunteering their services at La Clínica del Pueblo, there was never the notion that this health center would be needed for more than a couple of years. After all, their plan was to return to their country when the war was over.

Juan Romagoza Assumes Leadership (1988-1995)

With the arrival in 1988 of Dr. Juan Romagoza (himself a refugee from El Salvador and a victim of torture at the hands of the Salvadoran military) to become its director, La Clínica del Pueblo expanded the scope of its services to include mental health as well as health education, outreach, and prevention. Alternative approaches to medicine were introduced out of respect for prior experiences and expectations of patients who in their countries of origin had benefited from cures provided by local faith healers. A conscious effort was made to demystify the role of the doctor, and to impress upon patients that the physician was not the "god" in the white coat whose word was to be taken without question.

Concurrently, the definition of quality health services as a basic human right was expanded to include access to quality health care as a human right *and* a responsibility where the patient was encouraged to assume responsibility for her/his health care. During this period La Clínica patients, staff, and volunteers became actively involved in demonstrating against U.S. military policy in Central America. For many, both patients and staff, who had been victims of human rights abuses in their own countries, exercising their right to protest was therapeutic.

Slowly, La Clínica began to grow. La Clínica's supporters from Central America realized that, contrary to initial expectations, they were destined not to return to Central America but to settle in the greater Washington, D.C., metropolitan area. With small, and primarily discretionary, grants from local foundations, La Clínica was able to hire individuals to provide the backstop support needed to run the Tuesday night clinic. A 1989 grant from the Washington Office on Latin America (OLA), made it possible for La Clínica to initiate a program to provide HIV/AIDS testing and limited clinical services to Latinos with HIV/AIDS.

There were other opportunities for growth and diversification in services during this period. In 1990 La Clínica received its first federal multiyear contract, through the Catholic Archdiocese of Washington, to provide physicals to Vietnamese refugees. La Clínica was able to stretch this funding to cover some of its administrative expenses. In 1991, in keeping with its philosophy of the importance of prevention, La Clínica organized its first large health fair. By 1993 health fairs, held annually and coordinated by La Clínica, were attracting up to 3,000 participants.

In early 1994 La Clínica successfully mobilized, with the active participation of its patients, to exert pressure on CARECEN's board of directors to gain independence from CARECEN (which it had outgrown) and become its own 501(c) (3) non-profit entity. By mid 1995, when the split became official, La Clínica had an annual budget of $800,000; a paid staff of 25; and a phalanx of devoted volunteers. La Clínica had expanded its services to five days a week and was providing specialty clinics in HIV/AIDS, adult medicine, pediatrics, and alternative medicine.

Becoming an Independent Entity (1995 -2003)

The period was one of tremendous growth for La Clínica del Pueblo. Realizing that reliance on small foundation grants was not sufficient if it was going to move toward becoming a full-fledged medical clinic, La Clínica made the decision to also seek grants and contracts from the Federal and Washington, D.C., governments. During this period La Clínica's annual budget expanded to $4.6 million. Paid staff increased to approximately sixty. In 1996, it started establishing the infrastructure for what has become a comprehensive medical interpretation program. Also in 1996, Dr. Juan Romagoza was the recipient of the prestigious Robert Wood Johnson Community Health Leader award, which "recognizes individuals who overcome daunting obstacles to improve health and health care in their communities". With this award—the first of many for Dr. Romagoza, La Clínica's departments, and other La Clínica staff— came not only funding but recognition of La Clínica's accomplishments and increased offers of funding from other sources.

In the latter part of the 1990s La Clínica added health and health policy to its advocacy agenda. During this period La Clínica's leadership, staff, and patients joined forces with other private health clinics in Washington, D.C., through the Non-Profit Clinic Consortium, to pressure the D.C. government to provide health insurance to Washington, D.C.'s, underserved population. Their collective efforts paid off. In 2001 the D.C. government closed D.C. General Hospital and, with the revenue freed up, established the D.C. Health Care Alliance, an insurance program for low-income D.C. residents whose incomes are under 200% of the Federal Poverty Level. The D.C. Health Care Alliance also provided badly needed revenue to non-profit health clinics serving the poor. An important outcome of the D.C. Health Care Alliance legislation for the D.C. Latino population was that it opened up eligibility to undocumented D.C. residents to receive health insurance.

The period from 1995 to 2003 saw major changes in La Clínica's provision of medical services. For the first time La Clínica hired a full-time, paid, medical director. New medical staff was also hired, and the medical clinic began providing services on a daily basis. Collaboration was established with Howard University Hospital wherein La Clínica offered opportunities for Howard residents to rotate to La Clínica. In return, Howard University Hospital provided a steady source of funding, specialty care, and hospitalization services to La Clínica patients, free of charge. With the transition to a new medical director, La Clínica changed its focus from a specialty clinic model to a family practice model.

During this period, and in order to increase funding for patient care, La Clínica took the decision to accept reimbursement from Medicaid. This decision was taken after spirited debate among La Clínica's patients, staff, and members of the board. For those who were in disagreement with accepting reimbursements from Medicaid, the concern was that this meant that La Clínica would no longer, technically speaking, be a free clinic.

As the result of a decision to seek a federal grant, La Clínica's HIV/AIDS program expanded dramatically. In addition to serving HIV+ patients, La Clínica launched a large HIV/AIDS prevention program. Volunteer HIV promoters, trained by La Clínica, spanned throughout the city in search of Latino populations at risk of contracting AIDS. As part of this expansion in HIV prevention services, La Clínica began to provide innovative programming targeted at reaching high risk populations, including: Latino men who have sex with men and Latino transgender women, a bold initiative that has become incorporated as a routine and welcome part of its program.

In 1997, and after extensive mobilization where its patients played an active role, La Clínica was able to persuade the D.C. government to assist with the purchase of an old building in the neighborhood. The remainder of this period was spent undergoing a protracted capital campaign to raise money for a total renovation of the building for La Clínica's use. In 2000 La Clínica established a small social service department. This department is staffed by case managers who provide services primarily to La Clínica's HIV+ patients. Also in 2002 La Clínica was the beneficiary of two grants from the Substance Abuse and Mental Health Services Administration (SAMHSA) for its mental health program. With this significant infusion of funding, La Clínica's mental health department moved from depending primarily on volunteer therapists to having full-time therapists on its payroll.

Moving to a New Building (2003-2007)

In April of 2003, La Clínica moved to its current location on 2831 15th St., N.W. The new building was the culmination of many desired improvements. It offered ADA accessibility, an elevator, properly functioning heating and cooling (no more overcoats in the exam rooms), much more adequate space, and new equipment. It was wired for a computer network that would bring the modernization of patient and employee data management, and ready access to internet resources for doctors. The new space had a safe place for children to play while their families awaited appointments. It had, uniquely, a chapel, considered culturally and emotionally important to La Clínica's integrated approach to health.

During this period, La Clínica continued to improve its administrative and management systems, including: with its Board of Directors developing a Strategic Plan, instituting patient satisfaction surveys, and conducting an employee morale survey. La Clínica's Board of Directors took steps to improve its organization and structure, including moving to monthly board meetings, establishing term limits for board members, increasing its patient membership to more than one half of the board, and instituting a nominating committee for recommending board directors and officers.

Activism, an ever present part of La Clínica's identity, moved to a focus on specific health and related issues of concern to the Latino population: diabetes, obesity, and immigration policy. In addition, the directors of both the HIV/AIDS and the Interpretation Departments were very active, working within the coalitions that they belonged to, in pushing for improvements in services and policy in their areas. The medical clinic and the HIV/AIDS departments continued to grow and improve their services. The medical clinic added new medical providers and moved to an open access system which dramatically reduced the percentage of no-shows. The HIV/AIDS department became La Clínica's best financed department. Innovative prevention efforts, through paid and volunteer HIV promoters, expanded La Clínica's outreach to areas and localities of Washington, D.C., that it had not been to before.

Between 2003 and 2007 La Clínica's mental health department continued to provide one-on-one therapy. With funds from SAMHSA, the Mental Health Department organized and ran three innovative psycho-educational group therapy programs: for individuals with histories of alcohol and drug abuse; for the elderly Latino population (Mis Abuelitos); and for families who have experienced trauma (Mi Familia). In 2005 La

Clínica's interpretation department established a web-based database that made it possible to better coordinate interpretation services for 40 entities throughout Washington, D.C., mostly health clinics to whom it was, by now, providing interpretation services. In 2006 La Clínica made health education and outreach into its own department. In addition to being responsible for organizing and conducting health fairs (which, starting in the late 1990s, became smaller and more frequent), this department also initiated an innovative diabetes education program designed to provide comprehensive services (nutrition education, an exercise program, one-on-one home visits) to patients with diabetes. In the summer of 2007 La Clínica was advised that its request to become a Federally Qualified Health Center (FQHC) had been granted. Also in the summer of 2007, La Clínica's long-time leader Dr. Juan Romagoza announced that he would be resigning to return to El Salvador to continue with the medical outreach to the country's poor that he had begun in the late 1970s before he had to flee the country.

La Clínica as of December, 2007

As of December, 2007, the date that data gathering for this case study was completed, La Clínica had eighty-five individuals on its staff, over a hundred volunteers and a budget of $7 million from sixty-five different funding sources. During the 2007 calendar year, La Clínica's medical clinic, which operates under a family practice approach, had 15,858 client encounters; the mental health department had 4,975 client encounters; the HIV/AIDS department had 113,054 client encounters; the social services department had 5,102 client encounters; the interpretation department had 10,839 client encounters; and the education and community outreach department had 9,988 client encounters. In addition, La Clínica facilitated 2,365 referrals that made it possible for its patients to visit private doctors, hospitals, and other medical facilities to receive specialized services that were not available through La Clínica. As needed, the patients who received these referrals were accompanied by interpreters provided by La Clínica. These visits were either free of charge or covered under the D.C. Health Care Alliance or Medicaid.[3]

IMPACT ON PATIENTS, STAFF, VOLUNTEERS, AND LATINO COMMUNITY

Impacts on patients

Nineteen of the twenty-four patients interviewed for the case study commented on how their experience with La Clínica benefited them in their lives. Five patients (26 percent) indicated that La Clínica had given them the opportunity to grow/change their way of thinking. Five (26 percent) said that La Clínica had become like a second family. Four (21 percent) indicated that La Clínica, through the medical services it made available to them, literally saved their lives.

Two of these nineteen patients share their observations on how La Clínica has benefited them in their lives. In order to protect their privacy, these individuals have been given fictitious first names.

> *Lorena*: I owe my life to La Clínica. They detected my thyroid condition and made arrangements for me to go to a hospital to be operated. In addition, La Clínica is like my family, because this is what happens in a family. If you have a problem, they are there to help you. That's the way La Clínica is. They call me to let me know if there is something I need to do. My daughter needs to see a specialist. They give me the directions for getting to the specialist's office and put them in an enve-lope.
>
> >*Roberto*: My life changed completely, 360 degrees. Dr. Alma started by clarifying everything in my mind, she started putting all the things clear on the table. She is very direct in telling you the things, she doesn't hide anything. She told me that being gay isn't to be embar-rassed about, you have to be proud of your traditions, your culture, and what you have to offer to others and not because you are gay. All that matters is the kind of human being you are, to respect others, to love nature, to love yourself as a person, your family and all the people around you. She gave me those tools. She helped me to be strong, to be persistent.

Impacts on Staff and Volunteers

Over half of the twenty-seven La Clínica staff and volunteers that were asked about the impacts that La Clínica had on them mentioned two themes: the fact that through their relationship with La Clínica they have been given a special opportunity to both learn and grow (eighteen responses or 67 percent) and that, through their relationship with La Clínica, they have undergone personal change or improvement (fourteen responses or 52 percent).

In the words of two of La Clínica's staff members:

Brigida Guyot, emigrated from Bolivia in 2000. She has been affiliated with La Clínica since she arrived (first as a volunteer HIV promoter and subsequently as a member of La Clínica's HIV department):

> Someone gave me a hand and supported me. They didn't resolve my problems but at least someone took the time to open the door, to listen, listen and listen. I was given the opportunity to participate in a com-prehensive training course to be a health promoter. The course helped me to understand the multiple problems of immigrants: legal social, medical. As an immigrant I saw that I was a perfect person to talk to other immigrants.

Look at where I am. Sometimes people ask me, "What is it with La Clínica? With your capabilities you could obtain a better job at a better salary!" They don't understand that I fell in love with La Clínica and that La Clínica received me with a great deal of compassion and watched me grow. Sometimes I get home tired, with many emotions that I need to process. But I prefer this to coming home empty. This way I can give more to my family.

Dr. Madeline Frucht-Wilks is a family practitioner who has been working part-time at La Clínica since 2001; Madeline is currently the lead clinician at La Clínica.

I consider my position here to be a privilege. As a physician I feel that way in any setting when a patient confides in me, and shares a window of their life. The difference here is that I am also invited to share a culture. My patients and the staff have been wonderful teachers.

I have learned a new style of medicine. Where I was taught to maintain a completely professional relationship, I now know when it is appropriate to share my own stories, who needs to see a photo of my children before discussing their problems, and who I need to see with the extended family in the room. I have learned about how people make do with such limited resources. I have been welcomed into homes, and saw hammocks strung from walls, and now understand how so many people can comfortably sleep in one room. I will never look at the faces serving me in my community in restaurants, construction, and housekeeping the same way.

Impacts of La Clínica on the Latino Community Living in the Washington Area

While it was not possible to obtain numerical data to back up assertions—as had been the case with patients, staff, and volunteers—this case study would be remiss if it didn't remark on the impacts that La Clínica del Pueblo has had outside of its walls, on the hundreds of thousands of Latinos living in the Washington metropolitan area. La Clínica is cognizant of the fact that many Latino immigrants to the Washington area had never in their lives been to a doctor and of the importance of providing them with sufficient knowledge to permit them to detect and prevent chronic disease before these diseases become extreme. Accordingly, La Clínica has developed and maintained an extensive health outreach and prevention program that has, over the years, reached tens of thousands of Latinos living in the Washington area. These Latinos have been reached through multiple means:

- Through La Clínica's HIV/AIDS promoters who go to the far corners of Washington, D.C., to educate people on AIDS and to persuade them to get HIV/AIDS screening.
- Through the health fairs that La Clínica has sponsored on a continuing basis since 1991 (at the beginning, large yearly or semi-annual

events and now smaller health fairs conducted two or three week-ends a month in churches and other venues throughout the city in communities where there are large concentrations of Latinos).
• Through messages on preventive health and good health practices in the local Spanish media (including multiple appearances of its director, Juan Romagoza, and other staff on local television and radio programs broadcast in Spanish).

In addition, through its innovative interpretation services program, La Clínica has taken the initiative to train individuals, primarily from the Latino community, to accompany non-English speaking patients (primar-ily Spanish speaking) to appointments with specialists. Thanks to this program, which now incorporates forty service delivery organizations in the greater Washington area (most of them health clinics), thousands of non-English speaking residents have been able to be seen by medical specialists and walk out satisfied that they both have been able to have their concerns heard by the specialists and that they fully understand the guidance the specialists are providing to them.

Through advocacy efforts on behalf of the underserved Latino popu-lation living in the Washington area, La Clínica has opened opportunities for Latino immigrants to receive health services for which they might not otherwise be eligible.

Through its participation in the Non-Profit Clinic Consortium, which played a pivotal role in establishing the D.C. Health Care Alliance (a free health insurance program that covers all Washington residents who are at or below 200 percent of the Federal Poverty Level), La Clínica has been able to ensure the incorporation of undocumented Latino D.C. residents as beneficiaries. La Clínica has also, through annual community fora, drawn together La Clínica patients and others to provide feedback to the authorities responsible for administering the Alliance. La Clínica, as a member of the D.C. Language Access Coalition, has advocated for legis-lation that obligates government services to provide language access for non-English speaking patients. La Clínica has also played a lead role in holding the D.C. Department of Health accountable for appropriately channeling Ryan White HIV/AIDS funds to D.C. health clinics.

STRENGTHS AND CHALLENGES AS A MEDICAL SERVICE PROVIDER

La Clínica's Strengths

Ninety individuals interviewed for the case study commented on what they saw as La Clínica's strengths. There was remarkable agree-ment among those interviewed (patients, staff, volunteers, board mem-bers, individuals from outside of La Clínica who are closely familiar with its services) regarding La Clínica's strengths. The data from patients interviewed for the case study, who are included in this pool of ninety individuals, corroborate data from patient satisfaction surveys conducted by La Clínica in 2005 and 2007.

Table 1.1.   La Clínica del Pueblo's Strengths

Strengths mentioned by 10 or more interviewees	Numbers	Percentages
A caring and friendly environment	35	39%
Staff commitment to quality & professionalism	24	27%
Staff commitment to La Clínica's mission	20	22%
A sense of family/community	18	20%
An organization that is of and for the community	18	20%
Patients treated with dignity and respect	13	14%
Cultural sensitivity/in touch with the needs of the patients	13	14%
Openness to/acceptance of diverse populations	13	14%
Juan Romagoza as a leader and moral authority	13	14%
A place where one's views are listened to	10	11%

Two of the twenty-four patients interviewed on this topic comment on what they see as La Clínica's strengths. An important message that comes out in both testimonies is the dedication of their doctors to providing them with the best quality and most comprehensive care possible:

Teresa: I have gone to La Clínica when I am sick. Dr. Bombard took charge of doing the diagnosis. She tried to figure out what I really had. That is something very good. There are many doctors that do analyses and then say they don't know. She is concerned about me. The Patient Care Coordinators are very cooperative. Once I go into the exam room they give me advice, they are friendly, and they care. When I am waiting to see the doctor there are many people that come to do health education, to teach us how to keep from getting sick. There are other programs in the waiting room. This is very good, everything that happens around the doctor's visit.

Yanira: Dr. Meredith has fought by my side. She has worked hard to address what has happened to me. She is always on top of things. For example, when the medicine for my breast cancer was bothering my liver she stopped the medication for a month in order to observe me. She sent me to the oncologist to change the medicine. There came a time when I thought I was going crazy. She asked me what was happening. I was embarrassed to talk about my personal situation. She sent me to a therapist at La Clínica.

Also included in the pool of ninety interviewees was a volunteer doctor at La Clínica. Dr. Helen Burstin is the Senior Vice-President for Performance Measures of the National Quality Forum. She has served in a volunteer capacity as an internist with La Clínica since 2000. She is also the Vice-President of La Clínica's board of directors.

> *Dr. Helen Burstin*: What struck me when I first came to La Clínica was that it was a place with almost nothing but it did remarkable work with patients. They got great care. True primary care was delivered. Patients got the same doctor every time. The doctors bent over backwards to get meds, to have mammography done for their patients. It was a place that was able to do a lot with a little.

Kathy Freshley, Senior Program Officer at the Eugene and Agnes E. Meyer Foundation, and Sharon Baskerville, Executive Director of the D.C. Primary Care Association, were also in the pool of individuals interviewed. Having known and worked closely with La Clínica for many years, Freshley and Baskerville provide a special "outsider perspective":

> *Kathy Freshley*: La Clínica's strength is Juan himself. Because of his experience, his personal story, he has been a person that other immigrants and refugees have trusted. Many people knew he had gone through similar experiences. Juan talks about Liberation Theology, that poor people deserve health care, a home, jobs, a chance. There is that deep understanding and respect. There have been many people who have volunteered at La Clínica who have shared that vision.

La Clínica developed early specialty programs that were unique. They have a strong HIV/AIDS program and a mental health program. Their program in HIV/AIDS incorporates men who have sex with men and transgender women. They have been very innovative given the Latino culture. They have been not only bold but rare. They have put together a strong team of very committed volunteers and staff.

> *Sharon Baskerville*: La Clínica continues to see the holistic need in serving people. They appreciate that, without focusing on the entire person, better health is hard to achieve. They have begun a process of stabilizing their funding stream to something that is not solely philanthropy and contracts. They have a management structure that has worked up until now; it is not in its nascent phases. La Clínica is a complex, multipronged organization. The fact that they managed up until now without disaster says something is going right there. They have different departments that have grown in competency each with its own autonomy.

Challenges Faced by La Clínica

Patients, on the one hand, and La Clínica staff, volunteers, board members, and interviewees from the outside, on the other, had different perspectives on the subject of challenges and areas for improvement. As can be seen in the text box below, patients' concerns (which were not many) centered primarily on a desire for: (a) more and expanded services, and (b) a reduction in the waiting time for their appointments. La Clínica staff, especially those in the medical clinic, expressed concern over being overworked and overwhelmed. There was also concern about pending realignments in physical space in the medical clinic to accommodate an anticipated increase in volume of services under FQHC.

Table 1.2.   Challenges Faced by La Clínica del Pueblo

Challenges faced by La Clínica del Pueblo	Numbers	Percentages
La Clínica Patients		
N	24	
None	6	25%
Expand services/patients to be seen	6	25%
Reduce waiting time to see doctors	5	21%
La Clínica Staff/Volunteers		
N	55	
Staff overworked/overwhelmed	10	18%
Limitations in physical space	9	16%
La Clínica staff, volunteers, board members and individuals from outside La Clínica		
N	65	
Challenges to La Clínica's essence with growth/change	37	57%
Financial stability	19	29%
Need for improvements in internal management with growth	16	25%

The principal concern expressed by La Clínica staff, volunteers, board members and individuals from the outside had to do with the challenges to La Clínica's "essence" or "heart" associated with growth and change. This was followed by concerns regarding financial stability and the need for improvements in internal management with growth.

   Two interviewees, one a member of La Clínica's staff and the other an individual from outside who has worked closely with La Clínica over the years, comment on the challenges to La Clínica's essence with growth and with the two key transitions taking place at the time this case study was conducted: the departure of Dr. Juan Romagoza and La Clínica's becoming an FQHC.

   Member of La Clínica's medical staff: Change is around the corner, not just Juan's departure but the boon of becoming an FQHC also means more oversight and more regulations than before. My fear, and that of others, is that to meet the various requirements of FQHC, the spirit and reality of what La Clínica does is going to have to change in a way that will make us practice medicine differently. I believe that we ultimately will be required to increase the number of patients/day, which put us into a category of almost a managed care business. One of the strengths we have now is that we, the clinicians, are able to some degree more than other places actually hear our patients. Their needs are very complicated, their psychosocial needs are equally as important as their physical needs and the two, of course, are linked. We already over-stretch ourselves with our patients in the amount of time we have allotted. To imagine we will be required to squeeze more people with the same complicated issues into the same amount of time is an unhappy thought for both the provider and the patient.

A person from the outside that has worked closely with La Clínica over the years: FQHC is looked at as a way to achieve sustainability. La Clínica has money to move forward on their renovation. How are they going to get all this done? The competing priorities are enormous for staff that is already overwhelmed. How do they realistically do this with the current structure? Are they really sitting down and saying how are we going to get all this done? They want to plunge into a building in Ward 5 for which they will need $20 million but they haven't thought this out. It's almost like nobody thought they would get FQHC. My fear is that they will be compelled into taking decisions that aren't strategic. The critical piece is, are they seeing this as whole cloth, the strings required, and the UDS reporting, corporate compliance? The Feds will probably give them a couple of years to meet these requirements.

LA CLÍNICA'S "ESSENCE"

The fact that La Clínica's essence is challenged by change—the departure of Juan Romagoza and La Clínica's becoming an FQHC—is nothing new. La Clínica's essence has been under challenge since the day La Clínica was born nearly twenty-five years ago. Challenges have come from the need to look for funding to provide services to meet the evolving needs of patients. Many of these funding sources, like FQHC, have imposed requirements that have seemed to go counter to La Clínica's essence. The internal requirements of growth have added further challenges. And, yet, somehow La Clínica has been able to weather these challenges while maintaining its essence.

So, the question becomes, just what is La Clínica's "essence"? When asked to identify what they saw as being the key elements of La Clínica's essence, the individuals interviewed for this case study pointed to the following. Many, not surprisingly, mirror what they saw as La Clínica's strengths:

1. La Clínica was created by the Latino community for the Latino community: a large proportion of the staff has similar backgrounds to and "look" like the patients.
2. La Clínica staff deeply care about their patients and clients; they are committed to going the extra mile to meet their needs.
3. Patients and clients at La Clínica are treated as equals—with dignity, and respect. Part of treating them with dignity and respect is seeking out, listening to, and acting on their feedback and suggestions.
4. La Clínica provides a refuge, a secure and trusted place; for many, La Clínica is like a second family.
5. La Clínica provides health care that is culturally sensitive, relevant, and that evolves to meet the changing needs of its patients and clients.
6. La Clínica approaches its patients in a holistic manner: as beings that have physical, mental, emotional, spiritual, socio-cultural, and political needs.
7. The staff at La Clínica go out of their way to do everything possible to ensure that every patient/client knows that s/he has the right to adequate health care as well as the responsibility to make sure her/his health needs are met.
8. La Clínica's philosophy is based on the premise that advocacy, making one's voice heard, is fundamental: as a means of pushing for change, providing patients and staff with a vehicle for exerting their rights, forming community, and providing a therapeutic vehicle for many individuals whose rights have been violated.

Two patients share their views of La Clínica's essence:

> *Guillermo*: One of the most magical things that happens at La Clínica is that the structure isn't linear; once you walk in you are part of La Clínica. This is first thing you sense. If you have a complaint, you can raise your voice and Juan's or Alicia's door is always open. Through my years living here, who did I come to say I was jobless, when I didn't have money to pay rent? They immediately put me on an emergency fund to pay rent. They gave me food cards from the Safeway. Every time when I come with an emergency I sense I am as important as any other priority going on. I don't feel like I am being put aside. There is a sense of empowerment. It is important to love and safeguard this place—do what is in one's power to keep La Clínica running. This is my commitment.
>
> *Susana*: La Clínica is caring. It was created by and for the people. It has a familiarity with the culture of the people being served. The staff are invested in their patients. There is a bond with every patient. If the patient is not doing what he or she should be, there is a sense of a failure among everyone trying help the patient. They ask, "What is it that we aren't doing?"

Robert Hardies (Pastor of All Souls Unitarian Universalist Church and a member of La Clínica's Board of Directors) and Rebecca Muñoz (Communities of Faith Coordinator in La Clínica's HIV/AIDS Department who began as a volunteer in 1995), comment on what they see as the key ingredients that make up La Clínica's essence. In addition, Sara Coviello (management consultant who assisted La Clínica with its capital campaign in 2001/2002) provides an outsider perspective.

> *Robert Hardies*: La Clínica's essence lies in its radical commitment to its patients and its staff. Juan Romagoza has exemplified this radical commitment through his servant hood to his people. He is a values-based organizational leader who has a holistic commitment to his people. We are not talking about health care narrowly defined. We are talking about advocacy, work on the social justice level. What is phenomenal at La Clínica is a leadership that is not only culturally sensitive and devoted to its patients and staff but one that is willing to push the cultural bounds. It is amazing to see little old Salvadoran ladies and transgender Latinos in the same waiting room.

> *Rebecca Muñoz*: La Clínica is a place where we can accompany people in their pain, support those who have been abused. It isn't just that the patient comes to La Clínica, the doctor examines the patient, and give the patient medicine. When you interview patients who said that they have changed, they have another way of thinking. They now know they can be part of a family. This is due to the way that Juan has carried out his approach, to give life to the teachings of Bishop Romero. Advocacy is something that we as Latinos have a hard time doing. We come from countries where someone else's will is imposed, where we are not permitted to value our rights. The rich have the right to do what they want with the poor. La Clínica has taught us that we all have the right to health.

> *Sarah Coviello*: The care and concern they have for the people they serve is pervasive. I see this in other organizations, but La Clínica isn't as caught up in organizational pettiness. They seem so absolutely mission driven and constituency driven. I don't think they would care whether the organization continues as much as they would care whether their services continued and their constituents were served in the same manner with same quality of services. The deep caring is pervasive, and to me, this group walks the talk to a degree that others don't.

Opportunities and Challenges to La Clínica's Essence with the Transition to FQHC

Becoming an FQHC provides La Clínica with a number of opportunities that will also make it possible to grow and enhance its essence. With the stability of funding that will become available through FQHC, combined with the opportunity to increase its third-party reimbursements from patients that qualify for Medicaid, La Clínica will be able to serve an increased number of patients. Through FQHC, La Clínica will have access to a broad range of opportunities for training and technical assistance. With this assistance, La Clínica, among others, will be better able to track the quality of patient services and, with this information, have the potential of further improving the quality of its health care service delivery. Eventually, through an expected increase in third party reimbursements from Medicaid, La Clínica will have increased discretionary funding which will make it possible to maintain as well as expand culturally relevant/holistic programs.

Becoming an FQHC also presents challenges to La Clínica, especially to its essence. One challenge, referred to above, is the requirement that La Clínica institute a sliding fee scale, which goes against the philosophy that health care as a human right should be free. Another, which is a source of distress to a number of La Clínica's current medical staff, is the pressure to increase the number of patients per hour that doctors see with the potential of adversely affecting the culturally sensitive approach to treating patients that La Clínica prides itself on.[4] Increased requirements for data gathering and reporting, if not handled well, can take away from quality patient time. In addition, La Clínica will have to decide—with the financial benefit under FQHC of receiving increased reimbursements for patients on Medicaid—how to maintain the balance of the services that it currently provides to undocumented immigrants, a number of whom live in Maryland and Virginia, and who do not qualify for either Medicaid or insurance available under the D.C. Health Care Alliance. La Clínica is also beginning to see indications that private foundations, with the knowledge that La Clínica has become an FQHC, are contemplating withdrawing their small donations of discretionary funds that La Clínica has welcomed and depended upon over the years. Finally, with the adoption of FQHC, La Clínica becomes more dependent on yet to be seen U.S. government policies related to the provision of government-financed health care, something which was a source of concern to several of the La Clínica staff interviewed for this case study.

LESSONS LEARNED

There are a number of lessons to be learned from the La Clínica experience that are relevant for La Clínica as it expands its services and for community health clinics serving similar populations. In particular, these lessons are relevant for community health clinics in the U.S. and in other areas of the world where there are refugees that need health and related care. These lessons are also relevant for community health clinics that serve populations that live under tremendous stress and whose rights have been denied: be they economic rights, victims of abuse and domestic violence, or other forms of abuse.

1. *The importance of having at the helm a leader and moral authority that, while willing to accommodate to the pressure of change, maintains an eye on the "essence."* This role was played in an exemplary fashion for over twenty years by Dr. Juan Romagoza. A visionary but also a pragmatist, Romagoza recognized that with growth, and especially with accepting non-discretionary sources of funding, comes the need to compromise. His "can do" message, that "we can take on challenges as they arise but we will not change our identity," has been fundamental in moving the organization forward while maintaining its essence.

2. *The importance of selecting and nurturing a management team that buys into the essence and passes it on in their dealings with their department staff.* It is a tribute to Romagoza and to the individuals he selected to become part of his management team that the persons that run La Clínica are firmly committed to La Clínica's essence. For the most part, they exemplify this essence in the way they run their departments.

3. *The importance of having individuals on the staff of the health clinic who are committed and who care.* The doctors and other staff who are employed by La Clínica are not there for the money or because it is simply a "job." They are there because they deeply believe in what they are doing, because they want to serve people in need, and because they want to provide service with excellence.

4. *There are advantages to being a health clinic that was established by and for the community.* The fact that the majority of the La Clínica staff themselves come from similar backgrounds as their patients/clients has made it easier for them to be able to identify with their patients/clients and their needs and to provide them with health services that are culturally relevant. A special feature of La Clínica's medical program is the patient care coordinators, individuals trained as medical assistants who are from the Latino community. Their role extends beyond that of the traditional "medical assistant." They accompany the patient throughout the medical visit — doing intake, during the consultation with the doctor, and helping the patient with follow up after they see the doctor. Since they are of the community and speak the same language, they are able to establish relationships of trust with the patients that make it possible for them to learn things about the patients that doctors wouldn't ordinarily become aware of.

5. *The importance of being seen as a safe and trusted place, a "sanctuary," a home away from home.* Added to this is the importance, in this safe place, of establishing an atmosphere that respects the dignity of

each refugee; a refuge or sanctuary where patients can open up and express their multiple needs, and where the staff does the best that it can to see to it that these needs are addressed. This is particularly relevant for populations that have been or are being persecuted, be it because they are residing illegally in a country where they are not welcome or because they have another "identity" (men who have sex with men, transgender women) that is not accepted by their families and by broader society.

6. *There are benefits to taking the time to address the needs of the patient in a holistic fashion.* An important underpinning of La Clínica's "essence" is that patients need to be treated as human beings with a wide range of health needs that are interrelated: physical, mental, emotional, spiritual, socio-cultural, political. While all of us benefit from this type of approach, patients who are victims of trauma manifest the traumas they have experienced in many ways: emotionally, physically, in the way they relate to family members.

7. *There is much to be learned from the way in which La Clínica has incorporated volunteer service into its model.* The benefits are multiple: volunteers provide La Clínica with person power to run its programs (such as health fairs, community outreach) that do not required individuals with specific certification. They also permit La Clínica to identify potential new staff members. For the volunteers the benefits are: a feeling of belonging, the satisfaction of helping others, the ability to appropriately contribute their skills (especially applicable for volunteers with medical backgrounds who aren't certified to practice in the U.S.), the ability to acquire new knowledge and skills (for personal benefit and potentially for future employability). For some, especially those who have experienced trauma, volunteering can be therapeutic.

8. *It is important to adopt a proactive approach that involves constantly reaching out and consulting with one's clients, seeking client/employee input in decisions to be taken.* La Clínica has a patient committee that meets bi-monthly to provide feedback to the director and personnel of La Clínica. Community fora, open to La Clínica patients and the broader Latino community, provide individuals with another place where they can air health needs and concerns. Through its HIV/AIDS promoters who fan out throughout the Washington metropolitan area and through its health fairs, La Clínica is able to identify health trends and related needs in the Latino population that assist it in its programming. When an important decision is to be taken, such as instituting a sliding scale under FQHC or selecting Romagoza's successor, the views of patients and staff are actively sought out. By adopting this approach, La Clínica sends out the message to its patients and others that they are worthy of dig-

nity and respect, that they are equals, and that their views are valued.

9. *While it comes with risks, there are advantages to being "bold" and holding to one's values.* A continual theme that emerged in the interviews is that La Clínica has remained true to its values and what it sees as being the "right" thing to do, even when it means possibly ruffling feathers. La Clínica has been lauded, by individuals interviewed from the outside, for taking the risk of reaching out to Latino men who have sex with men and Latino transgender women and incorporating them alongside their broader patient population in their medical program. In being an active participant (and in some cases the leader) in successfully lobbying the D.C. and Federal government for change in health policies that impact on the Latino population, La Clínica has taken the risk of alienating the very agencies that, up to now, have helped finance its services.

10. *Approaching health as both a right and responsibility is tremendously empowering.* It makes sense from a patient health perspective to demystify the role of the doctor as the all-knowing authority upon whom the patient puts responsibility for his/her health care, and instead impress upon the patient that the primary responsibility for the patients' health care (especially with patients who have chronic diseases such as diabetes and high blood pressure) is with the patient. This approach, fundamental to La Clínica's essence, is also empowering, especially for Latino immigrants who have come from countries where they have few rights and where what the doctor says is "the last word."

11. *There is value to adopting a comprehensive approach to advocacy.* Advocacy in the La Clínica context involves individual advocacy by the staff on behalf of each patient. It also involves advocacy at a systemic and political level. Patients are encouraged to participate in events organized by La Clínica (protest marches, community fora with city authorities, and interviews with the media) in which they advocate for new and important health and other initiatives. In addition to being empowering, for individuals who have been traumatized, participating in a broader social cause can also be therapeutic.

CONCLUSION

La Clínica del Pueblo would not be what it is today without the vision and leadership of Dr. Juan Romagoza, who has been its director since 1988. Romagoza, a humble man who has led by example, has been more than a director of a community health clinic. He has also been a community activist and a community leader. As Dr. Romagoza prepares to re-

48 Marcia Bernbaum

turn to El Salvador he leaves behind a well structured organization, staffed by individuals at all levels who are committed to La Clínica's "essence."

Romagoza has been fundamental in defining La Clínica's "essence." Being the visionary leader that he is, Romagoza has also been instrumental in encouraging La Clínica to grow and to adapt to changing circumstances. As La Clínica has grown and changed, Romagoza has kept his eye on La Clínica's "essence," ensuring to the extent possible that this "essence" has not been excessively diluted or distorted.

Remaining to be seen is how La Clínica's "essence" will survive this latest transition to becoming an FQHC which moves it into the mainstream of the U.S. community-base health care delivery system. If La Clínica's history has anything to say and if the individual selected to be La Clínica's next Executive Director is someone with the same philosophical approach, then the bets are on that La Clínica will maintain its "essence" and, in so doing, continue to keep true to its mission which is "to provide culturally appropriate health services to persons in the Latino community regardless of their ability to pay."

It seems fitting to close this summary of the case study with a quote from one of the many interviews that took place with Juan Romagoza while undertaking the case study. In this interview Romagoza remarks on the importance of maintaining La Clínica's essence while at the same time adapting to make way for change:

> The spirit that motivated the creation of La Clínica was not only to respond to physical health needs but to create our own original model based on our culture and based on the reality of the countries we had come from. We were the artisans of our own project, with its own sauce and flavor. Our program wasn't only culturally sensitive where we used our own language, our own traditions, our own schedule, our own model. It was also based on the concept that health is not only to cure but to prevent, orient, promote, and most importantly to defend. We motivated the patients to take ownership of La Clínica, that this was their project; that they needed to take charge.
>
> In the early years we were on the defensive. That way we were able to maintain our model. We were convinced that we would be returning to El Salvador. There was little motivation to integrate our model into the broader medical mainstream. But as time went on, we saw that we could not continue to operate in a parallel fashion. We realized that we had to find points in common with the larger system. We began to establish contacts with other community clinics, to participate in coalitions.
>
> As time went on we started to become concerned. We saw that we couldn't survive only with funds from private foundations. We had a meeting of our Board. We were looking at how we were growing, a lot of things needed to take place before we could qualify for FQHC status. We decided not to apply for now. Our priority was to have a building;

we couldn't embark on two big projects at the same time. There was still resistance to FQHC.

Nevertheless, there was a lot of pressure from the Latino community for health services and limited resources to attend to their needs. Funds from private foundations are transitory. We said, providing health services is the work of the government, we have to walk together, we can't work parallel to the system. We decided to apply for FQHC status.

Some members of the Board asked me: "Are you prepared for this?" I said "We have to do it."

NOTES

1. 501c3 a category in the United States that provides federal tax-exempt granted to non-profit organizations seeking charitable, educational, health, environmental, and other social purposes.

2. This research was first drafted in the report "A Health Clinic for the People, by the People: a Case Study of La Clínica del Pueblo."

3. In terms of its population, 68 percent of La Clínica's patients were residents of Washington, D.C., 22 percent of Maryland, and 8 percent were from Virginia. The majority (58 percent) of the medical clinic's users were uninsured; 5 percent were on Medicaid; 1 percent were on Medicare; and 36 percent had other forms of insurance (the primary among them being the D.C.).

4. La Clínica's doctors currently see an average of two patients an hour. The target, under FQHC, is to expand to three patients an hour.

TWO

Hogar Immigrant Services: Serving Diverse Ethnic Groups

A Case Example of Interagency Collaboration

Patricia S. Maloof

António Guterres (2008), United Nations High Commissioner for Refugees from 2005 to 2015, refers to the twenty-first century as "a century of people on the move." While human populations have migrated throughout history, the world is now witnessing the greatest number of refugees since World War II along with large numbers of migrant workers moving across borders.[1]

Crossing borders is one thing, yet settling into a chosen new country and being able to actively participate in all sectors of the new society involves a complex process of "integration." While there are multiple definitions and terms with similar yet distinct meanings (e.g. acculturation, assimilation), today integration is seen in general terms as referring to the ability of immigrants and their children and grandchildren to "actively participate in a host society through equality of opportunity and absence of discrimination on grounds of ethnicity or national origin." Ghosh (2005) clearly summarizes the three main approaches to integration globally: (1) multiculturalism as seen in Australia, Canada, and the United States—the cultural contributions of different immigrant populations are "formally recognized and permanently accommodated;" (2) assimilation as seen in France—immigrants are expected to "adhere to the customs, characteristics, and cultural mores of the host country;" and (3) segregation as seen in the Gulf States, Japan, and certain communist countries in Central and Eastern Europe—where the model rests on ho-

51

mogeneity of ethnicity and culture. Each of these three general models can have several variants, depending upon whether the host society or immigrants bear the responsibility of adjustment; how much cultural diversity is viewed as acceptable in the receiving community; and what methods, if any, are used to encourage the acceptance of the foreign-born. While exemplifying a multicultural model, the last decades in the United States have seen a change from melting pot (which implies homogeneity), to salad bowl or orchestra (which more readily recognizes individual cultures), to tapestry to describe integration.

The United States ranks ninth out of thirty-eight countries on the Migrant Integration Policy Index (MIPEX, 2015) with a score of sixty-three, placing it in a "slightly favorable" range. MIPEX measures integration in thirty-eight countries (all EU Member States, and Australia, Canada, Japan, Iceland, New Zealand, Norway, South Korea, Switzerland, Turkey, and the USA) with 167 indicators and eight policy areas (access to nationality, anti-discrimination, education, family reunion, health, labor market mobility, permanent residence, and political participation).

When it comes to how to approach integration on a national basis, efforts by the United States in the past have often been described as "laissez-faire," relying on a "strong labor market and high-quality public education" (Jiménez, 2011).

There are several notable exceptions to the laissez-faire approach. For decades, a public private partnership has existed in the refugee resettlement program between the federal government (the Department of State and the Office of Refugee Resettlement in the Department of Health and Human Services), state governments, and the non-governmental sector. Resettlement stresses integration and self-sufficiency through early employment as new arrivals receive orientation, assistance with finding jobs and enrollment in language classes, and are linked with resources in their receiving communities. The agencies that resettle refugees are required to hold quarterly Stakeholder Consultations as part of their contract with the Department of State that include discussions of numbers and characteristics of arriving populations, ability to serve the projected caseload, best practices, and addressing issues that are a challenge to resettlement.

The US Citizenship and Naturalization Service (USCIS, 2015) includes integration as one of its six goals in its mission statement—"Supporting immigrants' integration and participation in American civic culture." From FFY 2009-2015, USCIS awarded $53 million in competitive grants through its Citizenship and Integration Grant Program, intended to build capacity in support of citizenship preparation with citizenship classes and assistance with naturalization applications.

On November 21, 2014, President Barack Obama, by presidential memorandum, established the White House Task Force on New Americans (2015). Assigned the responsibility to develop a federal interagency coordinated strategy to immigrant integration, the Task Force released its action plan in April 2015. The approach is based on three "pillars" of integration—civic, economic, and linguistic, and stresses the collaboration of all sectors—government (federal, state, and local), private and nonprofit sectors, educational institutions, community-based organizations, religious institutions, the business sector, and more. To support this strategic plan, in September 2015, the federal government announced the launch of the "Building Welcoming Communities Campaign" (Abramson and Rodríguez, 2015) as a way to encourage the development of the three pillars within local communities. It takes deliberate and coordinated efforts from multiple sectors of society to facilitate and support long-term coordination. The experience of the Catholic Legal Immigration Network, Inc. (CLINIC) has demonstrated that the faith-based sector can be particularly supportive of integration efforts as affiliated agencies have the trust of immigrant groups, have a long history of providing extensive services without discrimination or ability to pay, and are often the first to be consulted when a crisis or need presents itself.

The United States finds itself at a defining moment in its rich immigrant history. Millions of diverse people live within its borders, pray at various places of worship, make contributions in the economic sector, help children excel in school, and bring new traditions and languages to their neighborhoods. Faith and community-based organizations have made great strides in recent years on many of the most critical issues that impact immigrants, including citizenship and naturalization, domestic violence, human trafficking, and more. Faced with these immediate needs, some organizations have seen integration as a secondary concern. However, integration must be taken seriously—and addressed as purposefully—as other issues confronting immigrant populations. An integrated community offers its residents equality, security, a sense of belonging, and adequate access to resources.

Historically, the Catholic Church has been an immigrant church and has the capacity to offer coordinated leadership, guidance, and inspiration to dioceses and parishes across the nation on integration efforts. The Catholic Legal Immigration Network, Inc. (CLINIC) is attempting to address integration at the community level. Based in the D.C. metropolitan area, CLINIC has the largest charitable immigration legal service network in the nation. Through its daily interactions with affiliates around the country, CLINIC identified a great need for a coordinated and focused approach to increase the immigrant integration efforts within local communities. As a result, during 2013, it laid the foundation for its Center for Immigrant Integration. This chapter will address the Center's core approach, present characteristics of successful integration programs, explain performance measures, and offer a case example from Northern Virginia.

APPROACH—A COORDINATED SERVICE-DELIVERY MODEL

The Catholic Legal Immigration Network, Inc. (CLINIC) supports the largest network of charitable immigration legal programs in the nation. Its mission is to promote the dignity and protect the rights of immigrants in partnership with a dedicated network of community-based immigration legal programs, both Catholic and non-Catholic (35 percent). The goal of CLINIC and its network is to provide a full range of comprehensive legal and non-legal support services to the most vulnerable and disenfranchised migrants (e.g., children, refugees, asylum seekers, detainees, families in need of reunification, laborers abused in the workplace, victims of domestic violence, and survivors of human trafficking—regardless of age, ethnicity, gender, race, religion, or other distinguishing characteristics). Gaining a visa to enter the U.S. on a green card is, for the majority of immigrants, the first step toward integration. For others, adjustment of status (receiving a green card and work authorization) is a first and critical step for integration. Thus the legal immigration process and assistance given is a stepping stone to help make that transition.

Founded in 1988 with seventeen affiliates, CLINIC's network now includes more than 270 affiliates in more 400 locations in forty-seven states, the District of Columbia, and Puerto Rico. The network serves more than a quarter of a million people annually. CLINIC has four core areas of work: Advocacy, Capacity Building, Religious Immigration Services, and Training and Legal Support. Aware of the importance of being representative of the populations and communities served, CLINIC has seventeen languages on staff and at least 77 percent know a language in addition to English.

Through its daily interactions with dioceses around the country, CLINIC identified a great need for a coordinated and focused approach to increase the number of immigrant integration programs within Catholic communities. CLINIC officially launched its Center for Immigrant Integration in January 2015, although steps have been taking place since 2013 to prepare the overall framework. These foundational steps reflect the inclusion of integration into: (1) CLINIC's Core Standards for membership, (2) CLINIC's immigration program management curriculum, (3) the annual survey of affiliates, (4) the question guidelines for annual calls, and (5) a self-assessment tool for affiliates.

The Center is a web-based portal for integration-related resources for agencies offering charitable immigration legal services. The Center seeks to promote a purposeful, focused, and strategic approach to increase immigrant integration programming within its network.

As a Catholic organization, CLINIC builds on a history and presence of the Catholic Church and integration:

- Social teaching of the Church

- Long history as an immigrant Church
- Well-established programs serving myriad needs
- Large numbers of foreign-born parishioners
- National platform for advocacy

The Center uses the definition of integration put forth by Grantmakers Concerned with Immigrants and Refugees (GCIR)—*a dynamic, two-way process in which newcomers and the receiving society work together to build secure, vibrant, and cohesive communities* (Petsod, 2006, p. 25).

With inter-agency collaboration comes an approach that includes:

- Coordinated service delivery model—holistic assessment of needs and response
- Whole person focus—strengths and challenges are both recognized
- Agency priority—beginning with leadership direction and throughout the agency, integration is seen as a priority for inclusion in all agency policies and programs
- Strategic plan—integration is included in the agency's strategic plan
- Measurable goals—not always easy to identify, yet necessary in order to determine if integration is taking place
- Increased accountability—with all staff and programs including integration as part of work plans and strategic goals, all recognize their role and responsibilities

Funded in federal FY2016, CLINIC is developing the *Paving the Path to Citizenship and Integration for Refugees Project*, a three-year national citizenship capacity building effort with the goals of (1) increasing the number of refugees applying for naturalization and (2) increasing the number of refugee resettlement organizations authorized to provide naturalization assistance to their clients. The three-pronged approach includes: (1) the implementation of a Citizenship Navigator (CN) Training and Support Project to sponsor a network of refugee resettlement service providers educated in and encouraged to promote citizenship for refugees; (2) building the capacity of refugee resettlement offices and refugee mutual assistance associations (MAAs) nationwide by supporting and encouraging the development of authorized immigration legal service provision; and (3) establishing a Civic Messaging Campaign (Text4Refugees) to provide selected and easily accessible citizenship resources and information to refugee communities. Text messages and other materials will be available in the top five languages spoken by refugees in the United States, currently Arabic, Somali, Nepali, Sgaw Karen, and Spanish. This project will enhance existing efforts by creating access to standardized citizenship services to all refugee populations, eliminating gaps by geographical regions, language, and capacity.[2] This project is intended to build upon and enhance the current integration efforts of the Center.

CHARACTERISTICS OF SUCCESSFUL INTEGRATION PROGRAMS

Based on more than a quarter of a century of working with community-based organizations, sometimes implementing programs from the beginning and enhancing others, CLINIC staff have identified common principles that guide their work in working with local agencies to implement best practices in integration. These common principles include:

- Subsidiarity—based on Catholic social teaching, CLINIC's approach identifies need, builds on assets, and supports potential for growth within its affiliates. There is recognition and respect for the different roles and capacities of partner agencies and encouraging them to assume as much responsibility for newcomers as they can while allowing CLINIC to focus limited resources on needs that local programs cannot meet. With each point of intervention, CLINIC considers the balance of what it can do and what the partner can do. This helps to guide what types of resources CLINIC develops, the technical assistance that it provides, and how it judiciously assesses distribution of funds that can be distributed from the national office.
- Integration is a complex process—it takes place in multiple sectors of the community and across multiple immigrant populations who are dealing with integration on individual, family, and community levels.
- Integration requires time—as a process, it should be viewed as spanning more than one generation.
- Integration is a multi-dimensional process—it requires the participation and "buy-in" from all groups represented in the community.
- Integration takes place at the local level—even with technical assistance from the national office, the local community takes an active role in the identification of needs, approach, characteristics, ideals, and issues that are important to its members.
- Integration efforts should focus on what community members bring to the community—not what they lack. An assets or strengths approach provides a good start and a positive approach to dealing with identified needs or challenges.

In planning and implementing its approach to integration, staff have been guided by the work of successful programs sponsored by the Catholic Campaign for Human Development and presented by John Hogan (Hogan, 2003). Summarizing the main characteristics contributing to the success of these efforts with each appearing as a theme from the individual chapters, CLINIC staff includes such elements as (1) participation is key, (2) identify the crux of the issue, (3) get power (leadership) involved, (4) develop a vision and market it, (5) train leaders from the community, and (6) establish partnerships accessible to newcomers.

PERFORMANCE MEASURES

Integration programs will not succeed if the goal is to "fix" something. Instead, initiatives should strive to create a community in which the assets of all members are nourished and used to create a more cohesive society. Positive outcomes arise from programs that reflect the unique needs and assets of a community. Social cohesiveness is achieved through an effort to understand the inspiring nexus between American values and norms and immigrant aspirations for their lives in their adopted home. Social justice can be achieved by working to promote justice and fair treatment for immigrants and other vulnerable populations overall in the community. Strengthened families can result from offering immigrants various social services, including education, health advocacy, federal benefits, and increased access to quality child care. Civic participation, family unity, and quality result from promoting civic engagement, family reunification through immigration, and legal means to represent immigrants in their defense.

Successful programs in CLINIC's network have the following components: Common integration is part of the mission, objectives are clear to everyone, a Point Person assumes responsibility for maintaining a focus on integration, a timeline helps to keep everyone on track with objectives and activities, successes are highlighted, and attention is given to outcome measures. CLINIC has developed an integration self-assessment tool for immigrants (in English and Spanish) and for agencies. Local agencies can use it with clients to measure such indicators as having a bank account and a job; ability to communicate with their child's teacher; comfortable calling the police if help is needed; visiting the local library, public parks, or other public spaces; feeling that one's home town is a welcoming place to live; and more.

To measure their own capacity to promote integration, CLINIC's affiliates can use a self-assessment tool that looks at such indicators as—do all staff members understand the definition of immigrant integration; does the agency assist clients in pursuing citizenship, including offering immigration legal services, English as a Second Language and citizenship test preparation classes, and registering to vote; as an agency, do staff promote immigration as a benefit to the community; is immigrant integration included in the strategic plan, mission statement, and measurable goals; are immigrants represented on the Board; does the agency advocate for immigrants within the community at the local and state government levels; does the agency offer leadership development opportunities to immigrants; and does the agency ask the immigrant community what services they need or what support they would like in their efforts to become involved in their community.

On its website, CLINIC presents the following ideas to help facilitate and encourage integration within an agency and within programs:

Ideas for Agencies to Try (Speasmaker, 2015)

- Include immigrant integration goals and objectives in the agency's strategic plan;
- Align the goal of immigrant integration with the agency's overall mission statement;
- Deliberately seek to hire a workforce reflective of the members of the community;
- Ensure that members of the Board reflect members of the community;
- Create opportunities, such as focus groups or round table activities, for the immigrant community and the receiving community to let the agency know what services are needed;
- Proactively promote positive stories about new relationships between newcomers and the receiving community through media contacts;
- Host leaders from different sectors of the community in an informal meeting, such as a coffee and chat event, to get to know each other; and
- Establish partnerships with well-established organizations that are also focused on immigration integration (parishes, civic groups, Rotary clubs, etc.).

Ideas for Programs to Try (Speasmaker, 2015)

- Develop leadership training and opportunities for immigrants;
- Focus training programs on helping immigrants recover (or recertify) their profession in the U.S. or acquire new skills for a new career;
- Host events that provide the receiving community and the newcomers a place to communicate and learn about each other;
- Ensure that voter registration is widely available to naturalized citizens and registration is available at naturalization oath ceremonies;
- Help clients open bank accounts and other financial products at a local bank;
- Ensure that community leadership recognizes the needs and contributions of the newcomers and invite them to events. For example, invite the Chief of Police or the Mayor to speak at Citizenship classes;
- Actively break down barriers to newcomer and receiving community interactions. For example, offer a Cultural Companion program where a staff member, such as the English language teacher, goes to a client's house to assist in learning about the community and accessing needed services;
- Invite former clients back to volunteer; and
- Establish Lunch and Learn opportunities at various workplaces.

In addition to working nationally with its affiliates, CLINIC also conducts administrative advocacy at the federal level directed to encourage integration. For example, the President's Task Force on New Americans invited public comment to submit suggestions and ideas for consideration by the Task Force's plan for increasing and improving immigrant integration in the United States. On February 4, 2015, CLINIC submitted thirteen comments and suggestions along with an additional five comments for USCIS to consider for supporting and strengthening its naturalization policies and programs (*See* CLINIC, 2015).

As part of its State and Local Immigration Project, CLINIC (2013) has developed *Welcoming the Stranger Through Immigrant Integration*—a toolkit that describes five state-level legislative initiatives that can be enacted to build communities and make states stronger by educating and including immigrants. These integration measures recognize the economic, social, and cultural contributions immigrants make at the local and state levels. In addition, these integration measures have strategic importance because they counteract and neutralize anti-immigrant bills and give legislators positive bills to support in the often contentious area of immigration policy.

Integration initiatives have gained momentum throughout the U.S. in recent years. Each of these measures ensures that all residents can succeed and contribute to building stronger communities and stronger states. Examples include legislation that creates tuition equity for all, legislation that strengthens human trafficking laws, legislation that invests in English language instruction, using the budget process to integrate immigrants, and other legislation such as access to financial aid and protection against immigration consultant fraud. Under each of these categories, the toolkit contains components of successful laws, model language for the law, state models, when legislation is not an option, talking points, responding to common misconceptions, etc.

CASE EXAMPLE: HOGAR IMMIGRANT SERVICES, CATHOLIC CHARITIES OF THE DIOCESE OF ARLINGTON (VA)

According to the American Immigration Council, one in nine Virginians are immigrants; in 2013 Hispanics/Latinos comprised 8.6 percent of the population and 2.7 percent of voters; in 2014, their purchasing power amounted to $20.6 billion; and in 2007, Hispanic/Latino businesses registered sales of $5.9 billion and they had a workforce of more than 34,000 people.[3] Virginia is also a major state for refugee resettlement so diverse populations and languages are represented throughout the state. However, approximately 70 percent of the foreign-born population is settled in the Northern Virginia Metropolitan Statistical Area (Gunter, 2014).

According to its mission statement,[4] Hogar Immigrant Services "responds to the Catholic Church's call for social justice by welcoming the stranger to this country, regardless of ethnicity, religion, nationality, or ability to pay. Our goal is for immigrants to achieve self-sufficiency and participate fully in the greater community."[5] Founded in 1981 in recognition of the need, Hogar Immigrant Services is a program of Catholic Charities of the Diocese of Arlington (VA) and provides (1) legal immigration consultation and representation and (2) educational programs. Several languages are represented on staff. Approximately 95 percent of the clients are Spanish-speaking and most of the staff members speak Spanish. More than 91 percent of Hogar's clients live below the federal poverty level with services provided using nominal fees and fee waivers. Current and prior funders of services include the Community Foundation for the National Capital Region, Virginia Department of Education, the Virginia Literacy Foundation, and the U.S. Citizenship and Immigration Services (USCIS).

Hogar's legal services are largely family-based, serving to reunite families; help eligible immigrants to apply for citizenship or to become lawful permanent residents; and assist clients who are eligible for Deferred Action for Childhood Arrivals (DACA), Nicaraguan and Central American Relief Act (NACARA), Special Immigrant Juvenile Status (SIJS), T Visas, Temporary Protected Status (TPS), Violence Against Women Act (VAWA), and U Visas. Referrals are provided for cases not handled by the office such as applications for asylum, assisting persons in detention, and employment-based cases. Monthly naturalization workshops are held at various locations throughout Northern Virginia and staff conduct local area workshops on immigrants' rights for immigrants, immigration advocates, and service providers. The impact of Hogar's legal services is illustrated by the following example.

> A 12-year old from Mexico was reunited with his mother (a victim of domestic violence) and his siblings. Mother and son had been separated for 10 years. The reunion was a particularly emotional one because the boy's older brother had passed away during the prior year.[6]

Hogar has offered English for Speakers of Other Languages (ESOL) classes since it opened its doors. All staff members are certified in the Comprehensive Adult Student Assessment System (CASAS). Classes for adults are available at literacy, beginner, intermediate, and advanced levels. In the mid-1990s, Hogar began offering citizenship test preparation classes to prepare individuals to pass the naturalization exam. A nominal fee paid by students covers the textbook and other materials. Progress of the students and effectiveness of the classes are measured with pre- and post-tests. Computer literacy classes and other workforce development initiatives prepare immigrants to participate more fully in the workforce. "Know Your Rights" workshops educate immigrants about their legal rights regardless of their immigration status. Hogar is sensitive to the need to encourage integration in other areas as well and thus will occasionally offer classes on starting a business, financial literacy, and other subjects that the immigrant community identifies as important. Student satisfaction is measured with an annual survey and through the use of focus groups, which provide more in-depth qualitative information.

Volunteers are the backbone of the program, including pro-bono attorneys and volunteer teachers who receive extensive training. For FY 2015 (July 1, 2014 to June 30, 2015), Hogar served 3,003 unduplicated clients. Of these, Hogar assisted 1,315 unduplicated clients with immigration legal services and had an approval rate of 98 percent of the cases that were closed. There were 1,688 adults who attended classes and for those students who completed the naturalization interview, 95 percent passed. A total of 745 volunteers contributed over 26,399 hours to the program.

When it comes to integration, the citizenship classes do more than improve English proficiency or help prepare immigrants for the naturalization interview. Brooke Hammond Pérez, Program Director at Hogar, explains that these classes encourage the students to participate more actively in their communities, learn about their civic responsibility, and gain proficiency in expressing themselves in a new language. She emphasizes that one of the most important impacts from the ESOL classes is the effect on parents and that they indicate they are better able to and feel more comfortable communicating on the job, with health care providers, and with their children's teachers.

In discussing integration, Ms. Hammond Pérez states while the term is difficult to define, she thinks of the term as meaning "we" and not "us" and "them." "There is not a sense of me helping you; we talk as equals."[7] She mentions the "coffee and conversation" sessions once a week after class when students and teachers sit and chat, helping to encourage interaction and share ideas. Agency integration efforts are deliberate as students are encouraged to participate more fully in the workforce and with civic engagement.

Examples of the importance of Hogar's work can be seen in the following comments about the achievements of former clients:

> A father of four children took ESOL classes to improve his English and computer literacy classes to improve his computer skills. After graduating from Hogar's classes, he was then accepted into Northern Virginia Community College and received a promotion at work because of his enhanced computer and English skills. He is now able to better provide for his family.[8]

U.S. Citizenship and Immigration Services (USCIS) recognized Hogar's program as a "Promising Practice" on its website and describes the celebrations that are held as each student naturalizes (*see*, USCIS). A calendar records upcoming naturalization interviews for the students. Upon successful completion of the interview, family, friends, mentors, and other students join in the celebration at Hogar. The newly naturalized student speaks to the group about his or her experience. Students are able to ask questions and the insight gained from a peer who has just completed a direct experience with the interview goes a long way in encouraging other students who have not yet been interviewed.

CONCLUSIONS

CLINIC's Center for Immigrant Integration is building its technical assistance and developing resources for its network using specific examples of the three prongs from the President's Task Force on New Americans— civic (assistance with immigration legal status), economic (tax assistance), and linguistic (ESOL and citizenship tests). It has designed its approach to technical assistance and resource development to include certain critical components—inclusion; assets approach; collective impact with CLINIC as the backbone agency for the network and the local affiliates serving as the backbone in their area; participatory research for the local communities to identify what they think are the major challenges and how to address them; local adaptation of best practices from other agencies; and using a strategic and deliberate approach, not just thinking or waiting for it to happen.

> CLINIC is a highly recognized and regarded nonprofit in the sector of charitable immigration services and integration strategies. Its structure is a network of locally-governed nonprofits meeting the unique needs of their respective communities of native and foreign-born. The network is formed around similar mission statements and shared values overarching different sectarian, non-sectarian, and humanitarian origins. The network is increasingly diverse in the organizations represented in the network and the immigrants assisted. Even so, the nonprofits view immigrants less as a client seeking a particular service but as a whole person with short- and long-term integration needs with ambition and talents. Within and around social services offered, there is a growing effort to engage immigrants in shaping their own futures, legal and otherwise. As such, immigration and immigrant integration are intertwined, creating greater social solidarity in the U.S. overtime within ever widening social spaces.[9]

NOTES

1. Acknowledgment: Special thanks are given to Jeff Chenoweth, Director, Center for Citizenship and Immigrant Communities, CLINIC; Brooke Hammond Pérez, Program Director, Hogar Immigrant Services, Catholic Charities, Diocese of Arlington; and Leya Speasmaker, Field Support Coordinator and Integration Program Manager, Center for Citizenship and Immigrant Communities, CLINIC.

They assisted in the development of this chapter by providing inspiration, freely sharing their program information, and reviewing and commenting on its contents. The author of this chapter was formerly the Director of Development at CLINIC and is now the Program Director of Migration and Refugee Services at Catholic Charities, Diocese of Arlington.

2. This entire paragraph description of the new project is directly quoted from the original proposal submitted to the Office of Refugee Resettlement, written by the current author while working at CLINIC, and included in this chapter with permission from CLINIC.

3. All data in this sentence are from the American Immigration Council. (2015). Fact Sheet. "New Americans in Virginia: The Political and Economic Power of Immigrants, Latinos, and Asians in the Old Dominion."

4. See Hogar website at www.hogarimmigrantservices.org/. Information in this section based on interview with Brooke Hammond Pérez, Program Director, Hogar Immigrant Services on July 7, 2015 and unpublished program materials with data provided by her to this author.

5. *See* Hogar website. Tab: About. www.hogarimmigrantservices.org/#!mission-statement/c1kwn. Last accessed September 21, 2015.

6. Unpublished Hogar materials.

7. Personal Interview. July 7, 2015.

8. Unpublished Hogar materials.

9. Unpublished quotation from Jeff Chenoweth, Director, Center for Citizenship and Immigrant Communities, CLINIC. October 6, 2015.

REFERENCES

American Immigration Council. (2015). Fact Sheet. "New Americans in Virginia: The Political and Economic Power of Immigrants, Latinos, and Asians in the Old Dominion." www.immigrationpolicy.org/sites/default/files/docs/new_americans_in_virginia_2015.pdf. (October 3, 2015).

Abramson, Jerry and Rodríguez, León. (2015). "A More Perfect Union—Building Welcoming Communities Campaign to Strengthen Immigration Integration." The White House Blog. www.whitehouse.gov/blog/2015/09/17/more-perfect-union-join-white-house-building-welcoming-communities-campaign. (October 3, 2015).

CLINIC. (2015). https://cliniclegal.org/sites/default/files/task_force_on_new_americans_2-4-15.pdf. (October 3, 2015).

CLINIC. (2013). *Welcoming the Stranger through Immigrant Integration.* https://cliniclegal.org/sites/default/files/immigration_integration_toolkit_sept_2013.pdf. (October 3, 2015).

Ghosh, Bimal. (2005). "The Challenge of Integration: A Global Perspective." In *Managing Integration: The European Union's Responsibilities Towards Immigrants.* Rita Sussmuth and Werner Weidenfeld (eds.). Washington, D.C.: Migration Policy Institute.

Gunter, Meredith. (2014). "U. Va. Study: One in Nine Virginians is Foreign-Born." *UVA Today.* news.virginia.edu/content/uva-study-one-nine-virginians-foreign-born. (October 3, 2015).

Guterres, António. (2008). People on the Move: The Challenges of Displacement in the 21st Century. International Rescue Committee UK Annual Lecture. London: United Nations High Commissioner for Refugees, Royal Geographical Society, London, 16 June 2008. www.unhcr.org/48873def4.html. (September 21, 2015).

Hogan, John P. (2003). *Credible Signs of Christ Alive: Case Studies from the Catholic Campaign for Human Development.* Lanham, MD: Rowman and Littlefield Publishers, Inc.

Jiménez, Tomás R. (2011). *Immigrants in the United States: How Well are They Integrating into Society?* Washington, D.C.: Migration Policy Institute, p. 1. www.migrationpolicy.org/research/immigrants-united-states-how-well-are-they-integrating-society. (September 27, 2015).

Migrant Integration Policy Index (MIPEX). (2015). www.mipex.eu/usa. (October 3, 2015).

Petsod, Daranee (ed.). 2006. *Investing in Our Communities: Strategies for Immigrant Integration.* Grantmakers Concerned with Refugees and Immigrants, p. 25. www.gcir. org/publications/toolkit . (September 7, 2015).

Speasmaker, Leya. (2015). Citizenship: A Step on the Pathway to Integration. cliniclegal.org/news/citizenship-day-citizenship/citizenship-step-pathway-integration. (October 19, 2015).

USCIS. Citizenship and Integration Grant Program Archives. www.uscis.gov/archive/ archive-citizenship/citizenship-and-integration-grant-program-archives. (September 27, 2015).

White House Task Force on New Americans (2015) Strengthening Communities by Welcoming All Residents: A Federal Strategic Action Plan on Immigrant & Refugee Integration. www.whitehouse.gov/sites/default/files/docs/final_tf_newamericans _report_4-14-15_clean.pdf. (October 3, 2015).

THREE

Pluralistic Universe in Multicultural Medicine

Latinas Adapting Cultural Heritage in Medical Fields

Lucy M. Cohen

The growth of multicultural neighborhoods and communities in the U.S. has contributed to a renewed interest in community health programs and practice in these changing settings. Authors suggest that multicultural-ism differs from models in which communities have been characterized by tightly knit boundaries and organizations. Multiculturalism is the co-existence of several cultures rather than the blending of various traditions into one heritage or way of life (Kottak and Kozaitis, 2003). Interest in this model of community organization is an outgrowth of my anthropological research doing fieldwork in community centers in the Washington, D.C., metropolitan area serving several immigrant groups as well as long time residents. This includes studies of selected neighborhoods with long time U.S. residents as well as immigrants from several world regions: African Americans, West Africans, mostly from Nigeria, and Latinos from di-verse countries, particularly Mexico and El Salvador.

In the 1960s, I worked in Washington, D.C., at St. Elizabeth's Hospital, a psychiatric hospital which at that time had 7,000 patients, the largest in the United States. I was involved with the decentralization of that hospi-tal within the community. We hoped residents could understand former patients, with whom there had been a great deal of discrimination. It was a pioneer experience not only for the health fields, but also for anthropol-ogists involved. We must keep in mind that Washington had the charac-teristics of a Southern city of that period. Southern meant segregation:

black people lived here, and whites lived elsewhere. The interaction of blacks meant that services of health for blacks were offered in one locality, while whites went for services elsewhere. To understand the anthropology in Washington one has to consider that the city has had influence on inter-ethnic relations and it strongly shaped the work that anthropologists conducted then. When Elliot Liebow (1967) did his research among street corner black men in Washington, D.C., which resulted in his well known book, *Tally's Corner*, he made us consider seriously the possibilities of what we as anthropologists could do in Washington. Later, an increasing number of Latin Americans began to settle in Washington and outlying areas. I worked as a volunteer in the Spanish Catholic Center and other sites. We offered services but we wanted also to increase the awareness of their presence in the area.

As the Latino women settled in Washington, one of the first active groups was of Puerto Ricans, many of whom worked with the federal government. I became involved with a committee of Latinas in Washington.[1] There was no segregation of newcomers. However, there still was memory of legal segregation between blacks and whites. I believe that the Latinos contributed to the development of what we now call multiculturalism in the city. At present, there are community groups from various parts of the world living next to each other in the Washington, D.C., metropolitan area to such an extent that our communities are no longer made up of single cultures. It is important for anthropologists to understand these processes since they cast light on the development of public policies regarding social and cultural processes which are basic components in all societies. We need to understand the direction of these processes with special interest in getting to know the social power structures and cultural values which are in them.

Along with the increase of multicultural neighborhoods in the Washington, D.C., metropolitan area, particularly with the arrival of Latino immigrants from Central American countries, one of the most significant present-day trends is the central role played by women who have to reshape the character of life in this country as well as the structure of communities in their home countries. As I have written in other publications (Cohen, 1973; 1979), migration patterns of undocumented workers differ from those of legal immigrants, particularly in the case of women who cross borders without documents. Central American women do not usually bring young children with them, since this is considered too grave a risk and children in the home country tend to be cared for, almost exclusively, by the maternal grandmothers. Women who act as leaders in migration engage in careful planning, particularly with the caretaking of children left behind (Cohen, 1981).

This chapter focuses on ways in which Latino immigrants and their children settle in multicultural communities in the Washington, D.C., metropolitan area. Drawing on my research and advocacy work, I will discuss models associated with the management of multiculturalism in health settings in the United States and illustrate these dynamics with two cases on the circumstances of separation and reunification of parents and children from El Salvador (Cohen, 1999). In both cases, the parents were undocumented during at least some of their residence in the United States, even though the children themselves eventually came to the United States with "proper papers." Implications for policy formulation and health and mental health programs using multicultural medical resources for prevention and care are discussed.

MODELS AND CULTURAL COMPETENCE MANAGING CULTURAL DIVERSITY

The concept of multiculturalism refers to the view that various cultures in a society merit equal respect and scholarly interest. It has been an important force in American society as diverse communities such as African Americans, Latinos, and other ethnic groups have examined their own histories in the 1970s and 1980s. Anthropologists and other social scientists have proposed various theoretical frameworks to analyze multiculturalism as a social phenomenon that occurs in contexts of different forms of social contacts by focusing on the presence or absence of conflict between different ethnic groups. In a final report "Defining Multiculturalism" submitted by Clara M. Chu to the Multicultural Populations Section of the International Federation of Library Association (IFLA) (2005, p. 1), she defines multiculturalism as the "co-existence of diverse cultures, where culture includes racial, religious, or cultural groups and is manifested in customary behaviours, cultural assumptions and values, patterns of thinking, and communicative styles." With this coexistence, one cultural identity does not prevail over other identities. People participate in multicultural communities without denying or hiding their own cultural identities. The existence of ethnic diversity is recognized while ensuring the people's rights to maintain their own cultures. Multiculturalism emphasizes that individuals from social and cultural minorities should enjoy, as an alternative to assimilation, full access to participation in the society. As an official policy, multiculturalism benefits not only individuals, but also the society at large by diminishing inequality and, consequently, social conflicts.

Conrad P. Kottak and Kathryn A. Kozaitis (2003, p. 49) note that the concept of multiculturalism differs from assimilation and pluralism by recognizing a multiplicity of legitimate culture cores or centers acknowledging cultural criteria as the source of group formation, and by promoting democratization and equity among groups. As a new moral order, multiculturalism pushes society toward sociocultural equity seeing the various segments of population, along with their institutions, behavior,

and beliefs, as having legitimacy and value. In this respect, multiculturalism is manifest in policy and laws that seek to redress economic, political,
and social inequities while combating discrimination based on factors
such as origin, sex, and age.

Aung San Suu Kyi (1991) has suggested that it is important to take
into account the different understandings of the concept to evaluate how
multiculturalism operates in contemporary societies. Broadly speaking,
approaches managing cultural diversity are classified by this author into
three models. First, an individualistic model exemplified by the French
national policy that is based on the principle of *jus solis*; without political
recognition of cultural minorities in the country, French citizens enjoy
equal civic rights as individuals. Although this individualistic model
could have allowed France to integrate its immigrant populations until
recently, French policy has had difficulties to cope with ethnic and cultural diversity, particularly with the arrival of new generations of Muslim
immigrants. Second, a model based on *jus sanguinis* represented by German and Japanese national policies. In contrast to the French approach,
citizenship has been based on ethnic origin. For instance, a third generation of Turks born in Germany or Japanese-born Koreans can obtain German and Japanese nationalities.

And third, a multicultural model illustrated by Australian and Canadian national policies. In the evolution of this model it must be highlighted, as Aung San Suu Kyi (1991) did, that Australian society is composed of aborigines and English people, and later populated by different
waves of immigrants coming from European countries and recently from
Asian countries (Castles, 1992; Castles & Miller, 1993). The Canadian case
also has several indigenous populations and English and French settlers
with important political consequences in the development of multiculturalism in the country.

Along with these models, Aung San Suu Kyi (1991) links these approaches to practices that she classified as demographic-descriptive,
ideological-normative and programmatic-political usages. The demographic-descriptive application occurs when multiculturalism is used to
refer to the existence of linguistically, culturally, and ethnically diverse
populations in a given society or nation-state. In the second usage, the
ideological-normative, multiculturalism is adopted to manage and organize political actions as responses to ethnic diversity. The programmatic-
political usage of "multiculturalism" refers to the specific policies developed to respond and manage ethnic diversity. In a national public policy,
the multicultural model is, therefore, the opposite of the assimilationist
model, in which minorities are expected to abandon their traditions and
values, replacing them with those of the majority: promoting the affirma-
tion and practice of culture/ethnic traditions.

In a related article entitled "The Coming of Age of Multicultural Medicine," Gail McBride (2005) discusses this concept as an illustration of the

circumstances in Stockton, California, which is California's largest agricultural valley where some 100 different languages are spoken. She states that: "Acculturation is difficult in the best circumstances, but what happens when people with limited or no proficiency in English have a medical problem? Many United States hospitals are required to provide some manner of interpreter services for people with limited English proficiency—but do these services also bridge the cultural divide?" She notes further that "meeting the challenge of providing health care for multicultural population is now a major movement that affects health care in a number of countries, principally the United States but also in European nation-states and Australia" (McBride, 2005, p. 181). As she points out, although the bulk of studies and commentaries on this issue grew in the 1990s, the literature dates back much further with medical anthropologists, among other social scientists and health professionals, in the 1960s and 1970s. She suggests that the provision of quality health care to those who differ from a country's majority population in terms of language and culture is a challenging task that does not yield to easy or quick fixes, but rather to consistent and determined efforts at improvement.

McBride (2005, p. 182) states that "the most common term used in this effort is 'cultural competence,' essentially defined as respectful knowledge of an attitude toward people from different cultures that enables health professionals who work with people from another culture to develop and use standard policies and practices that will increase the quality and outcome of their health care." This issue is particularly important for anthropologists and other social and behavioral scholars studying the immigrants who live and work in Washington, D.C., as the center of major metropolitan area. Health care constitutes a dominant concern for professionals, and the public, as efforts are made to understand how immigrants and minority groups communicate and manage illness as they reformulate beliefs and practices through contacts with representatives of popular and professional medicine. In this respect, I have underscored (Cohen, 1979) that "field work calls for an understanding of denotative and connotative aspects of the language which patients use to describe symptoms; we consider that spoken language has not only denotative aspects (what words stand for) but also connotative aspects (what words suggest)."[2] On the other hand, it is also important to be sensitive to the specific language and assumptions on the part of providers of health care services. Professionals who deliver health care frequently assume that patients not only accept the professional's explanations about the nature of illness but that they also will comply with their advice. Effective cross-cultural communication in medical care depends on personnel who speak a language of the patient and understand his/her ideas about the cause and cure of illness.

LATINAS ADAPTING TO CULTURAL HERITAGES IN MEDICAL
FIELDS

Good health is highly valued by Latino immigrants. The typical phrase *vale más la salud que el tesoro* (health is worth more than treasure) underscores the central place of this theme in their lives. Most researchers agree that there is no single integrated Latino theory of disease. Latin American popular medicine is multicultural in character. An important characteristic of this belief system is its capacity to adapt practices from various popular and biomedical concepts: Spiritualism, patent medicine, homeopathic therapy, and the professional biomedical traditions are combined to form a dynamic system (Cohen, 1979).

The popularly held explanations for illness, the wide range of practitioners consulted for health problems, and typical curing approaches, reflect this multicultural character. This can be noted through examination of the types of practitioners Latinas use for various types of health problems, and the commonly found processes through which cultural traditions are combined during the course of management of illness. As Latinas settle in the new setting they draw on various popular and biomedical traditions to prevent and cure illness. Latinas may fuse various popular and biomedical traditions without conflict, to offer rational explanations for etiology and health practices which they may not fully understand (Cohen, 1981). Finally, as immigrants gain new information, they adapt old and new belief systems by reinterpreting and reclassifying symptoms as they fit in their new life situation.

Since little attention has focused on the children left behind and the processes of reunification with parents after long periods of separation I will illustrate how Latinas adapt drawing on two cases of children who reunited with the parents in the Washington, D.C., metropolitan area (Cohen, 1999). Prolonged separation of children from their parents needs to be addressed in order to prevent ill health and serious distress.

As mentioned earlier, women who cross borders without documents do not usually bring young children with them, since this is considered too serious of a risk. Such mothers bring their children to Washington subsequent to their own entry and only when they feel that their job and living situation are stable enough to permit it. Children in the home country who are in the stages of early and late childhood tend to be cared for, almost exclusively, by the maternal grandmothers. Thus, the availability of support by their own mothers has made it possible for women to lead the movements of families and communities into the United States. In the context of present-day international migration, the movement and settlement of many immigrants of Latin American origin are led largely by women. Moreover, most of these women had begun to establish their own households in their countries of birth prior to immigration, and thus they are separated from children, husbands, or other relatives. This growing proportion of women of Latin American heritage who have led their own and their children's transnational movements has received limited attention in the literature about immigrants and their health.

The next sections present two cases on the circumstances of separation and reunification of parents and children from El Salvador while discussing implications for health and mental health. For some young people separations from parents and caretakers can be fraught with difficulties. An issue of interest is how young people manage these circumstances as they make accommodations in the country of birth and the site of resettlement.

When Parents Become Strangers: The Case of Rafaela's Health Problems

When Rafaela Hernández, a twenty-four-year-old Salvadoran immigrant, first came to the Washington health center where I met her, she complained of headaches, palpitations, and chest pressures. The clinical evaluations were negative. Upon further assessment her symptoms were associated with periods when she recalled negative or tragic experiences in her life. She had been reunited with her family in Washington three years earlier and described separation from her mother in the following words:

> My mother gave me away when I was ten months old. I did not live with her again till I was nineteen, when she brought me to the U.S. I grew up with my grandparents and with an unmarried aunt. This aunt got a special job which provided for my monthly expenses and school till I reached the ninth grade. To me, my grandmother is my mother. She taught me principles, morals, and responsibility.

In addition to the care of Rafaela, the grandparents kept one of Rafaela's brothers. The grandparents took in an additional child, the daughter of another of Rafaela's aunts who had also emigrated, five years after Rafaela arrived in this household. Eighteen years after her separation from her parents, Rafaela's mother arranged immigration papers to bring her and her brother to the United States. Since her mother had entered the United States without "proper papers," it had taken her a number of years to locate an employer who was interested in sponsoring her entry to the country. Not until after these papers were processed and approved was her mother able to put in the request to bring her children to Washington.

Rafaela's early period in the parental household in Washington was strained.

In her words, "Our parents are strangers." Nonetheless, she made the resolution to "move forward." She wanted to work and learn English so that she could fulfill a dream of working in an office. However, her mother asked that she first repay the sum of $1,000.00, plus other expenses incurred to bring her to Washington. So Rafaela was not able to study until she repaid her mother for the expenses of this trip. She obtained a part-time job, and it took her two years to repay the money that her mother had claimed. In the meantime, her relationship with her mother was strained, so much so that upon completion of the repayment she decided to live independently, moving out to live with a family from whom she rented a room.

Her mother became upset about Rafaela's departure from the family home. As a consequence, she would not talk to her even when Rafaela visited other members of the family. Not until several months later, when Rafaela went back to her home country to visit her grandparents, did her mother contact her to send a parcel to the family. Rafaela's visit to El Salvador was a fruitful experience. Both her grandfather and her grandmother expressed affection and sentiments of "welcome home." The visit reassured her of her continued positive sentiments toward the grandparents and their solicitous interest in her. During this trip she also visited her aunt to thank her for the many sacrifices she had made in providing for her education while she was a child. Rafaela told her that she would send her remittances as frequently as she could. This was not to be seen as "repayment" but as a token of appreciation.

Upon her return from this trip, Rafaela's mother met her at the airport. Since then, their telephone communication is more frequent, and Rafaela visits her periodically, when invited. Rafaela has also made some friends in her language school and at work. From Rafaela's perspective, the care offered by her grandparents was not a substitute for parenting. Rafaela states: "My grandmother is my mother." Her grandfather, who is "like a father," has been a source of wise advice. The aunt who paid for her early years of education in El Salvador now merits her remittances, a sign of her reciprocity for sacrifices made on her behalf.

Rafaela's sentiments of estrangement from her biological mother were heightened by her demand for repayment for the expenses of her trip and the paperwork involved. Not until she moved to an independent household, separate from her mother, did she feel that she could begin to establish her identity and experience a decrease of the physical symptoms that had burdened her since her arrival in the United States.

Sufferings for the Children's Sake: Marlene Molina's Case

Marlene Molina, a native of El Salvador, had been in the United States for a year and a half. I met her when she came to the health center to seek relief for her headaches, nervous tension, and a skin rash. She wanted also to find health resources for her mother who had been diagnosed as a diabetic. Marlene was twenty-one years old when I first met her. She had been separated from her parents when she was six years old. Her mother first emigrated to the United States to join an uncle in search of improved economic resources for the family because Marlene's father, who was a heavy drinker, did not provide enough to support the family. Soon after her settlement in Washington, her mother made arrangements to bring over her husband and their son.

Marlene recalls that when their mother's remittances arrived every month, the aunts would threaten to take the money away from them. They were said to have made up stories such as: "Your mother has abandoned you." Marlene believes that they tried "to put these ideas in our heads so we could love them more than we loved our mother." "They also wanted us to obey their orders which were usually to work harder than their own children . . . " Marlene countered their aunts' stories by such statements as: "A mother's love is different from all others. That is why our mother emigrated so she could support us. She had to do this because our father has been very irresponsible about family support, and his relatives would not help her either." Marlene recalls that her aunts did not welcome her responses. As she states it: "They were afraid of me because I did not pay attention to them. They called me a rebel . . . " As Marlene maintained this positive image of her mother, her older sister continued to defend her younger siblings from the aunts' demands. The responsibility of protecting her younger siblings from adult demands was a constant source of worry. Marlene believes that for this reason this older sister developed a persistent headache problem.

When Marlene was eleven, their older sister sent an urgent message to their mother in Washington that their lives with the aunts had become increasingly difficult. In response, their mother returned from the United States and stayed with them until the older sister finished secondary school and was ready to go to San Salvador, the capital, to study pharmacy in the university. The mother helped to rearrange their caretaking arrangements so that the three sisters resettled in the capital, when Marlene and her younger sister attended high school, and the older sister studied in the university. Their older sister exercised her authority as needed, saying: "Obey me because I am the mother here. Our other mother is in Washington."

Marlene emphasizes that her mother's suffering with the struggle for her children and husband have been major contributions to her ill health, particularly the onset of diabetes. She summarizes these beliefs and sentiments with comments such as: "Our mother has suffered for our sake so we can launch our lives. She has worked so hard so that we can overcome difficulties." Marlene worries about her mother and spends time helping her with needed medical resources. Her mother's recent diagnosis of diabetes had led Marlene to link her mother's sufferings with the onset of this illness.

Narratives of past and present efforts to cope with family illness are drawn upon as examples of how her mother has overcome the difficulties of life. For example, Marlene believes that one of her mother's early sources of suffering was with a life threatening illness of unknown origin that her oldest daughter experienced in El Salvador when she was a baby. For reasons unknown to her, the baby's body became swollen and she was believed to be close to death. The mother's household employer offered to help telling her that if she "gave her" the baby in a permanent caretaking arrangement, she would be cured. The employer also guaranteed provisions for the future lifelong medical care for the baby, when needed. "Our mother responded that she would never give up her baby." She emphasized: "I would rather die than give a baby away." Marlene believes that her sister is alive, thanks to her mother's care. She administered a series of sunbaths until the baby's symptoms disappeared.

Another of Marlene's mother's sources of suffering has been her husband's long-standing problems with alcohol. After he emigrated to the United States he worked but his continuous alcoholism made employment increasingly difficult. He stopped work altogether. Periodically, Marlene's mother has had to "rescue him" from the street where he slept among the homeless. All of this stopped a year ago after he was assaulted and beaten so badly, that he lost all his teeth. Since this incident, he has stayed at home and has abstained from alcohol. He is now beginning to work again.

With regard to Marlene's mother's diagnosis of diabetes, one physician is reported to have told Marlene's mother that her problem is not due to heredity. Both Marlene and her mother are sure that this diabetes is associated with the suffering she has experienced throughout life. The linkage of illness with the burdens of suffering is part of a long tradition in El Salvador and in other Latin American societies. Suffering is not an explanatory concept for single incidents of illness. It is a core concept that reflects lifelong moral and physical pain. When Marlene's mother was asked by an employer whether she might not want to "give her child away" (*regalar la niña*), she touched on a deeply felt sentiment associated with the essence of motherhood. For the mother, there was a difference between "giving a child away" to her employer, a stranger, and the placement of children with her relatives, when the circumstances of migration forced the separation and dislocation of households.

Vulnerability and Resilience among Children Left Behind

In this discussion on pluralistic universe in multicultural medicine I have re-drawn on the cases of Rafaela Hernández and Marlene Molina to illustrate the relevance of using a multicultural model in order to address contrasting aspects of the lives of young members of immigrant populations that should receive increased attention in research concerned with vulnerability and resilience in child development. As in the cases of these Salvadoran children who, as a result of their mother migratory processes, were left in the home societies, age of separation as well as selection of caretakers are factors that deserve consideration.

Children's ability to actively draw on the memories of parents during separation may be influenced by the age at which their parents left them with substitute caretakers. Rafaela was ten months old at that time her mother placed her with substitute caretakers. She finds her relationship with grandparents and her aunt a major source of inspiration for her identity and ideals as a young woman in a new country. Marlene was six years old at the time her mother left her with her grandmother and aunts. While residing with these caretakers, she actively drew on her mother's image and received protection from her older sister to deal with the aunts' demands. Since reunification, she has strengthened bonds with her mother and other family members. She has come also to a new understanding of the difficulties her mother endured and her continuous struggles. Daughter and mother interpret problems of health and illness within a framework that views suffering as a pervasive life force and a state of being.

The mothers' selection of caretakers, on the other hand, influenced the experiences of the children left behind. In the case of Marlene, her aunts assumed an exploitative relationship. Her older sister became an informal caretaker as a "defense" against the aunts. Eventually, the older sister became the de facto caretaker. In Rafaela's case, both grandparents and the aunt assumed clear responsibility for her care and for that of her brother.

IMPLICATIONS FOR POLICY FORMULATION AND HEALTH PROGRAMS

As increasing proportions of Latino immigrants enter the United States, they reshape the character of life in this country, as well as the structure of communities in their home countries. Three areas should receive special consideration in policy formulation: the impact of female leadership in migration, the call for integrated medical and psychiatric outreach programs, and the multicultural character of sociocultural change.

One of the most significant present-day trends is that women play a central role in the international environment of peoples in the Americas. Yet, they have been neglected in deliberations of immigration policies in the United States. Latinas who enter as the relatives of an immigrant and those who lead in resettlement are committed to activity in full-time work soon after their entry. This is highly significant since they are in the labor force to a greater extent than either the Latinas left behind or women in the United States labor force. Stereotypes of the Latina as a dependent and passively-oriented female who does not work outside the home have led us to neglect the reality that she is an active self-reliant person who does not stay behind to wait for husbands and brothers to help her with moves to new countries.

A second point about the Latina's migration is that she resettles during her active child-raising cycle. To accomplish this, she relies heavily on her bonds with maternal kin for child care. For a Latina who enters as an undocumented worker, in particular, the selection of substitute caretakers is essential since she may leave children behind for long periods, or at least, until they reach late adolescence. Substitute caretaking is an institutionalized relationship which is central for Latinas who establish their ascendancy in pioneering immigrant roles. While the grandmothers coped with responsibilities of substitute caretaking in the places of origin, the immigrant mothers in Washington searched for ways to deal with anxieties and stresses that they associated with the course of the lives of absent children. To relieve symptoms of anxiety, they frequently sought a medical practitioner and medicines (Cohen, 1985, p. 207).

Dissatisfaction with the limited accessibility of medical and mental health services among Latinos has become acute enough to make their provision a subject of high priority in local and national programs. Recommendations have been made for the increased use of bilingual and bicultural personnel in the provision of these services. Limited attention has been given, however, to the strategic role which Spanish-speaking physicians in private practice play among immigrants who settle in our urban areas. Although handicapped by meager financial resources and lack of medical insurance, Latinos turn to these practitioners, nevertheless, for their health and mental health problems.

A crucial aspect in the use of physicians is that they are sought after for physical and psychological distresses whereas mental health resources, even when accessible, are not viewed with equal priority. Latinas closely link physical and psychological symptoms and they seek specialists to relieve them. The separate organization of our medical and psychiatric services is not attractive. The containment of feeling is also important; Latinas, for example, cope with stress-inducing situations through the practice of *controlarse* (control of the self) and *sobreponerse* (to overcome oneself). *Controlarse* is a central concept upon which Latinos draw to govern the management of stress. It is a central mechanism for the regulation of behavior. It enables a Latino to exercise discipline over unpleasant feelings, thoughts, and moods. Control of one's emotions and mood leads to various states, such as *resignarse* (to resign oneself), *no pensar* (not to think; in this context, to avoid thinking of a problem), or *sobreponerse* (to overcome oneself), that is the effort to overcome reactions to situations conducive to stress (Cohen, 1985).

Thus, these immigrants do not fit the prevalent stereotype to which people of Latin American heritage conform passively, to unkind fate. Instead, they contain their feelings, face difficulties, and work hard to master them. Those concerned with the design of services for adult and children of Latin American heritage should consider developing models of integrated or closely coordinated health and mental health care. There should be an increased use of bilingual and bicultural personnel to serve the needs of newcomers in human service agencies but a central aspect of their roles should be to serve as gatekeepers between systems.

Key primary care workers in public health agencies who work with Latinas and Latinos should be able to identify and work with the problems of psychological distress.

As advocates for newcomers, they should also be in positions of influence within their organizations, and in the communities where changes are sought. It should be clear, moreover, that since the tradition of private practice in medicine still plays a central role in the provision of ambulatory health services in the United States, we cannot neglect this sector in the assessment of services among minority populations. Mental health agencies, in particular, should seriously consider establishing linkages with Spanish-speaking physicians whom the Latinos choose as their first line consultants when they experience distress. Indeed, it appears as if we cannot properly identify what the unmet health and mental health needs of Latino immigrants are, until we draw on knowledge from the immigrants themselves, from the private sectors, and from our public health systems.

There is still another challenge in understanding the ways of life of immigrant women of Latin American heritage which should alter our conceptions of what it means to be a newcomer today. Multiculturalism is a complex reality which characterizes the countries of origin of these immigrants, as well as the areas in which they are resettling. Latino women and men come from complex societies which are in the midst of change to settle in cities in the United States where the unplanned crises of urban living threaten the stability of even the long-established residents. We cannot fully understand how Latinas view their host society and how they organize their thoughts and sentiments by simple descriptions of life in the "old country" and anecdotal experiences of the fortunes and trials of settlement.

I have offered illustrations of risk-taking behavior, of fusion, and of the reinterpretation and reclassification of belief systems in the health area to draw us closer to the tasks that immigrants face today as they successfully select, master, and control the alternatives in knowledge and practices found in their rapidly changing worlds. As we learn how Latinas accomplish these tasks, we should be better able to understand the dilemmas that we also share with these newcomers in our own transforming multicultural societies.

NOTES

1. The first President of our committee, Aida Berrio, was a Puerto Rican who had been a member of this group.
2. The connotative aspects of communication between respondents and caregivers were of great importance, since patients and professionals sometimes adopted postures of apparent self-confidence in their communication styles with each other without really understanding the different meanings attached to the language used (*see* Cohen, 1979, p. 134).

REFERENCES

Castles, Stephen. (1992). "Australian Multiculturalism: Social Policy and Identity in a Changing Society." In G. Freeman & J. Jupp (eds.). *Nations of Immigrants: Australia, The United States and International Migration.* Melbourne: Oxford University Press, pp.184-201.

Castles Stephen & Mark J. Miller (1993) *The Age of Migration: International Population Movements in the Modern World.* London: Macmillan.

Chu, Clara. (2005). "IFLA Section on Library Services to Multicultural Populations Adopts Ten Reasons to Offer Multicultural Library Services." *International Federation of Library Associations,* 1-2 http://libres.uncg.edu/ir/uncc/listing.aspx?id=2124 (October 5, 2015.)

Cohen, Lucy M. (1999). "Maintaining and Reunifying Families: Two Case Studies of Shifting Legal Status." In David Haines and Karen Rosenblum (eds.). *Illegal Immigration in America. A Reference Handbook.* Westport, CT: Greenwood Press, pp. 383-395.

Cohen, Lucy M. (1985). "*Controlarse* and the Problems of Life Among Latino Immigrants." In William A. Vega, William & Manuel R. Miranda (eds) *Stress & Hispanic Mental Health: Relating Research to Service Delivery.* Rockville, MD: National Institute of Mental Health (DHHS), pp. 202-218.

Cohen, Lucy. (1981)."Latinas Lead the Way." In Dolores Mortiner & Roy Bryee-Laporte (eds.). *Female Immigrants to the United States: Caribbean, Latin American, and African Experiences.* Washington, D.C.: Research Institute on Immigration and Ethnic Studies Smithsonian, pp. 179-202.

Cohen, Lucy M. (1979). *Culture, Disease, and Stress among Latino Immigrants.* Research Institute in Immigration and Ethnic Studies (RIIES) Washington, D.C.: Smithsonian Institution.

Cohen, Lucy M. (1973). "Gifts to Strangers: Public Policy and the Delivery of Health Services to Illegal Aliens." *Anthropological Quarterly,* 46: 183-195.

Kottak, Conrad P. and Kathryn A. Kozaitis. (2003). *On Being Different: Diversity and Multiculturalism in the North American Mainstream.* Boston: McGraw-Hill College.

Liebow, Elliot. (1967). *Tally´s Corner. A Study of Negro Streetcorner Men.* Boston: Little, Brown and Company.

McBride, Gail. (2005). "The Coming of Age of Multicultural Medicine." *PLOS Medicine,* 2(3): 62.

Suu Kyi, Aung San. (1995). "Introduction." In Multiculturalism: A Policy Response to Diversity. Sidney: UNESCO www.unesco.org/most/sydpaper.htm. (October 5, 2015).

FOUR

Latina Immigrants and Transnational Healthcare Adaptations

Marta S. Barkell

A massive influx of immigrants to the United States in the past decades led to changes in American society, noticeable in the nation's cities and a variety of institutions (Foner, 2003). Immigrants represent a rather special epidemiological subgroup, whose health status can be expected to differ from that of non-immigrants and that of the host population. Environmental changes, cultural values, altered social relations, and psychological burdens are some of the challenges which may reflect on their health (Monteiro, 1980; Menjívar, 2000).

Thousands of the immigrants who have settled in the United States are from Latin America, particularly from Mexico, Central America, and Caribbean countries. According to U.S. Bureau Census, in the Washington, D.C. metropolitan area there were 807,000 Latinos or Hispanics (16.4 percent of the total population) and most of them immigrants. Many Latino newcomers have settled in the metropolitan area of Northern Virginia, particularly in outer suburbs in the counties of Loudoun, Prince William and Stafford (*See* Map, Figure 4.1).[1]

Northern Virginia is an area of urban and suburban centers which in the past few decades has become a multicultural region with a diverse population of immigrants from Mexico, Central and South America, Asia, Africa, and the Middle East. The Latino population is considered one of the fastest growing in this region. According to data from the Bureau of the Census analyzed by the Weldon Cooper Center of the University of Virginia (2010), as of 2010 the state's population was over eight million people, of which more than 630,000 were of Latino origin, 62 percent of these Latinos live in Northern Virginia.

Anthropological studies among Latino refugees and immigrants, particularly from El Salvador, have focused largely on their lives in the context of work (Mahler, 1995; Repak, 1995), social networks (Menjivar, 2000), mental health and alcoholism (Porro Salinas, 1996), emotional processes and bodily experience (Jenkins and Valiente, 1996), health effects from violence and uprooting (Bowen, 1999), migratory settlement processes (Zentgraf, 1998), and immigration and transnational family networks (Sanchez Molina, 2006). While this research has contributed to an understanding of the culture and settlement processes of these refugees

Figure 4.1.   Map of Latino Population in Northern Virginia Source: U.S. Census Bureau, 2010

and immigrants in the United States, the experience of illness, disease and ways of healing among them has received limited attention.

My interest in the illness and health of Latina immigrants originated from my experience as a registered nurse and research for my doctoral dissertation. Through the years I came in contact with patients from other countries and from other ethnic groups. Because I speak Portuguese, German, and Spanish, I would frequently be called to interpret for patients who spoke one of these languages. Gradually I developed an interest in cultural differences while caring for patients from these different ethnic backgrounds. The Kaja Finkler books *Spiritualist Healers in Mexico* (1985) and *Physicians at Work, Patients in Pain* (2001), written in the context of rural and urban Mexican culture, social situation, and life circumstances, taught me that health, illness, and healing are much more complex than what I had learned in nursing school where patient education was heavily oriented towards "objective scientific nursing principles" about how to deal with illness.

In *Women in Pain*, a book focused on illness, life circumstances, gender, and the history of Mexicans in a social and cultural context, Flinkler (1994) points out that biomedicine views sickness as a physical breakdown where pathogens attack the human body, or there is wear and tear of the body through aging. If these interpretations cannot explain a disease, biomedicine can further rely on theories of heredity or behavioral risks such as diet. However, the broader perspective of biopsychosocial processes is viewed by many scholars (as well as healthcare providers) as more conducive to explanations of health and illness. Finkler (1994) argues that theories of life events, social support, and social relationships still tend to fall within biomedical paradigms because they divest individuals of their ability to evaluate and judge their own existence. In order to understand the complexities it is imperative to pay attention to life events within the context of a person's life, especially with respect to moral dilemmas and social interactions that must be braved in an individual's day-to-day existence. Based on these insights, I focused my research interests on Latina immigrants to attempt to uncover how they experience illness in a social and cultural context and how their life circumstances may or may not have impacted their health.

This chapter examines the transnational healthcare adaptations of Latina immigrants who live in a community in Northern Virginia.[2] In order to learn about these women's perspectives on health and healthcare I interviewed twenty Latinas who volunteered to participate. They frequented the Parent Liaison Office of an elementary school located in the heart of a Latino community, where I have volunteered since 2004. The women are the mothers of the school children, and they come to a trailer annex where the Parent Liaison Office is located. There, they receive assistance in understanding the American school system, interpretation of notices from the school, and any information that is connected with their children's schooling. In addition, they can also attend English language classes and a variety of information sessions with guest speakers such as health and healthcare information, tenant rights, legal aid, couples relationships, and parenting classes.

FIELDWORK RESEARCH AND PROJECT PURPOSE

There is a growing body of literature highlighting the health needs of Latina women in the United States, challenging healthcare providers to consider cultural and social issues such as language, health and illness, beliefs and practices, as well as cultivating compassion and caring human interest and kindness, and taking into account the financial situation of clients (Julliard et al., 2008; 2009). There also is a need to address how immigrants experience illness in the context of their lives, involving cultural dimensions, social relations, and their day-to-day existence. They brought with them their own culturally-based beliefs about illness and ways of curing. In addition, family relations, especially with mates and spouses, and economic problems, are also salient themes reflected in the lives and health of Latina immigrants. When they spoke about health and illness, they had their own conceptions about what health meant and what illness meant. Having energy to work in order to meet economic needs was an important dimension of health, and being tired, sad, and worried were perceived as agents of illness. Beliefs about illness, how to react to illness episodes, decisions about when, where, and from whom to seek care, are embedded in their culture (Kleinman, 1980; Janzen, 1987; Barkell, 2007).

In her study of Mexican women Finkler shows that women face harsh dilemmas, culturally constructed, which revolve around ideologies and practices of socialization. Women evaluate their life in terms of how they are expected to behave as well as how others (spouses, mates, and children) ought to behave. When others do not behave as culturally and socially expected, conflicts and contradictions are created that reflect on their health. From my observations in the Washington metropolitan area, Latina immigrants from El Salvador faced similar conditions, such as growing up in poverty, male dominance, conflictive spousal relationships, and the additional burden of civil war and emigration. The challenge lies in understanding the meaning of their particular circumstances from their perspective as Salvadoran immigrants and how these circumstances relate to their health.[3]

Moreover, with the recent immigration debates, their immigration status often produces fear and misconceptions that they will be deported if they use free medical services or if they register their American-born children for Medicaid or food stamps. There is even a perception that children who use legitimate available government help will be required to pay the government back when they turn eighteen years of age and start to work. During gatherings among Latino women in a trailer, they developed friendships, and established networks with other women from community organizations such as clinics and food distribution centers. These gathering places provide opportunities to network and gather information about organizations that can provide assistance, such as healthcare, legal aid, and language training. I noticed these kinds of networking among women while observing the waiting room of one of the clinics where I volunteered. There was much information being exchanged among women about home remedies for different ailments and about where to look for house cleaning jobs.[4] In other words, the trailer became a "cultural place and space" (Velez-Ibañez, 1997, p. 7).

The purpose of the project was explained to the participants, and they could refuse to participate at any time, and were not obligated to answer questions they did not feel comfortable answering. Names of participants were not collected. The interviews consisted of basic demographic data such as country of origin, age, years of schooling, and when they arrived in the United States. Following that were open-ended questions on how they took care of their health in their home country, and how they take care of their health in the United States. In order to better understand their conception of health and illness, I also asked how they define health and illness.

Participants in this study came from Mexico, Central America, and South America, with the majority being from Guatemala (6), Mexico (5), and El Salvador (5).

The others came from Colombia (1), Bolivia (1), Honduras (1), and the Dominican Republic (1). The majority arrived in the United States between 1986 and 2005.

One woman arrived in 1970, and one in 1986. Eighteen had an educational level between three and twelve years while two had one and two years of university studies respectively. Their ages ranged between twenty-six and sixty-five years old.

Ten of the women had no health insurance, three had health insurance from work, six frequented a low cost county clinic, and one became a member of a non-profit free clinic. One of the strategies used by uninsured women was to avoid going to the doctor as much as possible and consequently they relied on traditional folk remedies which they learned from their mothers and grandmothers, and prescription and non-prescription medicines sent by their families from their countries of origin such as of El Salvador. Over-the-counter medications were also bought in the United States. The medications sent from El Salvador were usually sent with a *viajero* (traveler), persons who travel back and forth between the United States and El Salvador, delivering money, videos or photos, packages of food, medicine, clothing, and other items (Barkell, 2007, p. 61). According to Salvadoran women informants, this system helps to defray the cost of medications, especially prescription medications which are much cheaper in El Salvador. As I talked with these women, they repeatedly discussed their economic situation and how this was one of their constant *preocupaciones* (worries) that they constantly had to deal with. They feared not being able to pay rent and losing their apartments, and not being able to pay *los biles* (the bills).

CONCEPTS OF HEALTH AND ILLNESS

Anthropologists and other scholars have produced a growing body of research on the cultural dimensions of health, illness and healing. Contemporary anthropological studies of illness and healing emphasize that people are steeped in their own culture and they are also "agents" in their cultural milieu. Their beliefs about illness, reactions to illness episodes, decisions about when, where, and from whom to seek care, are embedded in their cultures (Kleinman, 1980; Janzen, 1987). In recent decades anthropologists have conducted increased research on topics related to women's health with a focus on studies of the cultural and social nature of illness (Lamb et al., 2000; Ruzek, Olesen, and Clarke, 1997, Sargent and Brettell, 1996; Finkler, 1994).

Drawing on various theoretical frameworks, there is broad agreement that symptoms of illness have cultural and personal meanings. The culturally patterned ways people have learned to think and behave in the world also guide their understandings about how to manage illness; and as unique individuals, people harbor their own experiences and beliefs about their illnesses (Kleinman, 1988). Moreover, anthropologists and other scholars differentiate *illness* and *disease*. Finkler (1994, p. 11) states that illness refers to impaired function as perceived by the patient in a cultural manner, while disease refers to a biological and biochemical dysfunction. This differentiation in biomedicine is illustrated by signs, viewed as manifestations of disease processes, concrete pain and symptoms, understood by patients as subjective experience, without objective reality. In contrast to signs which can be measured using a variety of technologies, symptoms cannot be measured objectively, because they are intrinsically subjective. Symptoms place the focus on the person that is experiencing the pain. As we can identify from personal experience, pain and illness are a solitary and personal experience.

This research also addresses ways in which immigrants conceptualize health and illness, ways in which they manage illness in new settings and aspects of culture and social relations that interface with their symptoms. Following Kaja Finkler's theoretical perspective, I chose a phenomenological approach which encompasses the life world of a person. Each individual develops different ways of "being in the world," and ways to interpret it. Each individual's life story is unique. According to Drew

Leder (1990) in illness situations when we put aside the notion that the human body is a machine-like object, we are able to find the "lived body" and when the body is ill we do not have just a broken machine but a whole world transformed.

In order to learn how the participants viewed the concept of health and illness, I asked how they would define these concepts from their perspective. As each woman articulated a definition, it became clear that their definition of health and illness does not coincide with the common definition of the World Health Organization, namely: "Health is a state of complete physical, mental and social well being and not merely the absence of disease or infirmity."

While the women included some elements of this definition, they also had a more practical view of what health meant to them personally. Their definition included ideas of prevention which they had learned while in the United States, and centered on being able to work, to take care of oneself, to be able to do the activities of their daily life, and to be happy and not sad. On the prevention part they reiterated an adequate diet with portion control, not to lack food, exercise by walking forty-five minutes to one hour every day, recreation for mental health, and religion for spiritual well being.

The definition of illness was associated with physical ailments such as infection, fever, vomiting, pain, being in bed, as well as with not being able to work or perform daily activities. The definition was also associated with having a disease such as diabetes, cancer, anemia, or HIV. A mental dimension was also included characterized by low spirits, not sleeping well, and to be sad or depressed. Frequent comments were:

"If one is sick one cannot get ahead"
"Problems at home cause illness"
"Serious illness affects the whole family mentally and economically."

On the preventive side, the women reported that illness is related to not having medical checkups, not having vaccines such as for flu, and that mental health reflects on the body, indicating a selective knowledge of what promotes good health, preventive aspects such as medical checks, and social dimensions such as problems at home.

TAKING CARE OF HEALTH IN HOME COUNTRIES

A growing body of research on the cultural dimensions of health and illness has focused on ways in which new immigrants conceptualize health and illness, their practices associated with care, and cure in the country of settlement. This research also addresses ways in which they manage their illnesses in new settings and aspects of culture, social relations, family and work, which interface with their symptoms.

Chavez (1997) points out those issues often arise when immigrants come face-to-face with their own cultural beliefs and those of healthcare providers, an interaction where understanding each other's views about health and illness may be difficult.

Since the participants came from seven countries there was considerable variation in the responses to how they took care of their health in their home country. Access to healthcare depended if they lived in an urban area, small rural village, or on a farm. Ten informants lived in a city, nine in rural villages and one came from a farm. Virtually all of the participants stated that if they had an illness considered serious, such as persistent fever, an illness not resolving with home remedies, or had an accident, they would seek medical care at a nearby hospital or a government health post in their area.

For those in rural areas however, it often involved a long journey to a hospital in a city or to the health post. While government health posts were not available in all rural areas, the women relied on a repertoire of home remedies passed from generation to generation to treat illnesses and thus avoid a trip to the hospital or the doctor where money was essential to receive treatment. The home treatments consisted of herbal remedies, mostly in the form of teas, and pharmaceuticals obtained from local drug stores, including antibiotics.

As I have also highlighted in previous research (Barkell, 2007, p. 68), talking about the different curing strategies and remedies they used, most relied on remedies known from their country of origin, such as herbal products, and pharmaceuticals. At the same time they also used over-the-counter medications bought in local drug stores. The majority felt that they would only see a doctor if they thought the illness was grave (serious), especially if they did not have insurance. The cost of a medical consultation and the subsequent prescription was often the reason that going to the doctor was not an option. The women also revealed a trust in the medications from their home country because they were familiar with these medicines and had great faith in them. Language also was an issue, because here (in the United States) the information about medications is in English and they cannot read the instructions. The home remedies and pharmaceuticals used by the participants in this research from their home country were as follows (*See Table 4.1.*).

Besides the herbal treatments above, participants also described external treatments for various ailments and inhalation treatments such as boiling eucalyptus leaves to inhale the vapor for colds, fever, cough, headache, and chest congestion.

Another treatment for headaches consisted of raw potato slices tied to the forehead, or a cloth tied tightly around the head, or a plant heated over fire and covered with Vicks tied to the forehead for migraines. Cinnamon sticks soaked in alcohol were used as compresses for wounds, a

Table 4.1. Symptoms and Remedies/Treatments

SYMPTOMS	REMEDY/TREATMENTS
Stomach upset, pain	Chamomile tea, Anis tea, Mint tea, Wormwood tea, Baking soda
To relax and calm nerves	Cinnamon tea, Orange leaf tea
Fever	Lemon grass tea, Matjoram tea
Cough	Mint and honey tea, Ginger tea and Honey, Boiled onion and garlic tea
Tooth ache	Allspice seed tea
Flu and cough	Lemon and honey tea
Cold and fever	Linden tea with lemon
For Nerves	Rue and lettuce tea, Orange leaf tea
Fever, *Susto* (a), Diarrhea, Parasites	Epazote (tropical plant) tea
Ear ache	Garlic fried in oil as ear drops
Headache	Guava and lemon leaf tea
To regulate menses	Avocado leaf tea

a) A fright that can cause loss of soul.

wet cloth to the forehead and on the arm pits to reduce fever, and gargles with salt water for a sore throat were also mentioned.

Since pharmacies were often easier to reach in the rural areas, pharmaceuticals were often combined with home treatments. The more frequently cited medications were Advil or Tylenol for pain and flu, *Mejoral* (aspirin) for fever, flu and headache, Vicks for congestion and colds, *Novalgina* (dypirone), for fever and pain, and Tetracycline and Penicillin for infections, sore throat, wounds, and venereal diseases. In order to learn about possible health care adaptations the women underwent after migrating, I asked them how they took care of their health after they arrived in the United States.

The findings showed similar patterns of home remedies and teas, over-the-counter medications, and antibiotics obtained from local stores. But the women also reported an awareness of preventive measures such as a healthy diet with specific ideas about not drinking sodas, exercise, and consultation with a doctor. They also spoke about the importance of washing hands, having a flu vaccine, and a women's physical exam, including a pap test.

While the women availed themselves of the local healthcare system, they still relied on practices from their home country, such as the potato slices tied to the head for headache, Eucalyptus tea inhalations for cough and asthma, Chamomile tea for flu, stomach upset, menstrual regulation, to relax and sleep, hot lemonade for flu, and baking soda for stomach pain and upset.

Medications obtained over-the-counter in local United States drug stores consisted of vitamins, cough syrup, Zantac for gastritis, Aspirin for flu, and Tetracycline and Penicillin persisted in their use for treatment of infections and respiratory ailments. Advil and Tylenol proved to be the most popular medications for treatment of headaches, fever, pain, flu and cough. Some of the women also ordered medications from their home country and the most frequently cited were Panadol (Acetaminophen), Amoxicillin, and Tetracycline.

Even though only half of the women had either insurance through work or were members of a clinic, the ones that did not have any kind of insurance reported that if they were really sick they would seek medical help. They had learned how to obtain healthcare through low cost private physicians and in an emergency to go to a hospital emergency room.

The following comment illustrates how the women manage their health within their possibilities: "Here one is attended to if one has money or not, insurance or not, one can obtain a pay plan, or be eligible as a charity case." One woman said she has been saving money for one year and a half for a physical exam and blood analyses, with a private physician.

CONCLUSIONS

As these Latina immigrants have settled in their new environment, they draw on traditional and biomedical knowledge from their country of origin as well as from biomedical information obtained in the United States. They must negotiate different and often conflicting cultural expectations, and values and loyalties, regarding home and settlement societies. In the health domain they must learn to reconfigure cultural traditions and approaches to healthcare while learning to understand and negotiate the complex healthcare system of the United States. They must reconcile beliefs about health, illness, and curing, which they learned from their mothers and grandmothers, with the beliefs and culture of professional health providers. As the women spoke about their health and their illnesses, they also spoke about their past. They talked about strategies for cures that their mothers used when they were sick. Each woman has a repertoire of herbal remedies that she now uses, but also has the option of being able to consult with a physician if she feels that she is seriously ill.

NOTES

1. The metropolitan area of Northern Virgina includes Arlington, Fairfax, Loudoun, Prince William, Loudoun, Prince William, Stafford, Clarke, Fauquier, Spotsylvania, and Warren counties and the cities of Alexandria, Fairfax, Falls Church, Manassas, Manassas Park and Fredericksburg (see Figure 1). The counties of In Loudoun County with an 84.1 percent population increase between 2000 and 2010, Prince William County a 43.2 percent, and Stafford County a 39.5 percent (Singer, 2012).

2. This chapter is part of my Ph.D. Dissertation, *Illness Experience Among Salvadoran Women Immigrants* (Department of Anthropology at the Catholic University of America, 2007) and the research "Latina Immigrants and Transnational Healthcare Adaptations," which I presented at the 72th Annual Meeting of the Society for Applied Anthropology, "Bays, Boundiries, and Borders" held in Baltimore, Maryland, on March 28, 2012.

3. In Illness Experience Among Salvadoran Women Immigrants (Barkell, 2007), I explored the illness experiences of Salvadoran women immigrants in the context of culture, social relations, and life circumstances. I aimed to describe illness from the perspective of Salvadoran women immigrants in their social and context, and to show that their health problems reach beyond purely biological.

4. Cecilia Menjivar (2000) in her book evaluates the role of social networks among Salvadoran immigrants in San Francisco. She classifies social networks as composed of family, friends, and compatriots. These networks are expected to provide assistance to newcomers or persons in the community who need help. However, Menjivar found that relatives and compatriots often were unable to provide any assistance because they were barely able to survive themselves, or because of gender ideologies (*See also*, Barkell 2007).

REFERENCES

Bowen, Sara J. (1999). "Resilience and Health: Salvadoran Refugee Women in Manitoba." Master Dissertation, The University of Manitoba.

Finkler, Kaja. (2001). *Physicians at Work, Patients in Pain: Biomedical Practice and Patient Response in Mexico*. Boulder, CO: Westview Press.

Finkler, Kaja. (1994). *Women in Pain: Gender and Morbidity in Mexico*. Philadelphia, PA: University of Pennsylvania Press.

Finkler, Kaja. (1985). *Spiritualist Healers in Mexico: Successes and Failures of Alternative Therapeutics*. Salem, WI: Shelffied Publishing Company.

Foner, Nancy. (2003). "Introduction: Anthropology and Contemporary Immigration to the United States–Where We Have Been and Where We are Going." In Nancy Foner (ed.) *American Arrivals*. Santa Fe, NM: School of American Research Press.

Janzen, John M. (1987). "Therapy Management: Concept, Reality, Process." *Medical Anthropology Quarterly*, 1: 68-84.

Jenkins, Janis and Martha Valiente. (2003). "Bodily Transactions of the Passions: El Calor among Salvadoran Women Refugees." In Thomas Csordas (ed.) *Embodiment and Experience: The Existential Ground of Culture and Self*. Cambridge, U.K.: Cambridge University Press.

Julliard, Kell, Josefina Vivar, Carlos Delgado, Eugenio Cruz, Jennifer Kabak, Heidi Sabers. (2008). "What Latina Patients don't Tell their Doctors: A Qualitative Study." *The Annals of Family Medicine*, 6(6): 543-549.

Kleinman, Arthur. (1988). *Illness Narratives: Suffering, Healing, and the Human Condition*. New York: Basic Books.

Kleinman, Arthur. (1980). *Patients and Healers in the Context of Culture*. Berkeley, CA: University of California Press.

Lamb, Sarah, White Saris, and Sweet Manoges. (2000). *Agine, Gender, and Body in North India*. Berkeley and Los Angeles, CA: University of California Press.

Leder, Drew. (1990). *The Absent Body*. Chicago, IL: The University of Chicago Press.

Mahler, Sarah. (1995). *Salvadorans in Suburbia. Symbiosis and Conflict*. Boston, MA: Allyn and Bacon.

Menjivar, Cecilia. (2000). *Fragmented Ties: Salvadoran Immigrant Networks in America*. Berkeley, CA: University of California Press.

Ming-Chin, Yeh, Viladrich Anahi, Bruning Nancy, and Roye Carol. (2009). "Determinants of Latina Obesity in the United States: The Role of Selective Acculturation." *Journal of Transcultural Nursing*, 20(1): 105-115.

Monteiro, Lois. (1980). "Immigrants and the Medical Care System: The Case of Portuguese." In R. S. Bryce Laporte (ed.) *Sourcebook on the New Immigration Implications for the United States and the International Community*. New Brunswick, NJ: Transaction Books.

Porro-Salinas, Patricia M. (1996). Coping Responses and Adjustment Among Salvadoran Immigrants. Ph.D. Dissertation, George Mason University.

Repak, Terry A. (1995). *Waiting on Washington. Central American Workers in the Nation's Capital*. Philadelphia, PA: Temple University Press.

Ruzek, Sheryl B., Virginia L. Olesen, and Adele E. Clarke (eds.) (1997) *Women's Health: Complexities and Differences*. Columbus, OH: Ohio State University Press.

Sánchez Molina, Raúl. (2006). *Proceso migratorio de una mujer salvadoreña. El viaje de Maria Reyes a Washington, D.C.* Madrid: CIS/Siglo XXI.

Sargent, Carolyn F. and Caroline B. Brettell (eds.). (1996). *Gender and Health: An International Perspective*. Upper Saddle River, NJ: Prentice Hall.

Singer, Audrey. (2012). "Metropolitan Washington: A New Immigrant Gateway." In Enrique Pumar (ed.) Hispanic *Migration and Urban Development: Studies from Washington, D.C.* Bingley, U.K.: Emerald Group Publishing Limited, pp. 1-24.

Singer, Audrey. (2003). *At Home in the Nation's Capital: Immigrant Trends in Metropolitan Washington*. Washington, D.C.: Brooking Institution.

Velez-Ibanez, Carlos G. (1997). *Border Visions: Mexican Cultures of the Southwest United States*. Tucson, TX: The University of Arizona Press.

Weldon Cooper Center, University of Virginia (2010) *Creciendo Juntos*. Charlottesville, VA: University of Virginia.

World Health Organization. (2012). *Definition of Health*. Geneva, Switzerland: World Health Organization.

Zentgraf, Kristine M. (1998). "I come only with My Soul": The Gendered Experiences of Salvadoran Women Immigrants in Los Angeles. Ph.D. Dissertation, University of California.

FIVE

Waiting for a Job at 'New Corners'

Honduran Immigrant Men Day Laboring in Greater Washington

Raúl Sánchez Molina

As a global metropolis, Greater Washington, which includes the District of Columbia, Northern Virginia, suburban Maryland, and Jefferson County in West Virginia (District of Columbia Government 2011, p. 36), has become one of the major new immigrant gateways in the United States, transforming the area into one of the most multicultural metropolitan regions in the country.[1] With a vibrant economy, Honduran migrants, who have been suffering the consequences of the post-civil war period in Central America, natural catastrophes, violence, and political and economic crises, arrive in this metropolitan region fleeing from poverty and violence and seeking to improve their families' quality of life (Schmalzbauer, 2005a; Reichman, 2011; England, 2006). As a new gateway for immigrants, Greater Washington is one of the top metropolitan areas in the United States that offers high-skilled jobs in professional and business fields—such as scientific research, development services, or technical services (Center for Regional Analysis, 2004; Singer, 2003; 2012). Nevertheless, along with high-skilled foreign immigrants, many Central American workers settle in this region, filling the low-wage positions available in its ethnic- and gender-segmented labor market.[2]

While most Honduran women enter the reproductive labor market—as domestic workers, babysitters, or caregivers—men enter the construction and service industries, some of them to work as day laborers (Sánchez Molina, 2015). Gathering daily at street corners and store parking lots, they seek short-term and poorly-paid jobs with no access to labor unions or unemployment insurance (Valenzuela, 2003). With a long tradition in Washington, D.C. (Liebow, 1967), in recent decades, the day-labor market has expanded throughout this region, as well as many other U.S. regions (Mahler, 1995a; Hamilton and Chinchilla, 2001; Valenzuela, Kawachi, and Mar, 2002; Quesada et al., 2014; Meléndez et al., 2014), due to the increase in the number of contractors and homeowners seeking the inexpensive, hard-working, and trouble-free work that undocumented Latino immigrants are willing to do (Valenzuela et al., 2005).

Based on ethnographic fieldwork carried out with Honduran immigrants in this metropolitan region, this chapter analyzes how Honduran men enter this workforce by gathering at 'new corners' in different parts of the region.[3] Like other Latino immigrants, Hondurans use the term *esquinas* (corners) to refer to these public labor sites (street corners, storefronts, or parking lots), where many of them have to gather every day in order to find a job (Pinedo Turnovsky, 2006). In doing so, they have to challenge different kinds of social adversities caused by employers at work, local residents, and anti-immigrant groups who try to stop them from congregating in these public sites while waiting for a job (Cleveland and Pierson, 2009).

GREATER WASHINGTON AS A NEW DESTINATION FOR HONDURAN MIGRATION

After four months traveling by land, crossing the Guatemalan, Mexican, and the United States borders, Jairo, a thirty-six-year-old Honduran man, and Elvira, his thirty-five-year-old second wife by *acompañamiento* (or free legal union), arrived in Houston (Texas) in 2004. While he left an eighteen-year-old son with his first wife in Honduras, Elvira left two teenage children with her mother. Once in Houston, where Jairo's oldest brother has been living since the end of the 1990s, news about jobs available in Prince Williams County (Northern Virginia) led them to move to this county in Greater Washington. Once they had arrived in a town in this area—where Latinos made up 31.9 percent of its total population—they rented a little room in a house shared with other Honduran immigrants. Jairo began to work as a day laborer soon after arrival, gathering with other Central American immigrants at a nearby store parking lot, while Elisa found her first jobs cleaning private apartments and houses. As in other outer localities in Greater Washington, the highest concentration of Latino immigrant population has occurred in counties and cities of northern Virginia such as Prince William County.[4]

Early in the 2000s, Gustavo, a twenty-five-year-old electrician from southern Honduras, arrived in the United States, also by land, after crossing the U.S. border in Arizona, leaving a nine-year-old daughter in Honduras with his former wife by *acompañamiento*. From the beginning, Gustavo settled in Fairfax County in northern Virginia, an area where Latino residents made up more than 30 percent of the total population, and where other family members have settled since the end of the 1990s. Upon arrival in this outer suburb of Washington, D.C., one of his male family members took him to one of the store parking lots located in the vicinity where he found his first job.

Although Honduran migration to Greater Washington started several decades ago (Repak, 1995), following Salvadoran displacements to this region, and with the Hondurans settling in the neighborhoods where Salvadorans had begun to concentrate since the 1980s, the number of Honduran immigrants began to increase significantly in the metropolitan area after Hurricane Mitch in 1998.[5] Not only did thousands of Hondurans lose their homes, but also their employments, as agricultural fields were destroyed, infrastructures damaged and the country economy weakened (Oliver Smith, 2005; Kirchbichler, 2010; De Souza, 2011). Leaving hundreds of thousands of Hondurans homeless, the hurricane affected directly two million people—a third of Honduras' population (Fuentes, 2003).

After Hurricane Mitch, other structural conditions, such as the postcivil war economic crisis in Central America and political and economic crises in Honduras, especially after the coup against President Zelaya on June 26, 2009 (Booth, Wade, and Walker, 2010), have also forced Honduran women and men to migrate to Spain, Mexico, Canada, and especially to the United States to support their families (Schmalzbauer, 2005a; Zarrugh, 2007; Reichman, 2011). However, as is the case of other undocumented immigrants in the United States, because it is very difficult for Honduran citizens to obtain papers in order to migrate, they depend on the aid of their close social networks to migrate by land to the United States; long dangerous journeys, clandestinely crossing several national borders, Guatemala, Mexico, and the United States (Sládkovà, 2007; 2010), that make them vulnerable to different sort of assaults and exploitation (Blanchard et al., 2011).

According to the 2010 Census, there were 731,000 registered Honduran people living in the United States, constituting the eighth-largest population of Latinas/os in the country. Besides New Orleans and New York, which have the largest Honduran populations in the United States (Gorman, 2010; Chaney, 2012; England, 2006), Hondurans have been settling in other U.S. metropolitan areas, particularly in southern and northeastern states, with Greater Washington becoming one of their new destinations in the United States, especially after Hurricane Mitch.[6]

At present, there are Honduran women and men settled in the region coming from all regions of Honduras. The majority have settled in Fairfax and Prince William counties and the city of Alexandria in northern Virginia, and in Montgomery and Prince George's counties in suburban Ma-

ryland. Nevertheless, due to the increase of unauthorized Honduran immigrants in the United States, the Honduran population may very well
be undercounted in the 2010 U.S. Census, as they represent the greatest
overall increases in undocumented immigrants in the last decade.[7]

As soon as they arrive in Greater Washington, Honduran women and
men settle in nearby and outer metropolitan suburban neighborhoods,
and enter an informal workforce that is unregulated by law and without
labor benefits. Internationalization and economic expansion in Greater
Washington as well as social and economic changes in the United States
(Knox, 1991; Abbott, 1999; Singer, 2003) have created a significant labor
demand for immigrants from developing countries in an ethnic- and gender-segmented workforce (Pessar, 1995). While jobs available in the reproductive labor market, in domestic and care services, lured Latina immigrants to the Washington, D.C., metropolitan area from the late 1950s,
the growth of construction industry and related sectors in the area have
offered low-skilled work to Latino immigrant men since the 1980s. In
addition, both men and women could also find low-paid jobs in other
service sectors working as dishwashers, assistant cooks, busboys/girls, or
cooks (Repak, 1995).

Since then, the labor market boom in the metropolitan region has
continued to offer jobs to new immigrants who have been incorporating
into the region, especially from El Salvador, Mexico, Guatemala, Bolivia,
and Honduras (Singer, 2003). While most Honduran women start work
in the domestic or care sectors as housekeepers, child-care providers, or
care-givers, most Honduran men usually find jobs in construction, starting to work as day laborers. This labor market is undervalued by the
native population, because, among other factors, it is unregulated by
formal rules and without benefits—such as paid vacations, health insurance or the option of joining a union.

FROM INNER CITY TO OUTER SUBURBAN AREAS

While Mauro, a thirty-five-year-old Honduran immigrant, was waiting
at a corner in the District of Columbia a couple of years ago, a U.S.
citizen in charge of a big building in suburban Maryland hired him and
four other Central American men, to move out and clean several apartments. When they finished this job, which lasted several days, the employer asked Mauro to work permanently with him at that building.
Mauro is from Olancho, a department in eastern Honduras with one of
the highest rates of immigrants who live in the United States (Reyes,
Torres, and Isaula, 2012). After arriving in Miami (Florida) in 2000, he
moved to Washington, D.C., three years later because, according to
him, he was told that there were more available and better paid jobs.
—*Fieldnotes*, August 15, 2012

In the beginning of the 1960s, Elliot Liebow (1967) started to meet with African American migrant men from the Southern states (Alabama, Georgia, Virginia, and the Carolinas), who used to gather daily at a street corner while waiting for a job in downtown Washington, D.C., —a street corner that was re-named by Liebow *Tally's Corner*. A decade later, Lucy M. Cohen (1979) would describe in her book *Culture, Disease, and Stress among Latino Immigrants* the case of Juan Cortés, a Latino immigrant man who was invited by "the janitor in his apartment building" to join him "on the line." According to Cohen (1979, p. 108), between the District of Columbia and Maryland there was a day-labor site where African American men used to congregate hoping to find "work with some construction crew." In Logan Circle, also in the District of Columbia, Central American men used to gather everyday at a store parking lot that was very close to the house where I was living with a Salvadoran family in 2002 (Sánchez Molina, 2005). A few years later, day-laborers who used to gather there had to move to other *esquinas* (corners) in the inner city since a brand new apartment building was constructed on that exact site.

While old street corners in the inner city are no longer available for day workers in the District of Columbia, mainly due to processes of gentrification (Williams, 1988) that have intensified in the city in the last decade (*see also* Prince, 2014), other 'new corners' have proliferated in close and outer suburban areas attracting the attention of anthropologists and other social scientists (Valenzuela et al., 2005; Ibáñez-Holtermann, 2011; Pierson, 2009; Bianchi et al, 2013). At present, there are still several day-labor sites in the city where Latino immigrants gather daily while waiting for a job. In the case of Hondurans, and other Central American immigrants, they usually gather at specific public sites located at street corners and/or store parking lots in the capital and in close and outer suburban neighborhoods in both Maryland and northern Virginia.

A decade ago, there were, according to Valenzuela et al. (2005), about sixteen day-labor sites throughout the metropolitan region (including Baltimore) where immigrants,[8] most of them from Latin American countries (94 percent), and especially from Central America (67 percent), used to wait for a job (*see also* Theodore et al., 2008). The proliferation of these day-labor sites in the region had to do with the rapid growth of the economy in the region that increased the employers' demand, especially in the construction industry. Along with this economic factor, and as in other metropolitan areas in the United Sates, these authors also highlighted the significant growth of undocumented immigrants in the region as a result of the lack of a migratory reform. A political factor which, according to other scholars (Gomberg-Muñoz, 2010; Fussell, 2011), has intensified the vulnerability of these day-labor immigrants' in their new destinations in the United States. Valenzuela et al. (2005) state that the day-labor market in Greater Washington is distinct from other areas in the United States, on the one hand, because most day-workers are Latino immigrants, especially from Central America, and, on the other hand, because most of them are hired by contractors and subcontractors from construction companies.[9]

Potential employers usually pass by day-labor sites located throughout the region seeking to hire immigrant workers, individually or in groups, for doing moves, painting, carpentry, and landscaping, among other jobs related to the construction industry. Another feature of the day-labor market in the region, according to this research team, is that most of the Latino day workers settled in the region have basic and also higher education. As Marie D. Price (2012) also underscores in the case of Bolivian immigrants settled in northern Virginia, this is a new employment niche for Honduran men with university education who work as day laborers. While Gustavo came to the region with professional training as an electrician, Jairo studied engineering at a university in Tegucigalpa, the capital of Honduras.

CORNERS AND LABOR CONDITIONS IN A GLOBAL METROPOLIS

> Then, I began to realize the other story of the United States, since the United States is portrayed to us (*nos lo pintan*) as a country with a lot of opportunities, as a hospitable country, as a humanitarian country, as a country where people open their doors . . . But it was nothing like this!
> —*Gustavo*

Like Gustavo, many Honduran immigrants came to the United States hoping to fulfill the mythical "American dream" having imagined the United States as a country full of labor opportunities and economic success for all immigrants willing to work hard; this *imaginaire* that is usually reinforced by the mass media, and by other migrants and kin in their home societies (*see* Mahler, 1995b; Schmalzbauer, 2005b; Rosser, 2008). Even so, starting to work as a day laborer in the United State, doing jobs that they have not done before in their home societies, may be a very hard experience, as Gustavo expresses when he remembers the first time that he was hired at a corner in northern Virginia:

> That day, an American man passed by and said to me: "I want a person to do this . . ." And I followed him without knowing him. He chose several people and drove us to a place in order to open holes with a bar (rod) all day long . . . When we finished, my hands were bleeding! . . . And since then, I've gone back daily to the same *esquina* (corner).

As other informants reemphasize, once they start to work as day-laborers, they usually go to the same *esquina* (corner) where they meet other Latino immigrants who can also inform them about jobs, potential employers and community services in Spanish. Gathering with other Latino workers at these public sites, they can build a sort of community by socializing, participating, and sharing personal and family experiences helping them to face different kinds of social and cultural barriers during their process of incorporation into the host society. In this sense, day-labor sites become, as Liebow (1967) had pointed out regarding the "inner-city carry out shops" in downtown Washington, D.C., "outpost institutions" where they communicate with each other in Spanish and exchange information and advice about available jobs, housing, social services, and other social resources.

Although the labor conditions with which they have to deal are very tough, they gather at these public sites hoping to find more stable jobs that prevent them from having to go back to the same *esquinas* (corners). Above all, considering that some of the construction work that many of them have to perform, often without proper training, theirs are considered the highest risk jobs in the United States (Walter et al., 2002). According to some of my informants, not only are these labor conditions very hard, including heavy and risky work, but some employers also mistreat and exploit them by stealing their salaries or threatening to take advantage of their migratory status. Some of my informants offered accounts of being swindled at work: how "an American man stole $800 from me" and keeping a bounced check as a memento, how "a French man did not pay me $700," and also how Latinos swindle them. [10] These labor conditions make them much more vulnerable if, as was the experience suffered by one of them, they decide to ask for labor rights:

An American woman who lives in R. stole $600 from me and threatened me, saying:

> –I am going to have you deported!
> And I answered her:
> –I am not frightened of you deporting me.
> She continued:
> –You are an illegal alien and we are going to expel you.
> And I responded:
> –And, I am going to take you to court because you are hiring illegal immigrants because you do not want to pay taxes. What you are doing is more of a crime.

During his first year in Fairfax, Gustavo was hired by a homeowner to work at his house sawing wood. According to him, the saw did not work very well and he had an accident with it, cutting off two fingers of his right hand. Although his employer took him to a clinic, paying the bill that day, he stopped paying his salary. And although this employer had promised him more jobs, he did not hire him anymore. Since he was not able to work for three months, he looked for a lawyer's help, taking this employer to court, who then lost the case and had to pay all his medical bills. Even so, this kind of response to labor exploitation is not very common among Latino immigrant day-laborers. Although federal legislation establishes specific rules for high-risk jobs, frauds, and injuries at work, covering and protecting undocumented immigrants (Walter, Bourgois, and Loinaz, 2004), many of them are reluctant to accuse their employers because of their migratory status, and other social and cultural obstacles such as language or ignorance of the U.S. legal system (*see also* Cohen, 1973). As is the case among the Latino immigrants studied by Elizabeth Fussell (2011) in New Orleans, since most of them are afraid of deportation, they usually refuse to take their employers to court, becoming, consequently, much more vulnerable to labor abuse and exploitation (*see also* Meléndez et al., 2014). These labor conditions are, therefore, key factors in understanding how these Honduran men incorporate into and adapt to the United States since, as Lucy M. Cohen has highlighted (1979, p. 123), these first labor experiences provide new immigrants "with a microcosm" of the host society at large:

> For most immigrants low-status work did not entail simply an evaluation of their knowledge and skills against the requirements of specific jobs. Work was the avenue through which they established key relations with representatives of the larger society. And it was on the job that they learned how *buen trato* and *mal trato* function in American society.[11] (Cohen, 1979, p. 256)

The challenges that undocumented Latino day laborers have to face daily at work may drive them to despair, as Quesada et al. (2014) have shown. Based on research with Latino immigrant day laborers in the San Francisco metropolitan area, these authors use the Spanish concept of *desesperación* (desperation) as a cultural idiom of distress. Since most of them support families in their country of origin, particularly children, their feelings of distress may intensify when they cannot find jobs and, consequently, send remittances to their homes. As Bustamante and Aleman (2007, p. 76) underscore in their analysis of transnational fatherhood practices among Mexican guest workers in the United States, remittances are a major strategy used by these immigrant fathers not only for providing their children financial stability, but also to compensate for their "spatial-temporal separation." As in the cases of Jairo, Gustavo, and Mauro, many of them have left their children in their home societies and regularly send remittances to support them.[12] When they leave their children in Honduras under the care of their mothers, as some of my informants have done, pre-migratory family reconstitutions require, nevertheless, few changes (*see* Debry, 2010). In addition to these labor and family conditions, Quesada et al. (2014, pp. 3-4) also emphasize that feelings of desperation increase among day laborers when they face experiences of discrimination at work, particularly when they are accused of lawbreaking and threatened with deportation.

EXCLUSIONARY POLICIES AND REGIONAL DISPLACEMENTS

Jairo and Elisa did not have many problems finding jobs during the first three years that they lived in Prince Williams (Northern Virginia) since — according to them—there were a lot of jobs available for both of them. The problems came when county legislation against undocumented immigrants was released. Since then, their situation began to get worse. They had to move to the District of Columbia because, according to Jairo, the legislation in Washington, D.C., was much more tolerant of undocumented immigrants, and community organizations that help Latino immigrants were much more organized. Once in Washington, D.C., Elisa found a job cleaning houses and Jairo continued to gather with other Latino immigrants at the *esquinas* (corners) in the inner city and nearby suburban areas.

Trying to expel Latino immigrants from some *esquinas* in outer suburban localities, in both Northern Virginia and Maryland, some residents and organizations from these places began to press local governments to enact ordinances prohibiting them from gathering in public sites, forcing many of them to leave these jurisdictions. Along with these local political initiatives, many of them began to experience different kinds of harassment (such as verbal abuse and photographing) while gathering at the day-labor sites (*see* Claffey, 2006). These social reactions against day-laborers contributed to their identification as troublemakers and potential criminals (Quesada, 2011; Pinedo-Turnovsky, 2006), causing some local governments to release other ordinances against undocumented immigrants, such as requiring the police to check migratory status.[13]

> Montgomery County officials yesterday announced the planned opening of a new employment center that will offer a range of services to prospective day laborers. Just a block from where the new center is scheduled to open by the end of next month in Wheaton, several dozen people, mostly Latino immigrants, congregate each workday behind a paint store on Viers Mill Road, waiting for employers to show up to hire them (Partlow, 2005).

In response to these anti-immigrant reactions, civic and faith-based organizations from suburban localities have tried to support these immigrant workers by establishing formal day-labor centers (*see* Leitner and Strunk, 2014). These centers provided Latino day workers facilities, such as restrooms and shelters, labor organization, assigning, for instance, jobs through a lottery system to potential employers, and labor protections against work exploitation (Rodriguez, 2008; Cleaveland, 2011). As in other U.S. metropolitan areas, these labor centers were established in the region trying to stop labor, health and safety law violations occurring in the day-labor market while acting as labor mediators between workers and employers (Meléndez et al., 2014). Even so, since these day-labor centers were supported by municipal councils with public funds, they had to be closed due to pressures from local anti-immigrant organizations that argued that public resources could not be used to support undocumented immigrants. [14]

One social consequence of these local exclusionary policies was the displacement of undocumented immigrants to other metropolitan areas, seeking social and political support in inner and nearby suburban metropolitan neighborhoods. In this social context, Jairo and Elisa had to move from Prince William County to Washington, D.C., in 2009. [15] This specific regional displacement drew the attention of some social scientists who named this phenomenon the "Prince William effect" (Capps et al., 2011). The growth of anti-immigrant reactions in outer suburban localities in Greater Washington has been explained by pointing out local structural conditions such as the rapid increase of undocumented Latinos in these new destinations in the last decade. These localities have neither the historical trajectory nor the social resources, such as schools, healthcare delivery services, and worksites, to incorporate new immigrants. While the District of Columbia, Arlington, or Alexandria have had a longer trajectory and infrastructures receiving immigrants, new destinations such as Prince William or Loudoun counties in Northern Virginia have neither the experience nor the necessary resources to face rapidly increasing high concentrations of immigrants (*see* Singer, Wilson, and DeRenzis, 2009).

This sort of exclusionary local ordinances against day laborers was not, however, a new phenomenon in U.S. metropolises, having occurred, as shown by Sarah Mahler (1995a) and Hamilton and Chinchilla (2001), in Long Island and Los Angeles during the 1980s. According to Sarah Mahler (1995a, p. 118), two main reasons explain the rise of anti-immigrant reactions in the United States: Economic insecurity, as a consequence of global economic restructuration, affect the rise of unemployment rates and cuts in labor benefits, and the increase of immigrants in suburban localities produces higher budget spending in social services while putting at risk residents' investments in real estate. These social conditions have made immigrants, particularly undocumented immigrants, much more vulnerable in the United States (De Geneva, 2002). It has caused them to become, as has happened in other historic periods (Higham, 1955; Sanchez, 1997; Chavez, 2008), scapegoats for economic crises.

These exclusionary local policies against undocumented Latino day-laborers contrast, however, with other more inclusionary policies developed and implemented by other local governments in the region. For this reason, scholars analyzing these anti-immigrant reactions in the region have argued that, along with demographic, economic, and historical factors, other political factors at the federal and local levels must be underlined (Leon et al., 2009; Rodriguez, 2008; Bernstein, 2011). In doing so, they have shown how the development and implementation of inclusionary policies at the county level in other suburban areas have been more positive in helping undocumented immigrants to become incorporated into their own jurisdictions. These scholars, for instance, underscore local policies supporting community and organization networks that provide basic social and cultural services to new immigrants as a key factor. Although organizations serving Latino immigrants have increased throughout outer suburban areas, most of them continue to be concentrated in the District of Columbia and the inner suburbs in Northern Virginia and Maryland. They are important social service providers filling the void left by governments helping the new immigrants to incorporate and adapt in the host society (Leon et al., 2009). In these efforts, immigrant organizations have played an important role by local policies in their own jurisdictions in the development and implementation of inclusionary policies, among others, in Washington, D.C., Arlington, and the city of Alexandria in Northern Virginia, or Takoma Park in suburban Maryland (Leitner and Stunk, 2014).

These local inclusionary policies explain, on the other hand, immigrants' displacements to other areas in the region—as was the case of Elisa and Jairo—who sought protection and social support. In addition to the need for more inclusionary local policies, scholars have also pointed to the lack of a comprehensive federal migratory reform. The absence of migratory policy reform has not only affected the rise of anti-immigrant social and political actions in different regions in the United States (Singer, 2012), but also the expansion of the day-labor market in the Washington, D.C., metropolitan area as well as other metropolitan regions in the country (Theodore et al., 2008).

CONCLUSIONS

If globalization has developed an ethnic- and gender-segmented labor market for immigrants in a global metropolis such as Greater Washington, low-skilled workers from developing countries have received little official support either to migrate or adapt to the host societies. As some scholars have stressed, while nation-states maximize production by lifting borders and welcoming the flow of capital, information, and labor, they simultaneously close these borders when it comes to the permanent incorporation of immigrants and refugees; particularly after the terrorists' attacks occurred on September 11, 2001 (Mabee, 2009; Bender, 2002; Ahmad, 2002). This political exclusion make immigrants much more vulnerable to other sorts of social exclusion and marginalization in their processes of incorporation and adaptation to the host societies (Aranda, Hughes, and Sabogal, 2014; Bonilla-Silva, 2006).

In the case of undocumented Honduran workers in Greater Washington, the lack of migratory political reforms at a federal level has been one of the main factors which has contributed to the growth of both undocumented immigrants and day-labor market in the region. Under these circumstances, some local governments have tried to facilitate new immigrants' incorporation by supporting, among other policies, multicultural communities and organizations. In these efforts, immigrant advocacy has played, as pointed out by Helga Leitner and Christ Strunk (2014, p. 11), an important role by acting as cultural brokers through public social strategies of "claims and actions" challenging dominant discourses that stereotypy or reify undocumented immigrants.

NOTES

1. An earlier version of this chapter was presented at the Society for Applied Anthropology, 75th Annual Meeting, March 24-28, 2015 in Pittsburgh (Pennsylvania). I would like to thank Nancy Anne Kovalinka, Peter Watkin, and Asdrubal Mencía for their insightful comments and suggestions.

2. Since the 1980s, the *labor market segmentation* theory has tried to overcome the *dual labor market* theory proposed in the United Stated during the 1970s (*see* Piore, 1979). The concept of "segmentation" was introduced by Michael Reich, David Gordon, and Richard Edwards (1973) to emphasize how political and economic factors have perpetuated in the United States segmented labor markets by sectors (as the *dual labor market* theory highlights), ethnicity, and gender. However, while emphasizing local characteristics in segmented labor markets, these theories have not paid enough attention, according to Michael Samers (2011, p. 53), to the international character of labor markets in globalized urban localities and how many migrants enter to work in specific sectors depending, for instances, on their countries of origin and migratory status.

3. I carried out ethnographic research with Honduran immigrants settled in the Washington, D.C. metropolitan area from 2007 to 2015. The data were collected through participant observation and informal and in-depth interviews in different social contexts: At day labor sites, communities, and my informants' homes (*see also* Sánchez Molina, 2015).

4. According to the 2010 Census, there are 81,460 Latino people registered in Prince William County, accounting for 20.3 percent of its 402,002 residents. Along with Prince William County, cities in this area in Northern Virginia also register some of the highest percentages of Latino population in the Washington, D.C. metropolitan area: Manassas Park (32.5 percent) and Manassas (31 percent) (U.S. Census Bureau, 2010; *see also* Singer, 2012).

5. Civil wars in several Central American countries during the 1980s also prompted Honduran migration to the United States, especially Hondurans living close to the border with El Salvador (Gallardo, 2006). Following Salvadoran migratory networks, Honduran immigrants began to settle in Washington, D.C. and its surroundings, especially in those neighborhoods where Salvadorans were settling in Northern Virginia, particularly in Alexandria City and Fairfax County, and suburban Maryland (Petrozziello, 2011; Sánchez Molina, 2015).

6. The reported number of Honduran immigrants in the United States has tripled in the last decade, according to the 2010 Census, making them the eighth largest Latino community in the country. Mostly arriving in the United States since the 1990s, they are mainly concentrated in Southern states (59 percent), particularly in Florida (18 percent) and Texas (14 percent), and also in Northeastern states (21 percent), especially in New York (12 percent) (Motel and Patten, 2012).

7. It is difficult to calculate the number of Hondurans residing in the United States due to the increase in undocumented immigration which intensified after Hurricane Mitch; in fact, Honduran immigrants represent the greatest overall increases in undoc-

umented immigrants in the United States (*see also* Motel and Patten, 2012). According to Hoefer, Rytina, and Baker (2010) there were about 320,000 Honduran undocumented immigrants in the United States, constituting the national group with the greatest overall increase (95 percent) in undocumented immigrants.

8. At present, there are at least three new day-labor sites in the Washington, D.C., area.

9. From Guatemala 25 percent, Honduras 22 percent, and El Salvador 20 percent, while immigrants from Mexico accounted for 14 percent and from South American countries 12 percent (Valenzuela et al., 2005).

10. According to Theodore et al. (2008), a day-labor immigrant in the region used to earn between $10 and $12 per hour; around $200 per day working in landscaping, or $150 per day cleaning snow in the winter season. At present, day-laborers in the Washington metropolitan area can earn, according to my informants, around $14 and $15 per hour and $120 per day.

11. In the context of labor relationships, Lucy M. Cohen (1979, p. 122) translates *buen trato* as "proper and good treatment" and *mal trato* as "ill treatment, or lack of consideration."

12. After Hondagneu-Sotello and Avila (1997) proposed the concept of "transnational motherhood" as an analytical tool to explain current migrant women's kinship relationships with their children living in their home societies, ethnographies focusing on transnational families, mothering, and children have significantly increased (Salazar Parreña, 2001; 2005; Bryceson and Vuorela, 2002; Schmalzbauer 2005a; Boehm 2008; Sánchez Molina, 2004; 2006). However, not until more recently have scholars paid attention to "transnational fatherhood" as a social phenomenon to take into consideration (Pribilsky, 2004; 2012; Bustamante and Aleman, 2007; Dreby, 2010; Schmalzbauer, 2015). Social and cultural expectations based on gender related to identity constructions and expectations of masculinity/femininity and fatherhood/motherhood affect and distinguish transnational kinship relationships among parents and children.

13. In Prince William County was enacted the Illegal Immigration Enforcement Ordinances in 2008 requiring, among other measures, local police to ask about migratory status in order to reduce the number of undocumented immigrants in the county, crime, public disorder at day labor sites, and save public funds in social services. In addition to this legislation, the 287(g) agreement, authorizing local police to enforce immigration law, with the Immigration and Customs Enforcement (ICE) federal agency was signed (*see* Leitner and Strunk 2014).

14. These were the cases of day labor centers opened in Herndon (Fairfax in Northern Virginia) and Gaithersburg (Montgomery County in Maryland) during the 2000s that had to be closed due to the pressures led by anti-immigrant local groups such as Help Save Herndon and the Herndon Minutemen in Fairfax (Singer, Wilson, and DeRenzis, 2009) and Help Save Maryland in Montgomery County (Cleaveland and Pierson, 2009).

15. According to Leitner and Strunk (2014: p. 6) there were at least 15 local jurisdictions in new immigrant destinations in outer suburbs in Greater Washington that have passed exclusionary immigration ordinances since 2005 seeking to increase local enforcement of federal immigration legislation or limit the access of undocumented immigrants to housing, employment, or social services.

REFERENCES

Abbott, Carl. (1999). *Political Terrain. Washington, D.C., from Tidewater Town to Global Metropolis*. Chapel Hill and London: The University of North Carolina Press.

Ahmad, Muneer. (2002). "Homeland Insecurities: Racial Violence the Day after September 11."*Social Text 72*, 20(3): 101-116.

Aranda, Elizabeth M., Sallie Hughes and Elena Sabogal. (2014). *Making a Life in Multiethnic Miami: Immigration and the Rise of a Global City*. Boulder, CO: Lynne Rienner Publishers, Incorporated.

Bender, Steven. (2002). "Sight, Sound, and Stereotype: The War on Terrorism and Its Consequences for Latinas/os." *Oregon Law Review*, 81: 1153-74.

Bernstein, Hamutal. (2011). "Stranger or Neighbor? Explaining Local Immigrant Policymaking in Washington, D.C. and Madrid." Ph.D. Dissertation, Georgetown University.

Bianchi, Fernanda, Carol A. Reisen, Felisa A. Gonzales, Juan C. Arroyo, Maria Cecilia Zea, and Paul J. Poppen. (2013). "Sex with Sex Workers among Latino Day Laborers in Suburban Maryland." *Archives of Sexual Behavior*, 42:835–49.

Blanchard, Sarah, Erin R. Hamilton, Nestor Rodríguez and Hirotoshi Yoshioka. (2011). "Shifting Trends in Central American Migration: A Demographic Examination of Increasing Honduran-U.S. Immigration and Deportation." *The Latin Americanist*, 55(4): 61-84.

Boehm, Deborah A. (2008). "'For My Children:' Constructing Family and Navigating the State in the U.S.-Mexico Transnation." *Anthropological Quarterly*, 81(4): 777–802.

Booth, John A., Christine J. Wade, and Thomas W. Walker. (2010). *Understanding Central America. Global Forces, Rebellion, and Change*. Boulder, CO: Westview Press.

Bonilla-Silva, Eduardo. (2006). *Racism Without Racists: Color-blind Racism and the Persistence of Racial Inequality in the United States*. Lanham, MD: Rowman & Littlefield Publishers.

Bryceson, Deborah and Ulla Vuorela eds. (2002). *The Transnational Family: New European Frontiers and Global Networks*. Oxford: Berg.

Bustamante, Juan José, and Carlos Alemán. (2007). "Perpetuating split-household families: The case of Mexican sojourners in mid-Michigan and their transnational fatherhood practices." *Migraciones Internacionales*, 4(1): 65-86.

Capps, Randy, Marc R. Rosenblum, Christina Rodríguez, and Muzaffar Chishti. (2011). *Delegation and Divergence: A Study of 287(g) State and Local Immigration Enforcement*. Washington, D.C.: Migration Policy Institute.

Center for Regional Analysis. (2004). *The Employment Sectors of Washington, D.C. and the Downtown Business Improvement District*. Washington, D.C.: School of Public Policy, George Mason University.

Chaney, James. (2012). "Malleable Identities: Placing the Garínagu in New Orleans." *Journal of Latin American Geography*, 11(2): 121-144.

Chavez, Leo R. (2008). *The Latino Threat: Constructing Immigrants, Citizens, and the Nation*. Stanford, CA: Stanford University Press.

Chavez, Leo R. (1994). "The Power of the Imagined Community: The Settlement of Undocumented Mexicans and Central Americans in the United States." *American Anthropologist*, 96, 1: 52-73.

Chavez, Leo R. (1991). *Shadowed Lives. Undocumented Immigrants in American Society*. San Diego, CA: Harcourt Brace College Publishers.

Claffey, James. (2006). "Anti-Immigrant Violence in Suburbia." *Social Text*, 24: 73–80.

Clark-Lewis, Elizabeth. (1996). "'For a Real Better Life' Voices of African American Women Migrants, 1900-1930." In Francine Curro Cary (ed.) *Urban Odyssey: A Multicultural History of Washington, D.C.* Washington, D.C.: Smithonian Institution Press, pp. 97-112.

Cleaveland, Carol. (2011). "Borders, Police, and Jobs: Viewing Latino Immigration Through a Social Spatial Lens." *Family in Society*, 92(2): 139-145.

Cleaveland, Carol and Leo Pierson. (2009). "Parking lots and police. Undocumented Latinos' tactics for finding day labor jobs." *Ethnography*, 10(4): 515-533.

Cohen, Lucy M. (1979). *Culture, Disease, and Stress among Latino Immigrants*. Washington, D.C.: Smithsonian Institution.

Cohen, Lucy M. (1973). "Gifts to Strangers: Public Policy and the Delivery of Health Services to Illegal Aliens." *Anthropological Quarterly*, 46(3): 183-195.

De Genova, Nicholas. (2002). "Migrant 'Illegality' and Deportability in Everyday Life." *Annual Review of Anthropology*, 31: 419–47.
De Souza, Sarah. (2011). "Honduras: The Debate between the United States Immigration Crackdowns." *Social Sciences Journal*, 10(1): 16-19.
Dreby, Joanna. (2010). *Divided by Borders: Mexican Migrants and their Children*. Berkeley, CA: University of California Press.
District of Columbia Government. (2011). *Indices: A Statistical Index to the District of Columbia Services*. Washington, DC: The District of Columbia Government, vol. XV.
England, Sarah. (2006). *Afro Central Americans in New York City: Garifuna Tales of Transnational Movements in Racialized Space*. Gainesville, FL: University Press of Florida.
Fuentes, Vilma Elisa. (2003). "The Political Effects of Disaster and Foreign Aid: National and Subnational Governance in Honduras after Hurricane Mitch." Ph.D. Dissertation, University of Florida.
Fussell, Elizabeth. (2011). "The Deportation Threat Dynamic and Victimization of Latino Migrants: Wage Theft and Robbery." *The Sociological Quarterly*, 52: 593-615.
Gallardo, Glenda (eds.). (2006). *Informe sobre Desarrollo Humano Honduras 2006. Hacia la expansión de la ciudadanía*. San José, Costa Rica: Programa de las Naciones Unidas para el Desarrollo (PNUD) Honduras.
Gomberg-Muñoz, Ruth. (2010). "Willing to Work: Agency and Vulnerability in an Undocumented Immigrant Network." *American Anthropologist*, 112 (2): 295-307.
Gorman, Leo B. (2010). "Latino Migrant Labor Strife and Solidarity in Post-Katrina New Orleans, 2005-2007." *The Latin Americanist*, 54 (1): 1-33.
Hagan, Jacqueline, Karl Eschbach, and Nestor Rodriguez. (2008). "U.S. Deportation Policy, Family Separation, and Circular Migration." *International Migration Review*, 42 (1): 64-88.
Hamilton, Nora, & Chinchilla, Norma S. (2001). *Seeking Community in a Global City: Guatemalans and Salvadorans in Los Angeles*. Philadelphia: Temple University Press.
Higham, John. (1955). *Strangers in the Land: Patterns of American Nativism, 1860-1925*. New Brunswick, New Jersey: Rutgers University Press.
Hondagneu-Sotelo, Pierrette, and Ernestine Avila. (1997). "I'm Here, but I'm There: The Meanings of Latino Transnational Motherhood." *Gender and Society*, 11(5): 548-571.
Ibáñez-Holtermann, Esther (2011) "La Parada: Explaining Ixil Day laborers in Virginia Illegality, Loss, Hope and Community." Ph.D. Dissertation, American University.
Kirchbichler, Elisabeth. (2010). "Those Who Never Make It and the Suffering of Those Left Behind: The Fate of Honduran Missing Migrants and their Families." *Encuentro*, 87: 61-74.
Knox, Paul L. (1991). "The Restless Urban Landscape: Economic and Sociocultural Change and the Transformation of Metropolitan Washington, DC." *Annals of the Association of American Geographers*, 81(2): 181-209.
Leitner, Helga and Christopher Strunk. (2014). "Assembling Insurgent Citizenship: Immigrant Advocacy Struggles in the Washington, D.C. Metropolitan Area." *Urban Geography*, 35(7): 943-964.
Leon, Edwin de, Matthew Maronick, Carol J. De Vita, and Elizabeth T. Boris. (2009). *Community-Based Organizations and Immigrant Integration in the Washington, D.C. Metropolitan Area*. Washington, D.C.: The Urban Institute.
Liebow, Elliot. (1967). *Tally's Corner. A Study of Negro Streetcorner Men*. Boston: Little, Brown and Company.
Mabee, Bryan. (2009). *The Globalization of Security State Power, Security Provision and Legitimacy*. New York: Palgrave Macmillan.
Mahler, Sarah. (1995a). *Salvadorans in Suburbia. Symbiosis and Conflict*. Boston: Allyn and Bacon.
Mahler, Sarah. (1995b). *American Dreaming. Immigrant Life on the Margins*. Princeton, NJ: Princeton University Press.

Massey, Douglas S. and Karen A. Pren. (2012). "Unintended Consequences of US Immigration Policy: Explaining the Post-1965 Surge from Latin America." *Population and Development Review*, 38 (1): 1–29.

Meléndez, Edwin J., M. Anne Visser, Nich Theodore, and Abel Valenzuela. (2014). "Worker Centers and Day Laborers' Wages." *Social Science Quarterly*, 95(3): 835-851.

Motel, Seth and Eileen Patten. (2012). *Hispanics of Honduran Origin in the United States, 2010*. Washington, D.C.: Pew Hispanic Center.

Oliver-Smith, Anthony. (2005). "Communities after Catastrophe: Reconstructing the Material, Reconstituting the Social." In Stanley E. Hyland (ed.) *Community Building in the Twenty-First Century*. Santa Fe, NM: School of American Research Press, pp. 45-70.

Orozco, Manuel. (2007). "Central American Diasporas and Hometown Associations." In Barbara J. Merz, Lincoln C. Chen, and Peter F. Geithner (eds.) *Diasporas and Development*. Cambridge, MA: Harvard University Press, pp. 217-55.

Partlow, Joshua. (2005). "Montgomery Plans to Open Second Day Laborer Center." *Washington Post*, Tuesday, February 1; Page B02 www.washingtonpost.com/wp-dyn/articles/A52562-2005Jan31.html (October 29, 2015).

Pessar, Patricia R. (1995). "The Elusive Enclave: Ethnicity, Class, and Nationality among Latino Entrepreneurs in Greater Washington, DC." *Human Organization*, 54 (4): 383-92.

Petrozziello, Allison J. (2011). "Feminised financial flows: how gender affects remittances in Honduran-US transnational families." *Gender & Development*, 19 (1): 53-67.

Pierson, Leo. (2009). "'We're Just Not Blended Yet': The Case of Latino Day Labor in Prince William County." Master Dissertation, George Mason University.

Pinedo-Turnovsky, Carolyn. (2006). "A La Parada: The Social Practices of Men on a Street Corner." *Social Text*, 24 (2): 55–72.

Piore, Michael. (1979). *Birds of Passage: Migrant Labor and Industrial Society*. Cambridge, U.K.: Cambridge University Press.

Price, Marie D. (2012). "Hispanic Entrepreneurship in a Global City: The Bolivian Diaspora in Washington, D.C." In Enrique Pumar ed (2012) *Hispanic Migration and Urban Development: Studies from Washington, D.C.* Bingley, U.K.: Emerald Group Publishing Limited, pp. 133-153.

Price, Marie and Audrey Singer. (2008). "Immigrants, Suburbs, and the Politics of Reception in Metropolitan Washington." In Audrey Singer, Susan W. Hardwick, and Caroline B. Brettell (eds.) *Twenty-First Century Gateways. Immigrant Incorporation in Suburban America*. Washington, D.C.: Brookings Institution Press, pp. 137-68.

Prince, Sabiyha. (2014). *African Americans and Gentrification in Washington, D.C. Race, Class, and Social Justice in the Nation's Capital*. Burlington, VT: Ashgate Publishing Company.

Pribilsky, Jason. (2012). "Consumption Dilemmas: Tracking Masculinity, Money and Transnational Fatherhood between the Ecuadorian Andes and New York City." *Journal of Ethnic and Migration Studies*, 38 (2): 323-343.

Pribilsky, Jason. (2004). "*Aprendemos a convivir*: Conjugal Relations, Co-parenting, and Family Life among Ecuadorian Transnational Migrants in New York City and the Ecuadorian Andes." *Global Networks*, 4 (3): 313-324.

Quesada, James (2011) "No soy welferero: Undocumented Latino Laborers in the Crosshairs of Legitimation Maneuvers." *Medical Anthropology*, 30 (4): 386-408.

Quesada, James, Sonya Arreola, Alex Kral, Sahar Khoury, Kurt C. Organista, and Paula Worby. (2014). "'As Good As It Gets': Undocumented Latino Day Laborers Negotiating Discrimination in San Francisco and Berkeley, California, USA." *City & Society*, 26 (1): 29-50.

Reichman, Daniel R. (2011). *The Broken Village. Coffee, Migration, and Globalization in Honduras*. Ithaca, N.Y.: Cornell University Press.

Repak, Terry A. (1995). *Waiting on Washington. Central American Workers in the Nation's Capital*. Philadelphia: Temple University Press.

Reyes, Wilmer, Pedro Torres, and Raquel Isaula. (2012). "Migration, Remittances and Natural Resource Management in Olancho, Honduras." In Susanna Hecht, Susan Kandel, and Abelardo Morales (eds.) *Rural Livelihoods & Natural Resource Management*. El Salvador: International Development Research Centre (IDRC) of Canada, Ford Foundation, and Fundación PRISMA, pp. 147-170.

Rodríguez, Cristina M. (2008). "The Significance of the Local in Immigration Regulation." *Michigan Law Review*, 106: 567-642.

Rosser, Ezra. (2008). "Immigrant Remittances." *Connecticut Law Review*, 41:1-62.

Salazar Parreñas, Rhacel. (2005). *Children of Global Migration. Transnational Families and Gendered Woes*. Stanford, CA: Stanford University Press.

Salazar Parreñas, Rhacel. (2001). *Servants of Globalization. Women, Migration, and Domestic Work*. Stanford, CA: Stanford University Press.

Samers, Michael. (2011). "The Socioterritoriality of Cities. A Framework for Understanding the Incorporation of Migrants in Urban labor Markets." In Nina Glick Schiller and Ayşe Çağlar (eds.) *Locating Migration. Rescaling Cities and Migrants*. Ithaca and London: Cornell University Press, pp. 42-59.

Samers, Michael. (2009). *Migration*. London & New York: Routledge.

Sanchez, George J. (1997). " Face the Nation: Race, Immigration, and the Rise of Nativism in Late Twentieth Century America." *International Migration Review*, 31 (4): 1009-1030.

Sánchez Molina, Raúl. (2015). "Caring While Missing Children's Infancy: Transnational Mothering among Honduran Women Working in Greater Washington." *Human Organization*, 74 (1): 62-73.

Sánchez Molina, Raúl. (2008). "Modes of Incorporation, Social Exclusion, and Transnationalism: Salvadoran's Adaptation to the Washington, D.C. Metropolitan Area." *Human Organization*, 67 (3): 269-280.

Sánchez Molina, Raúl. (2006). *Proceso Migratorio de una Mujer Salvadoreña. El viaje de María Reyes a Washington, D.C.* Madrid: Centro de Investigaciones Sociológicas/ Siglo XXI.

Sánchez Molina, Raúl. (2005). *"Mandar a traer."Antropología, migraciones y transnacionalismo. Salvadoreños en Washington*. Madrid: Editorial Universitas.

Sánchez Molina, Raúl. (2004). "Cuando los hijos se quedan en El Salvador: Familias transnacionales y reunificación familiar de inmigrantes salvadoreños en Washington, D.C. Madrid: In *Revista de Dialectología y Tradiciones Populares*, 59 (2): 257-276.

Schmalzbauer, Leah. (2015). "Temporary and Transnational: Gender and Emotion in the Lives of Mexican Guest Worker Fathers." *Ethnic and Racial Studies*, 38 (2): 211-226.

Schmalzbauer Leah. (2005a). *Striving and surviving: a daily life analysis of Honduran transnational families*. New York: Routledge.

Schmalzbauer, Leah. (2005b). "Transamerican Dreamers: The Relationship of Honduran Transmigrants to the American Dream and Consumer Society." *Berkeley Journal of Sociology*, 49: 3-31.

Singer, Audrey. (2012). "Metropolitan Washington: A New Immigrant Gateway." *In* Enrique Pumar ed *Hispanic Migration and Urban Development: Studies from Washington, D.C.* Bingley, U.K.: Emerald Group Publishing Limited, pp. 1-24.

Singer, Audrey. (2003). *At Home in the Nation's Capital: Immigrant Trends in Metropolitan Washington*. Washington, D.C.: The Brookings Institution.

Singer, Audrey, Jill H. Wilson, and Brooke DeRenzis. (2009). "Immigrants, Politics, and Local Response in Suburban Washington." *Metropolitan Policy Program at Brookings*, Washington, D.C.: The Brookings Institution.

Sládková, Jana. (2010). *Journeys of undocumented. Honduran Migrants to the United States*. El Paso, TX: LFB Scholarly Publishing LLC.

Sládkovà, Jana. (2007). "Expectations and Motivations of Hondurans Migrating to the United States." *Journal of Community and Applied Social Psychology*, 17(3): 187-202.

Sládková, Jana, Sandra M. García Mangado, and Johana Reyes Quinteros. (2012). "Lowell Immigrant Communities in the Climate of Deportations." *Analyses of Social Issues and Public Policy*, 12(1): 78-95.

Reichman, Daniel R. (2011). *The Broken Village. Coffee, Migration, and Globalization in Honduras*. Ithaca and London: Cornell University Press.

Rosser, Ezra. (2008). "Immigrant Remittances."*Connecticut Law Review*, 41: 1-62.

Theodore, N., A. Valenzuela, E. Meléndez, and A. L. González. (2008). "Day Labor and Workplace Abuses in the Residential Construction Industry: Conditions in the Washington, DC Region." In A. Bernhardt, H. Boushey, L. Dresser and C. Tilly (eds.) *The Gloves Off Economy: Workplace Standards at the Bottom of America's Labor Market*. Ithaca, NY: Cornell University Press, pp. 91–109.

U.S. Census Bureau. (2010). *United States Census 2010*. Washington, D.C.: U.S. Department of Commerce.

www.census.gov/prod/www/decennial.html (June 6, 2015).

Valenzuela Jr., Abel. (2003). "Day Labor Work." *Annual Review of Sociology*, 29: 307–33.

Valenzuela Jr., Abel, Ana Luz Gonzalez, Nik Theodore, and Edwin Melendez. (2005). *In Pursuit of the American Dream: Day Labor in the Greater Washington D.C. Region*. Los Angeles, CA: Center for the Study of Urban Poverty University of California.

Valenzuela Jr., Abel, Janette A. Kawachi, and Matthew D. Marr. (2002). "Seeking Work Daily: Supply, Demand, and Spatial Dimensions of Day Labor in Two Global Cities." *International Journal of Comparative Sociology* (IJCS), 43 (2): 192-219.

Walter, Nicholas, Philippe Bourgois and H. Margarita Loinaz. (2004). "Masculinity and undocumented labor migration: Injured Latino Day Laborers in San Francisco." *Social Science & Medicine*, 59: 1159–1168.

Walter, Nicholas, Philippe Bourgois, H. M. Loinaz, and Dean Schillinger. (2002). "Social Context of Work Injury Among Undocumented Day Laborers in San Francisco." *Journal of General Internal Medicine*, 17: 221-229.

Williams, Brett. (1988). *Upscaling Downtown: Stalled Gentrification in Washington, D.C.* Ithaca, NY: Cornell University Press.

Zarrugh, Laura H. (2007). "From Workers to Owners: Latino Entrepreneurs in Harrisonburg, Virginia." *Human Organization*, 66 (3): 240-248.

SIX

Latin Women Organizers in Faith-Based Communities in West Virginia and Maryland

Tadeusz Mich

The growth of Latino communities in the United States is a reality of American society and the Catholic Church (Matovina, 2012). As several studies indicate, Latinos represent around 25 percent of the entire Catholic community in the United States (Perl et at. 2006; Suro et al., 2007; Lugo et al. 2008). They constitute not only the largest minority, over 16 percent of the total population in the United States, but also a large and growing portion of the Catholic Church. According to Suro et al. (2007: 12), one-third of all Catholics in the United States are Latinas/os religious denomination is going to grow. In addition to these demographic factors, these authors also underscore that the Latino population is transforming the U.S. Catholic Church's "religious landscape." Indeed, most Latino Catholics in the United States, around 68 percent, are foreign born. In addition, they represent a complex cultural diversity rooted in twenty-three different countries in Latin America. Around 55 percent have Spanish as their primary language (Suro et al., 2007, p. 9).

Scholars studying migration and globalization have focused on immigrants' religions to analyze how faith-based institutions affect their adaptation to host societies. This academic interest has, nevertheless, precedent in the United States with research focused on how Catholic institutions facilitated or prevented Irish, Italian, and Polish immigrants from assimilating to mainstream U.S. culture (Hirschman, 2004). However, not until the 1990s, did religion start to become a more relevant topic in migratory studies in the United States (Odgers Ortiz, 2009), paying a

particular interest from a transnational perspective on the role that religious communities plays in the contemporary immigrants' processes of
incorporation and adaptation (Levitt, 2001; Mahler and Hansing, 2005).

Since the late 1990s, new ethnographic approaches began to focus on
the role played by Christian churches among Latin American immigrants
in the U.S. in building community and identity (Hirschman, 2004; Odem,
2008). Research carried out in the Washington, D.C., metropolitan area
highlights how Catholic and Protestant Pentecostal churches help Central
American immigrants to face structural conditions in their processes of
incorporation into the host society while building transnational communities (Menjivar, 1999; Vásquez, 1999; Sánchez Molina, 2009). Although
there are a significant number of studies of Latino immigrants in the
United States, nevertheless, most of them have concentrated on the major
urban centers of the United States. A growing number of Latino immigrants, particularly from Mexico, are moving into a new "territory" in
distant suburbs, such as Jefferson County or Columbia Maryland in the
Washington, D.C., metropolitan area. On the other hand, little attention
has been given to faith-based organizations at the parish level and the
role that immigrant women play constructing communities in the host
societies (Peña and Frehill, 1998; Kemper and Adkins, 2005; Palmer-Boyes, 2015).

Like elsewhere in the Unites States, there are a growing number of
Latino communities in West Virginia and Maryland. They have to face
numerous challenges in their processes of becoming part of American
society and the Catholic Church in the United States. According to the
pastoral plan established by the U.S. Conference of Catholic Bishops,
Hispanic communities in Catholic parishes in the United States are part
of the American parish (U.S. Catholic Conference, 2001). Based on "Unity
in Diversity," this pastoral plan underscores that Latinos do not form a
separate parish or an independent community outside of the parish. This
model of working with diverse ethnic groups differs from other faith-
based organizations where Latinos have established their own communities separate from American communities.

Based on data from my extensive fieldwork in Catholic Latino Communities in West Virginia and Maryland from 2007 to 2015, this chapter
focuses on the implementation of this plan in these communities to analyze the role played by Latino women in the process of organizing Latino
communities in five parishes in these states. Data was collected in St.
James in Charles Town (Jefferson County) and in St. Joseph, in Martinsburg (Berkeley County) in West Virginia; St. Timothy in Walkersville
(Frederick County), St. John in Columbia (Howard County), and St. Joseph in Hagerstown (Washington County) in Maryland. Data collection
consisted of participant observation and interviews of many members of
these five Latino communities, particularly women. A significant part of
the data was gathered during group meetings that were dealing with

some critical issues related to the organization of the Latino Community in the American Catholic Parish. In addition to these meetings, I have participated in the celebration of baptisms, First Communions, marriages, Sunday services, and celebrations of *Quinceañeras* (a girl's celebration of her 15th birthday).

LATINO IMMIGRANTS IN CATHOLIC PARISHES IN WEST VIRGINIA AND MARYLAND

In the diocese of West Virginia, there are two Catholic parishes that have established Hispanic communities in American parishes: St. James in Charles Town and St. Joseph in Martinsburg. According to the 2010 Census data, Charles Town, a city located in Jefferson County, has a population of 4,062 inhabitants. Latino population accounts for 8.8 percent (359 residents) of its total population. Martinsburg in Berkeley County has 13,321 inhabitants and there are 731 Latinos, accounting for 5.4 percent of its population (U.S. Census Bureau, 2012). Due to the increase of Latino population in West Virginia, the number of Latino communities in Catholic parishes has been growing since the 2000s. According to the U.S. Census Bureau (2010) Latino population has increased significantly in Jefferson County due to the arrival of new immigrants from Mexico (1.5 percent) and U.S. citizens from Puerto Rico (0.7 percent).[1] As an informant at St. Joseph parish (Martinsburg) expressed it, "just ten years ago there were very few Hispanics at St. Joseph."

When I started my ethnographic research in 2007, there was no full time priest assigned to these Latino communities. However, as of 2015 both communities have a full time Spanish-speaking priest. Usually a priest would cover more than one Latino community in the area. This is an important factor to take into account in the process of organizing the Latino communities within the American parish. The constant absence of a Spanish-speaking priest in Hispanic communities helps them to organize themselves and, consequently, to become more self-sufficient.

With respect to Maryland, according to 2010 Census data, there are 470,632 Hispanics or Latinos, accounting for 8 percent of its total population. Out of 5,800 individuals in Walkersville town in Frederick County, 236 residents are Latinos, 4.0 percent. Columbia in Howard County has 99,615 inhabitants and 7,884 Hispanics or Latinos, accounting for 7.9 percent of its total population. And Hagerstown, a city in Washington County, has 39,662 inhabitants and 2,232 Hispanics or Latinos, who consist of 5.6 percent of the entire population (U.S. Census Bureau, 2012). Most Latino population in Frederick, Howard, and Washington counties in Maryland also come from Mexico and Puerto Rico (U.S. Census Bureau, 2010).

The Archdiocese of Baltimore Hispanic Ministry has a long history of its presence and also has a strategy to engage the Latino population in the state.[2] According to a Pastoral *de Conjunto* (Communion in Mission) strategy, cultural enrichment is a basic principle of the coexistence between Latinos and Americans in the same American Catholic parish. Before 1992, only several parishes in the Baltimore metropolitan area offered weekly Masses in Spanish; some of these date back into the 1970s. In 2003, there were sixteen parishes with Hispanic communities with an increasing number of Hispanic priests and others able to minister in Spanish (Office of Hispanic Ministry, 2003, p. xi).

An assimilation model encourages members of the Latino communities to give up their language, traditions and customs and be assimilated into mainstream American society. The cultural enrichment model does not promote a Latino community isolated from the American members of the parish. It is a model that promotes "unity in diversity." However, the reality in Catholic parishes in Maryland is different from the ideal model of mutual enrichment. There is a consistent pattern of confusion on both sides. On one side, Latino community members insist on a separate service in Spanish, and would like to have their own Latino organizational structure within the American Catholic parish. On the other side, American parishes usually expect them to eventually be assimilated (Office of Hispanic Ministry, 2003). American parishes have different rules and regulations, and this creates tension and conflict between the two communities (Palmer-Boyes, 2015). It is important to take into account cultural models of local faith based communities in order to understand how "cultural" approaches work in faith-based organizations and community development—as Kemper and Adkins point out (2005, p. 97).

FIRST STAGE OF ORGANIZING A LATINO COMMUNITY: SERVICE IN SPANISH

Linda, a twenty-six-year-old married immigrant woman with three young children arrived in Martinsburg in Berkeley County (West Virginia) in 2010.[3] They came from Mexico to the United States by land. While her husband started to work in a local construction company upon arrival, Linda began to work later in a local factory. From the beginning of her life in the United States, Linda had to face a lot of challenges because they were undocumented, and because she did not speak English well and, according to her, she could not understand the "American way of life." Linda says that one of the things she missed the most was a sense of community. She remembers the first years in Martinsburg as a time of isolation and loneliness. Linda left behind members of her extended family who still live in her "pueblo" (village). Due to mental health problems,

Linda's husband committed suicide leaving her with her children on her own. As a consequence, she needed personal support, a community, and social connections. When Linda remarried she needed, according to her, "to fix my life and my social relations, including my relationship with God. I need to go back to church." Under these circumstances, Linda was intentionally looking for a community and for a church that she helped to organize. Many Latino immigrants in Maryland and West Virginia seek a community at the Catholic parish for basic religious services, support and social connections.

With the increase of Latino immigrants in the area the need to establish a Latino community in the local American Catholic parish has emerged. So, demography became a major factor to take into account as was the case in the five parishes studied. Latino Catholics did attempt to attend English Sunday services at American Catholic parishes but because there is a different cultural language in the service they do not continue participating in American services at the parish. Many of the Latino participants would describe their experience in an American service as different and something they could not identify with. As an informant expressed it, the service in Spanish would make them "feel like home:" *"para mi la iglesia es como casa."* In this respect, as Palmer-Boyes (2010: 317) states, Latino immigrants try to incorporate into U.S. Catholic parishes aspects of religious life from their own country of origin in worship practices beyond language (*see also* Menjivar, 1999).

A Cultural Latino Space: More than Language

In the case of St. Joseph in Hagerstown, Latinos who attended English services were fluent in English. However, the need for Sunday service in Spanish is not defined just by the fluency in English. There is a need of more than language. There is a need of a different cultural environment in a parish, a cultural Latino space when they can socialize with each other and develop other social activities such as fundraising, cooking, and prayer groups (Palmer-Boyes, 2015). In this parish a Sunday liturgy is done in a Latino way that includes familiar songs and homelike liturgical style. In addition, for the members of a Latino community a cultural Latino space means that during Sunday service there are announcements about job openings, birthdays, and Latino community events outside the church. Inasmuch as the growing number of Latinos in the area is a first and basic condition in the process of establishing a Latino community within an American parish, the emerging leaders of Latino Communities have to go through the process of making a case with the American priest of the parish.

Before an American priest of the parish would be contacted about a possible service in Spanish, there would be a long process of selecting leaders within the community. In all these parishes, the critical role in this process of selecting leaders had been played by women. As Peña and Frehill (1998) underscored, Latinas play central roles organizing faith-based communities and shaping religious practice and beliefs. In Charles Town, it was a married woman from Mexico who came to the United States by land with her husband. They came hoping to establish a small business. A mother of three children, she has two older children studying in a college in the United States. For her, a Latino community in Charles Town was an important place to keep her Mexican identity. In her case, Mexican identity means to belong to a community and be Catholic.

In Martinsburg, a Colombian Josephine Sister has been playing a critical role in the formation of the Latino Community in the area.[4] Sister Mary was in her fifties with a lot of experience of working in both communities, American and Latino, in a parish environment. The presence of Sister Mary was important in the development of the Hispanic Community. In most of the Latino communities main activities take place during a weekend. There is no full time person available for the members of the Latino Community. Sister Mary was available during the week for the members of the Latino Community. She was a friendly counselor whom Latino members trusted and liked to talk. In one of the informant's words: "Sister Mary reminds me of my country and childhood. We always had *una Hermanita* (a Sister) in our church in my country."

In the case of St. Joseph, Hagerstown it was a married woman from Puerto Rico. She was a college educated, bilingual, and well connected with the American community at the parish. Her connections with American members of St. Joseph played an important role in the process of making a case for the Spanish service. In St. Timothy in Walkersville it was a group of Latino women. Two of them were from Mexico, college educated, and bilingual. Both women were in their fifties; their children were already grown up and had families. The two of them did not personally need a Sunday service in Spanishm they were fluent in English, but they had a sense of a strong Latino identity and commitment to the service of their community. Some of them are married to American men, such as Liz, a retired woman, who is married to Steve who also attends Sunday services in Spanish. The same pattern is seen in the case of St. John in Columbia. It was a married woman from Argentina who lost her daughter in a tragic way thirty years ago. Since then, she has been engaged in establishing and developing the Latino community in Walkersville (Frederick County). In the initial stages of organizing a Latino Community in all these parishes, in both states West Virginia and Maryland, married women usually involve their husbands in the process.

Latino women married to American men play, consequently, an important role organizing these Latino faith-based communities. They become a cultural bridge between the Latino and American communities in the parish. It is helpful for making a case for Spanish services when a Latino woman married to an American man approaches an American priest. These couples are full members of a parish and participate in both services in that parish. In many cases they break stereotypes about American and Latino cultures. It is through a very basic experience of mutual interactions they improve their ability to speak both languages and become more bicultural. Most of the married women are from Mexico, educated, with residence or citizenship, and usually integrated into mainstream American society in a deeper level than the rest of the Latino Community members, especially those who have arrived recently.

In all communities where research was conducted, there were multiple events where members of both communities could interact and socialize sharing food and worship together. However, most of the parishioners interviewed expressed a fear of rejection and misunderstanding that had prevented them from getting closer and accepting each other. As an informant pointed out, "I was afraid that at in an American parish I would be rejected because of my way of talking, dressing, for being different." At the leadership level of a parish it is critical for the priest to be aware that at least some parishioners are members of the American community and at the same time attend services in Spanish.[5] They are often active members of the Latino community. In most of the cases they have been in the United States for a very long time, usually twenty to thirty years, and some of them are married to Americans.

CELEBRATION OF *QUINCEAÑERA*

Another cultural bridge in the parish is the Latino members of the youth groups. Most of them are teenagers that are more fluent in English than in Spanish. About 85 percent of all teenagers prefer to attend American youth groups. In the words of one Latino teenager: "My parents are Mexicans, I am not Mexican. I have never been to Mexico. I am an American and would like to participate in an American youth group." It is important in making a case for a Spanish service to mention that there is a group of teenagers interested in joining a youth group.

Elba is sixteen years old born in Columbia, MD. Her parents came to the United States from El Salvador twenty years ago by crossing a border between Mexico and the United States. Both parents have been working two or more jobs to pay bills. Their daughter has been having problems with her identity and suffered depressions. Through the participation in the *Quinceañera* celebration she learned about a Latino youth group at St. John's, Columbia. She joined the group that became for her an important space to share her challenges of growing up in American society. It is interesting to see Latino teenage girls who actually want to have a *Quinceañera* celebration. Even though most of them do not understand well the history of this tradition, they want their *Quinceañera* to be celebrated in English. *Quinceañera* is a girl's fifteenth birthday celebration that in Latin America, especially in Central America, it is customary to celebrate. This celebration traditionally marks a girl's coming of age and afterwards she is considered a mature person who is ready to assume family and social responsibilities.[6] This is the case in Latin America. However, in Latino communities in the United States, a girl who celebrates the *Quinceañera* is not expected to assume social responsibilities. In this respect, in many of the Latino communities in the studied area, this celebration is a symbolical indicator of the Latino cultural identity of the girl. For this coming of age celebration a Latino teenage girl invites her American classmates. Many of them are not Catholic and have little understanding of the celebration. In the process of preparing the celebration and participation in it, a bridge is built between these two communities. The argument used by Latino leaders in the process of negotiating a permission to celebrate the *Quinceañera* at the parish is that this would attract teenagers to attend the church. Most of the participants of this social event normally do not attend church. The celebration, therefore, brings to the church adult members of the local Latino Community who normally would not attend the church. Some of them act as *padrinos* or *madrinas* of this ritual.[7] The average expenses related to *Quinceañera* celebration in the area of West Virginia and Maryland is between $ 5,000.00 and $8,000.00. And in some cases, it's more than that. Since many parents of the girl who celebrates her fifteenth birthday are not able to pay for all related expenses, such as food, dress, music, and limousine, the institution of *padrinazgo* was created. The parents of the girl select from extended family members, community, or church somebody who can sponsor a specific expense. So, there is a *padrino* of the dress, a *padrino* of the food, and so on.

This social event is a pastoral challenge for most of the American Catholic priests. It is a Latino tradition they are not familiar with. *Quinceañera* is not a sacrament. So, for the priests the question is: "Where does it fit in the church theology?" "What do I do with this?" "Why should I do it?" It requires another service and in most of the cases priests have to be bilingual to celebrate it. Even so, the priests engaged in Latino ministry accept to celebrate *Quinceañera* and use it as a way to attract young people to the church. Whether they organize a *Quinceañera* celebration or not, married Latino women also play a leading role in creating a need for Spanish services in American Catholic parishes.

As previously mentioned, opting for a service in Spanish is linked not only to the language barrier but to the perception of profound cultural differences in the traditions of American versus Latino religious services. Most of the interviewed members of the five communities (85 percent) felt that Latino services helped pull people together and make the participants feel more at home. To make a case at an American parish for the presence of Latino community, organizing leaders have to present specific reasons. There are several justifications for the Spanish service. First, more than 80 percent of the members of the community do not speak fluent English. Second, the American Sunday service is done in what many members of the community define as *Misa Gringa* (American-style Mass) which means service is in a different liturgical style. It does not include celebration of elements of Latino popular religiosity such as celebrations of patron Saints, Our Lady of Guadalupe, and processions.

The third reason for organizing a Latino service in an American Catholic parish is the need of sacraments. More than 75 percent of the members of these Latino communities in Charles Town and Martinsburg in West Virginia come from different countries in Central America, particularly from small towns and rural areas. For many of them the sacrament of Christian initiation, baptism, is a critical element in the spiritual and physical wellbeing of their child. More than 95 percent of requested baptisms services are done by mothers of both communities. This is another reason to organize a Hispanic Community in an American parish: "The wellbeing of the children."

SECOND STAGE OF ORGANIZING A LATINO COMMUNITY: MEETING A PRIEST AND ADVERTISING A SERVICE IN SPANISH

María was a college educated woman in her thirties when she emigrated from Puerto Rico because she could not get a job there after graduation. She got a good job in Hagerstown in the computer company. María got married after college and had one child. Her husband is also from Puerto Rico, a college educated and U.S. citizen. She was an active member of the American Community at St. Joseph in Hagerstown in Washington County (Maryland). María was fluent in both languages English and Spanish. According to her, she felt "a call to help *mi gente* (my people)." With time, Maria became a cultural broker for both American and Latino communities. With her husband she organized a first formal meeting between a pastor of St. Joseph and a leader of the Hispanic Community. María enjoyed a position of being in the leadership role in Latino Community. María was well connected in the Latino Community in Hagerstown through personal relations she has developed. She could use her extensive social network to market service in Spanish at St. Joseph in Hagerstown.

The participants in the first stage of the organization of the five Latino Communities did not used formal assistance from the church. They did not ask a priest or nun to help them make connections in the parish or coordinate the creation of the community. It was done within the community and led by women who insisted on having a *Misa en Español* (Mass in Spanish). In all five cases, the first formal contact with the priest from the American parish was initiated by women. They speak English, so they can be a bridge between the American community and the Latino group in formation.

Gender also played a very important role in the process of connecting with an American priest since the door keepers in the parishes are the secretaries. In all five parishes, the female who started the organization of the Latino Community stated that "it was easier to deal with secretaries that were women." As one of the informants put it: "They are women like us and they understand us well." It was less intimidating and they felt understood. After several meetings with the priests and parish administration, the women received a positive response. This meant that the parish council approved the request and the priest was willing to support a Spanish service. This is where the next stage of the organization of the Latino Community begins.

Once this positive response is received from the American Community, the next step is to advertise the service in Spanish and locate a priest who speaks Spanish. The Spanish service is advertised in all English services, local Latino newspapers, Latino businesses, and among friends. In 85 percent of the cases, it was done by Latino women. A critical part of the "marketing" of the service in Spanish is a network of Latino families in the area. An important part of the process in organizing a Latino Community is the first church service which is a test to determine if there is a real need for a service in Spanish. At the first service in all five communities, thirty to fifty Latinos participated. However, this number of participants would not justify having a service in Spanish.

As it was mentioned before, there is a shortage of priests in the Catholic Church in the United States, especially Spanish speaking priests . There are just 3,000 Spanish speaking priests in the United States for more than thirty million Catholics in the country (Hoge and Okure, 2006). There is another reason based on a budget capacity of the American parish. At the beginning of the process, the number of participants during Sunday service is usually low. That means that the Latino Community is not self-sufficient. Most of the members of the Latino Community do not contribute to the church a significant amount in donations. That means that a small Latino Community would not be able to maintain financially the costs of facility, salaries of administrative staff and so on. Even so, during the following three to six months, the number of participants had grown to more than one hundred in two of the five communities. This moves the community to the next stage of organization.

THIRD STAGE OF ORGANIZING A LATINO COMMUNITY: WOMEN LEADERSHIP

Rosa is a middle age married women with three children from Mexico who came to the United States by land. Her husband, who also came from Mexico without papers, is an owner of a small landscaping company where some members of the Latino Church Community work. Rosa is a stay-at-home mother with a few years of a high school education. Her social position in the Latino Community is the one of prestige. Her husband owns a company, they are now U.S. citizens and all members of the Latino Community respect them as a family. Rosa is in a perfect position to assume a leadership space in the process of organizing a service in Spanish.

In St. Joseph, Martinsburg (Berkeley County), and St. James, Charles Town (Jefferson County) in West Virginia, there was no permanent priest assigned for the Sunday service. Each of these communities had a priest who would come from outside the parish just for Sunday service. This helped members of the community to further organize themselves. During the first few months of the Spanish service at the American parish there are some basic organizational issues to resolve within the Latino community. First, the coordinator of the Latino Community has to be elected. In the case of Charles Town, a Mexican female member was elected as coordinator. As already mentioned Linda was elected as a coordinator. In Martinsburg, Sister Mary, the Colombian nun who became a member of the parish council was chosen to coordinate the Spanish Ministry. For the Spanish service, there is a need to establish some key leaders of different ministries such as liturgy, music, prayer group, Bible study, and preparation to receive the sacraments.

In the five communities, more than 70 percent of the leadership positions within the Latino Community were filled by women. There is another common pattern in most of the Latino Communities in the diocese of West Virginia: Latino women bring male members of their families to church. In some of the leader positions, the community would have a husband and wife as coordinators of the group. However, the main work would be done by the women. Coordinators of the Latino Communities play a critical role in the Community. They coordinate all major activities in the community: Celebration of the Sunday service (if necessary, find a priest to do it), preparation of all sacraments and social events at the church, and feasts of patron saints. An example of one of the most important annual celebrations is the Celebration of the Feast of Our Lady of Guadalupe on December 12th. This celebration is an important element in the process of creating Latino identity in the United States (Medina, 2009; Rodriguez, 1994; Odem, 2004). The Celebration of the Feast of Our Lady of Guadalupe in all five communities includes preparation of the food for all members of the Latino Community and a procession with the statue or a picture of *La Guadalupana*. The procession usually takes place from the parking lot to the church. An exception was a procession in Martinsburg which took place from St. Joseph Church to a parish school. In addition, women usually prepare a reenactment of the story of Guadalupe and the main celebration consists of a Celebration of the Eucharist in honor of Our Lady of Guadalupe.

Coordinators of the Latino Communities are mediators between the American parish and the Latino Community. In a typical American parish there are a lot of rules and regulations related to church teaching and the sacraments. Coordinators play an important role as bridge builders and negotiation of exceptions from the rules. This is a critical capacity for the Latino Community to be able to grow. There is a consistent need to negotiate exceptions from rules to baptize children, receive a First Communion or other sacraments in the church. A typical example is age requirement for the sacrament of his or her baptism. In most of the American parishes candidates who are six or seven years old have to go through a long formation process. There are many cases of the Latino children that do not fit into this age group. One of the main characteristics of the Latino Communities under study is their mobility. They move frequently and their children are not able to finish formation programs or receive all the sacraments of the church. First Communion is done in the Catholic Church when a candidate is between seven and nine years old. In all five communities there were a lot of children much older who did not celebrate their First Communion.

With these newly acquired organizational and leadership skills, Latino women from Latino communities in Charles Town (Jefferson County), Martinsburg (Berkeley County) in West Virginia, and Hagerstown (Washington County) in Maryland expanded their work outside the church with faith-based social service organizations. In Martinsburg several Latino women worked with Catholic Charities and used government social services agencies such as Department of Social Services in Martinsburg and Department of Health and Human Resources. In Hagerstown, Latino women engaged with such government agencies as Healthy Family and Faith Hope and Charity. Social workers from Healthy Family did use the churches Sunday services to make announcements about services provided for the Latino families.

CONCLUSIONS

As in other parts of the United States, Latino immigrants are transforming the religious landscape of Maryland and West Virginia. In the case of the Catholic Church, they are contributing to the growth of parishes. Due to this growth, archdioceses have expanded religious services for the Spanish-speaking. It is estimated that there are around 53 million Latinos in the United States and it is projected that they will to reach 122 million by 2050 (Malavé and Giordani, 2015). However, in their processes of incorporation, the Latino population has to face major challenges regarding dominant social and cultural structures in the host societies. One of the main challenges is a tension between assimilation and multicultural-ism. Latino Communities at American parishes can help members of their communities not only to incorporate and adapt to American society, but also to create a multicultural American parish.

A significant number of women in the Catholic Church in the United States are in leading positions on both the diocesan and parish levels. In five cases cases of Hispanic Communities in West Virginia (Martinsburg and Charles Town) and in Maryland (Hagerstown, Walkersville, and Co-lumbia), women played a critical role in the process of organizing the Latino Community within the American parish. They followed the three stages involved in the creation and organization of the Latino Commu-nity. In the first stage, they were leaders in the process of establishing a group of Latinos who would articulate the need and the reasons to have a Spanish service in an American Catholic parish. The five women con-tacted the leaders of the American Community. In the second stage, Lati-no women met a priest of a parish and advertised the services in Spanish in the local community, using social networks. They also played a pivotal role in organizing the initial service in Spanish and developing the lead-ers for the key ministries within the community. In the third stage the five women were leading all the main ministries of the Latino commu-nity. This includes a prayer group and preparation for the sacraments. In addition, the five women have developed the leaders for the key minis-tries within the community. As Peña and Frenhill (1998, p. 621) have pointed out, although Latino/a communities have given Latinas affirma-tion as leaders, especially at the grassroots level, they rarely have the same level of representation on the parish pastoral council as men. It has been a challenge in the Catholic Church, the reality of the leadership of women on a grass root level with a male dominance of the hierarchy of the church.

NOTES

1. Berkeley County (West Virginia) has a population of 104,169 inhabitants. Ac-cording to 2010 Census data, there are registered 3,961 Hispanics or Latinos; account-ing for 3.8 percent of its total population (U.S. Census Bureau, 2012).

2. The Archdiocese of Baltimore comprises the City of Baltimore and Allegany, Anne Arundel, Baltimore, Carroll, Garrett, Harford, Howard, Washington, and Frede-rick Counties.

3. All the informants' names in this chapter are not real names.

4. Colombian Josephine Sisters are a Catholic religious order dedicated to work with the poor. Josephine Sisters work at St. Joseph Catholic parish in Martinsburg. American members of this order have been supporting the Latino Community for several years. Some of them attend service in Spanish they speak fluent Spanish. Josephine Sisters play an important role of creating a bridge between American mem-bers of the parish and the Latino Community.

5. It means that they formally filled up a membership to be parishioners at American English speaking parish.

6. The historical roots of Quinceañera celebration go back to the initiation ritual among the Aztecs in Mexico. When a girl was fifteen years old, after going through initiation ritual, was ready to get married and have a family (Alvarez, 2007). Most tribal societies in Latin America have had male and female intiation rituals as a way to introduce a young members of their communities to an adult life (*see* Mich, 2011).

7. In this context for Spanish speakers "padrino" or "madrina" means sponsor.

REFERENCES

Alvarez, Julia. (2007). *Once Upon a Time Quinceañera. Coming of Age in U.S.A.* New York and London: Viking Penguin.

Hirschman, Charles. (2004). "The role of religion in the origins and adaptation of immigrant groups in the United States." *International Migration Review*, 1206-1233.

Hoge, Dean and Aniedi Okure. (2006). *International Priests in America. Challenges and Opportunities.* Collegeville, MN: Liturgical Press.

Kemper, Robert and Julie Adkins. (2005). "The World as It Should Be, Faith-Based Community Development in America." In Stanley E. Hyland (ed.) *Community Building in the Twenty-First Century.* Santa Fe, NM: School of American Research Press, pp. 71-100.

Levitt, Peggy. (2001). *The Transnational Villagers.* Berkeley, CA: University of California Press.

Lugo, Luis, Sandra Stencel, John Green, Gregory Smith, Dan Cox, Allison Pond, Tracy Miller, Elizabeth Podrebarac, Michelle Ralston, Andrew Kohut, Paul Taylor and Scott Keeter. (2008). U.S. Religious Landscape Survey. Washington, D.C.: A Pew Research.

Malavé, Idelisse and Esti Giordani. (2015). *Latino Stats: American Hispanics by the Numbers.* New York, NY: The New Press.

Matovina, Timothy. (2014). *Latino Catholicism: Transformation in America's Largest Church.* Princeton, NJ: Princeton University Press.

Medina, Néstor. (2009). *Mestizaje: (Re)Mapping Race, Culture, and Faith in Latina/o Catholicism.* Maryknoll, NY: Orbis.

Mahler, Sarah J. and Katrin Hansing. (2005). "Toward a transnationalism of the middle: how transnational religious practices help bridge the divides between Cuba and Miami." *Latin American Perspectives*, 121-146.

Menjivar, Cecilia. (1999). "Religious Institutions and Transnationalism: A Case Study of Catholic and Evangelical Salvadoran Immigrants." *International Journal of Politics, Culture and Society*, 12 (4): 589-612.

Mich, Tadeusz. (2011). *Initiation Into The Amazon: Yucuna Yurupari Myth and Ritual.* Saarbrücken: VDM Verlag Dr. Muller.

Odem, Mary E. (2004). "Our Lady of Guadalupe in the New South: Latino immigrants and the politics of integration in the Catholic Church." *Journal of American Ethnic History*, 26-57.

Odgers Ortiz, Olga. (2009). "Religión y migración México-Estados Unidos: un campo de estudios en expansión." In Juan Carlos Ruiz Guadalajara and Olga Odgers Ortiz (eds.) *Migración y Creencias.* San Luis: El Colegio de San Luis y Miguel Ángel Porrúa, pp. 13-29.

Office of Hispanic Ministry. (2003). Pastoral Plan for Hispanic Ministry. Baltimore, MD: Archdiocese of Baltimore.

Palmer-Boyes, Ashley. (2010) "The Latino Catholic parish as a specialist organization: Distinguishing characteristics." *Review of Religious Research*, 302-323.

Peña, Milagros and Lisa M. Frehill. (1998). "Latina religious practice: Analyzing cultural dimensions in measures of religiosity." *Journal for the Scientific Study of Religion*, 620-635.

Perl, Paul, Jennifer Z. Greely, and Mark M. Gray. (2006). "What proportion of adult Hispanics are Catholic? A review of survey data and methodology." *Journal for the Scientific Study of Religion*, 419-436.

Rodriguez, Jeanette. (1994). *Our Lady of Guadalupe: Faith and Empowerment among Mexican-American Women*. Austin, TX: University of Texas Press.

Sánchez Molina, Raúl. (2009). "Pentecostalismo y transnacionalismo: Inmigrantes salvadoreños y la Iglesia de los Apóstoles y Profetas en Washington, D.C." In Juan Carlos Ruiz Guadalajara and Olga Odgers Ortiz (eds.) *Migración y Creencias*. San Luis: El Colegio de San Luis y Miguel Ángel Porrúa, pp. 59-77.

Suro, Roberto, Gabriel Escobar, Gretchen Livingston, and Shirin Hakimzadeh. (2007). Changing faiths: Latinos and the transformation of American religion. Washington, D.C.: Pew Research Center, 1-151.

U.S. Catholic Conference. (2001). *Welcoming the Stranger Among Us*. Unity in Diversity, A Statement of the U.S. Washington, D.C.: Catholic Bishops.

U.S. Census Bureau. (2012). Maryland: 2010. *Summary Population and Housing Characteristics*. Washington, D.C.: U.S. Government Printing Office.

U.S. Census Bureau. (2012). West Virginia: 2010. *Summary Population and Housing Characteristics*. Washington, D.C.: U.S. Government Printing Office.

U.S. Census Bureau. (2010). *United States Census 2010*. Washington, D.C.: U.S. Department of Commerce. www.census.gov/prod/www/decennial.html (June 6, 2015).

Vásquez, Manuel. (1999). "Pentecostalism, Collective Identity, and Transnationalism Among Salvadorans and Peruvians in the U.S." *Journal of the American Academy of Religion* 67; 3: 617-635.

SEVEN

Educational Outcomes for Latinos in Washington, D.C. Elementary to Higher Education

Shaun Loria

Latino educational outcomes in Washington, DC closely mirror national trends and demonstrate a pressing and often unspoken problem. While there are some positive trends across K–12, nonprofits, and Higher Education, overall Latinos in Washington, D.C. are not currently achieving educational success proportionate to their demographic representation.[1] Looking towards the future and projecting current academic success rates to match the increasingly Latino demographics of the United States makes the severity of the situation quite clear.[2] Current methods have resulted in a lack of success, indicating that changes in our delivery of education to Latino students must take place.

Though the problem is pressing, this chapter will discuss solutions for Latinos that exist and can be addressed. Across the K–12, nonprofit, and Higher Education spectrum there are best practices and solutions that are making a difference, and it will be important to highlight the solutions that have scalable potential. As we discuss what the most effective charter schools, or privately run schools publically funded, Higher Education institutions are doing, we will also present ideas for implementation across the community. Sharing knowledge regarding solutions, and increased collaboration among policy makers, educational institutions, and the communities they serve will be a critical step moving forward. We must acknowledge that this is a problem that requires everyone to become involved, and fund scalable solutions in order to reverse current trends. The political scientist Robert Putnam (2015: 189) states in his most recently published book:

> As the twenty-first century opened, a family's socioeconomic status (SES) had become even more important than test scores in predicting which eighth graders would graduate from college. A generation earlier, social class had played a smaller role, relative to academic ability, in predicting educational attainment.

My experience in education has been working in elementary, middle, and high schools, as well as establishing a nonprofit that supports college students. I have witnessed the crushing effects of poverty, as well as the vast human potential that is underdeveloped by schools. My experiences as teacher, coach, and nonprofit director have deepened my resolve to continue to advocate for cost-effective solutions for low-income students. I continue to work with a range of community organizations because the potential I have witnessed, the resolve of the families with whom I work, and also because I am convinced that a nation that prides itself on innovation is capable of doing better than our current situation. After witnessing so many of my former students become incarcerated or drop out of high school and college, I began to wonder how K through twelve schools, nonprofits and Higher Education can all work together towards improving outcomes. Latinos still have the highest dropout rate from High School in the United States. Latino enrollment in college is up, but less than 10 percent of low-income students graduate from college. I am convinced we can do better, and fortunate to know organizations that are already making a difference.

COMPARING CHARTER AND PUBLIC SCHOOLS IN K THROUGH TWELVE EDUCATION

Minnesota was the first state to pass a charter school law in 1991—Washington, D.C. followed shortly after in 1994. In 1996, the first year of operation, 160 students enrolled in charter schools in Washington, D.C. (OSSE.DC.GOV, 2015). By 2014, approximately 39,000 elementary and High School students were enrolled in Charter schools (OSSE.DC.GOV, 2015). According to the Office of the State Superintendent of Education of the D.C. Government (OSSE.DC.GOV, 2015), the number of students enrolled in Public Schools has significantly decreased since 1996 until the present while the number of students enrolled in charter schools has been growing. As the home to the Federal government, the long standing debate between public and charter schools has a special symbolic and magnified importance in the city. Though the city is run by a local governing body, there are few other places where the Chancellor (or Superintendent) would be featured on the cover of *Time* (Ripley, 2008) and *Newsweek*

(Thomas, 2008) magazines. Michelle Rhee, a former Chancellor, was featured on *Time* in a famous incident where she was holding a broom in the classroom. Her message was simple, things need to improve for both charter schools and public schools.

Charter schools are publicly funded, privately run schools operating at the pre-kindergarten through High School grades. Charter schools are free to attend and have open enrollment so they technically must admit any student who applies (charter schools are frequently criticized for not taking students during the year or in certain grades), but they can select their own curriculum and target certain communities based on their approach, neighborhood location, and staff demographics. Why do parents choose charter schools and why have they been increasing in popularity?

Aside from the variety of interesting options at charter schools (such as bilingual classes) the most common answer is a lack of confidence in the city's public schools. In this regard Washington, D.C. reflects national trends of urban school districts which do not perform well as measured by graduation rates or percentage of students earning advanced scores on standardized testing (indicating college readiness). However, as we will see while comparing schools, charter schools have shown a range of success and quality—while remaining opposed by many policy makers, union groups, and educators.

Part of the difficulty extracting information in these areas is that data demonstrate vastly different conclusions depending on the presenting organization. For example, research presented by the Washington, D.C. Public School board and FOCUS, D.C., an advocacy group for charter schools in Washington, demonstrate different conclusions. The Public School Board inflates advanced proficiency by highlighting the change in percentage, but less than half of the students are rated even "proficient" in reading, and barely over 50 percent are labeled advanced in Math. On the other hand, FOCUS highlights data that indicates charter schools outperform public schools, one of the frequent debate points between the two groups of schools. When we discuss the problems with Latino education, images such as these should serve as reminders that education entities highlight the positive and mask the negative.

These numbers are highlighted by a yellow arrow with the percentage increases in each category (reading +13, math +23) distracting someone from the 51 percent overall as the highest mark, one of the two out of eighteen categories the schools achieved at least half of the students passing a test. Meanwhile, FOCUS demonstrates statistics by comparing their schools to public schools in an attempt to contrast the outcomes. It highlights relatively low gains in performance and features a contrast in performance.

According to an annual report on the conditions on education in the United States led by Kena et al. (2015, p. 178) between 1990 and 2013, the overall dropout rate declined from 12 to 7 percent, with nearly the entire

128 *Shaun Loria*

Table 7.1. Percent Proficient or Advanced from 2007 to 2014

Year	Reading	Math
2007	35%	28%
2008	43%	39%
2009	46%	45%
2010	44%	44%
2011	43%	44%
2012	43%	46%
2013	47%	50%
2014	48%	51%

NAEP and TUDA (District pf Columbia, 2015)

decline occurring after 2000 (when it was still 12 percent). During this time, Latinos went from over 30 percent drop out to approximately 12 percent. They remain the group with the largest drop-out rates but also the group that has made the most gains relative to earlier academic performance.

PUBLIC SCHOOLS AND SPATIAL SEGREGATION IN WASHINGTON, D.C.

Mirroring a national trend, public schools in Washington, D.C. produce a large achievement gap,[3] between schools located in wealthy areas with predominantly white populations, versus low-income areas where African-American and Latino students are the majority.[4] As Robert Putnam (1025: 163) notes, "residential sorting by income over the last 30 to 40 years has shunted high-income and low-income students into separate schools." Given neighbor segregation, two types of schools emerge. Schools in low-income areas have disproportionate minority rates and low academic performance numbers, whereas schools in wealthy areas that lack ethnic or socioeconomic diversity but perform well academically. Local public schools receive funding from local taxes and supplement these funds with donations from parents. Top performing schools have higher quality and more experienced teachers, offer more advanced classes, and more extracurricular opportunities. Let us compare demographics and student outcomes at Anacostia High School, Columbia Heights Education Campus, Cardozo Education Campus, and Woodrow Wilson High School.

The table below shows the tale of two very different education systems, each with different outcomes. The lack of ethnic diversity is marked, as are the expectations and results per school. At Anacostia High School, about one in five students are proficient in reading and math, and less than four out of ten students will graduate high school. It is 100 percent black, and 99 percent low-income. In 2013-2014 0 percent of students earned Advanced Placement (AP) credit, compared with only 4 percent the previous year. The quality of education delivered is the opposite at Woodrow Wilson High School, in an area where median household income is over four times higher than Anacostia. At this school, 55 percent of students earn AP credits and 67 percent of students graduate. Approximately seven out of every ten students are proficient in reading and math, far higher results than Anacostia High School. 35 percent of

Table 7.2. Student Demographics and Educational Outcomes at Various Public High Schools

School	Anacostia High School	Colombia Heights Education Campus	Cardozo Education Campus	Woodrow Wilson High School
Demographic by percentage	White (0%) Hispanic (0%) Black (100%) Other (0%)	White (1%) Hispanic (65%) Black (32%) Other (2%)	White (3%) Hispanic (43%) Black (53%) Other (1%)	White (25%) Hispanic (20%) Black (43%) Other (11%)
Ward Median Household	$33,964	$63,098	$63,098	$130,220
Percent Low Income	99%	86%	99%	35%
Percent English Language	0	31	33	6
Percent of Students Proficient	Math (22%) Reading (20%)	Math (57%) Reading (44%)	Math (31%) Reading (30%)	Math (69%) Reading (70%)
Advanced Placement Performance	0%	30%	0%	55%
Percent Graduation Rate	39%	84%	41%	76%

District of Columbia Public Schools, DCPS, 2015

students are low-income. As the two schools in Columbia Heights demonstrate, Latino schools are exhibiting the symptoms of low academic expectations and high levels of poverty.

The achievement gap between socio-economic classes begins in elementary school and grows each year so that by middle school and high school the gap between what wealthy students know and what low-income students know is seemingly insurmountable. As Latino students are concentrated in low-income areas, they attend lower quality schools and attain lower academic results. Approximately one in three Latino children are born into poverty, beginning kindergarten with a lower level of reading readiness than white students. Whereas white students graduate on time 78.4 percent of the time, Latinos graduate on time 57.6 percent. While 38 percent of Americans age twnety five to thirty four have earned an associate degree (two years of college), only 18 percent of Latinos ages twenty five to thirty four have achieved this level of academic success (Ryu, 2010). Public schools fit into larger gentrification patterns seen in the city, and reflect patterns in performance between ethnic and socioeconomic groups that result in disparity in education.

CHARTER SCHOOLS AND LATINO PARENTS CHOICES

"Nevertheless, compared to low-income schools, schools in affluent areas are characterized by greater engagement and support from parents." (Putnam, 2015: 167).

Charter schools exist in theory to provide choice to parents and eliminate the achievement gap created by neighborhood public schools. However, there are several questions that need to be answered: Have they solved the achievement gap? Do Latino parents take advantage of the choices provided by charter schools? Do charter schools actively recruit students from around the city or do they target specific neighborhoods? Do non-profits help match the best students to the best schools, provide transportation, or explain complex issues to parents in a number of languages? Do parents make informed choices? Are charter schools more diverse and more academically successful?

School choice is a slightly misleading idea, as selecting a charter school does not mean you are guaranteed enrollment. For many families, the charter school selection process is difficult to navigate, especially if the school is far away, the parents do not use electronic communication, or if the parents do not speak English. The most successful charter schools have extensive waitlists, so forgetting to submit a form on time can easily result in losing a place on the list and being bumped to lower quality schools. Well prepared, tech savvy parents who understand how to navigate the system have an advantage over parents who rely on their children to translate or only feel comfortable walking to a school to talk to members of the staff about their programs. I have worked with many parents who do not understand transfer policies, waitlists, or how to obtain a transcript for their students.

The factors these parents have identified as most important for enrollment are proximity to the house, enrollment for the entire family, and familiarity with the school. I have worked with Latino families who refused to put their children in an advanced curriculum at a different school because that meant separating him from his younger siblings. Consequently, their children remained in the low performing school. Proximity to home may result in choosing schools that are geographically close to low-income neighborhoods. Much like neighborhood public schools, these charter schools are usually underperforming. Selecting a school where a wide range of family members can attend narrows the list to a handful of choices and eliminates some of the highest performing schools. Furthermore, in order to simplify carpooling and to continue with a trusted network of existing contacts, families that are friends communicate with one another regarding schools instead of school personnel who typically do not speak the same language. Since Latino students are enrolled in underperforming schools, this leads to continued enrollment in low performing schools.

The end result is that many Latino parents do not make the wisest choices for their student's long term academic success. What may be convenient in the short term is often not ideal in the long term, as the more years spent in low quality schools the further a student falls behind. The District of Columbia Public Charter School Board (PCSB) was established in 1996 as a result of the District of Columbia School Reform Act of 1995 as a government agency to oversee charter schools. The Board provides excellent online resources, but very few community forums hosted by bilingual representatives to provide information to parents who do not speak English and do not have access to a home computer. In essence, it is difficult to navigate a complex process (charter school enrollment and selection) even if one is proficient in English and able to use computers. Without a common language or access to technology, it is harder for Latino families, particularly immigrant families, to make informed choices for their children.

Whereas Latino parents generally make uniformed decisions, wealthier parents follow an interesting pattern of enrollment in both public and charter schools. Elementary schools are the most diverse, and High Schools the least diverse, as approximately one out of every three families chose to withdraw their students from public and charter schools before High School. The exodus happens during the middle school years (Brown and Clement, 2014). This effect is noted at schools where a range of grades are offered, such as th well performing Capital City Public Charter School. Capital City is 20 percent white and 35 percent Latino at the elementary school level, 7 percent white and 46 percent Latino at the middle school level, and 0.9 percent white and 56 percent Latino at the High School level. According to a D.C. Public Charter School (2015) report, more than half, 56 percent, of the elementary school students come from disadvantaged economic situations whereas 78 percent of the high school families are economically disadvantaged (which just so happens to be quite close to the 20 percent white drop in enrollment).

If you dial into the main number of Capital City Public Charter School, a Tier One school that serves a large number of Latino students, the recorded message is played first in English, and then in Spanish.[5] Each office manager and attendance person is bilingual. While not every staff member speaks Spanish, the school makes an active effort to recruit staff members who reflect the demographics of their diverse student body. That accessibility is more than just a nice gesture on the telephone, it provides a feeling of comfort and familiarity with the school. Materials that go home with students are printed in two languages and parent meetings are often held in Spanish. Capital City Public Charter School has three schools, an elementary, middle, and high school, and all are Title One or Tier Two status for top performing academic schools.

It is a best practice to offer bilingual staff members, or at least a recorded phone message, as Capital City demonstrates. Surprisingly, these policies are not the norm but the exception. Few schools print materials in multiple languages or feature bilingual staff members. Few provide parent nights with Spanish speakers alternating with English speakers describing the school curriculum. There are also differences between how charter schools recruit families and where they recruit. A different top performing D.C. Charter school with 6 percent Latino enrollment, compared to Capital City's 56 percent follows a different recruiting pattern. They host chess tournaments, featuring wine on rooftop parties in wealthy parts of the city, and advertise in McLean and Georgetown. McLean, (Northern Virginia) is not a part of the city but has a private school operated by the same company. The median family income of McLean is $180,000, and the population is 79 percent white and 4.9 percent Latino. Georgetown's median family income is $118,000. There is no Spanish recorded message at this school, no current outreach efforts in heavily Latino areas such as Colombia Heights, (median family income $63,000) (U.S. Census Bureau, 2010). These schools exemplify different ways to attract different kinds of families. The unnamed high-performing charter school has no outreach programs in low-income areas and vague plans to prioritize that in the future.

Through passive decisions such as recruitment efforts, to active decisions such as bilingual communications, staff demographics, and school location many school personnel do not make a tremendous effort to work with the Latino community. It is difficult to imagine requiring charter schools to balance their recruiting efforts or ensuring economic diversity through laws, yet if they are receiving tax money there could be ways to incentivize balanced recruitment efforts and diverse student bodies. Capital City Public Charter School serves as an example of how to work with a Latino population and ensure it bridges the language gap with parents. Other schools offer slightly higher quality academic models as measured by not only how many students are accepted into college, but how they do once they are enrolled in college. It is not out of reach to merge a culturally relevant school with an academically rigorous school that provides long term success for its Latino students, but a consistent answer to this problem has not been found.

K–12 Summary

"Even more shocking, high-scoring poor kids are now slightly less likely (29 percent) to get a college degree than low-scoring rich kids (30 percent). The last fact is particularly hard to square with the idea at the heart of the American Dream: equality of opportunity" (Putnam, 2015, p. 190).

Due to the quality of neighbor public schools, enrollment patterns at charter schools, and higher concentration in poverty, Latino students are disproportionately enrolled in underperforming schools throughout the K–12 process. Latinos have the lowest graduation rates and earn the fewest advanced degree credits. Males in particular struggle with the education system and underperform female students. Latino males have the lowest degree attainment, followed by African American males, then Latino females. According to Census data analysis by Diversity Data (2015), 46 percent of Hispanic or Latino adults over twenty-five have less than a High School education, compared 7 percent overall.

The discrepancy between K–12 school success across different residential zip codes is a problem that has not been solved by charter schools. Education efforts on helping parents navigate the enrollment process and

Table 7.3. Share of Adults Age 25+ Without a High School Diploma or Equivalency

Group	Gender	Percentage with Less Than A High School Education
Non-Hispanic White	Male	7%
	Female	7%
Hispanic	Male	46%
	Female	39%
Black	Male	19%
	Female	18%

2000 Census Summary File 3 (Diversity Data, 2015)

the benefits of working with Tier One schools could make a big difference by ensuring parents enroll their students in the top schools. Top
down efforts to increase the quality of the schools Latino students enroll
are also needed. High Schools have long celebrated what percentage of
their student body is accepted into or enrolls in college, but that view is
shortsighted. Graduating underprepared students sets them up to fail at
the next step in their education career: College.

HIGHER EDUCATION — EXPANDING THE FOCUS FROM ENROLLMENT TO COMPLETION

"At the 200 colleges that are most difficult to get into, only 15 percent of
entering students in 2010 came from families in the bottom half of
incomes in the US (under $65,000). Nearly seven in ten students on
those campuses come from the top income group (above $108,000). The
result is the US higher education system is becoming less of a meritocracy. In the last decade, the percentage of students from families at the
highest income levels who got a bachelor's degree has grown to 82
percent, while for those at the bottom if has fallen to just 8 percent."
(Selingo, 2013, p. 6)

Compared to the K–12 process, there are fewer bright spots in Higher
Education for Latino students. According to the National Center for Education Statistics, in 2013 approximately 40 percent of whites ages twenty-
five to twenty-nine had a bachelor's degree or more, compared with 15
percent of Latinos and 20 percent African Americans (Kena et al., 2015).
As previously discussed, Latinos in poverty enter kindergarten academically behind wealthy peers. In similar fashion, Latinos who graduate
from low-performing High Schools enter college underprepared and behind their peers from better schools. This means many students are not
entirely prepared for the difficulty of Higher Education classes, let alone
the high cost of college. Academic difficulty plus economic strain leads to
persistently low graduation rates. There has been much attention recently
celebrating higher than ever enrollment numbers, but college completion
remains an underlying issue. Barely 50 percent of Pell Grants, a small
sum of money awarded to students in the lowest quartile of income
earners, complete college. Only 51 percent of Latino students who enroll
in college actually finish college. Enrollment numbers do not capture the
story, graduation numbers are very low. An important shift in how
Washington, D.C. funds education helps explain the higher education
problem.

Education is taxpayer supported, so at K–12 public schools students
are not charged tuition. Public Higher Education institutions are still tax
supported, but a percentage of the cost shifts to the student as schools
charge tuition. Schools go from costing a student no money to costing an

average almost $20,000 a year (U.S. Department of Education, 2015). There is a high range of college quality, but low quality college still charge high tuition. Coming from lower quality High Schools means Latino students have fewer earned college credits and lower Scholastic Achievement Test (SAT), a test that students take at the end of High School before enrolling in college, and hence are accepted into lower quality schools.[6] But that's just the start, as being accepted into college is the easiest part of the college process. Starting with a sample population of students who enroll in college, the majority of Latino students in the Washington, D.C., area who enroll do not finish college.

Programs such as Pell Grant for low-income students or the District's Tuition Assistance Grant, which provides up to $10,000 for students to attend out of state colleges cover a portion, not the entirety of, tuition. The point is this, most students must pay for a portion of their college costs and usually do so through loans. Tuition is not only part of the money spent during college, as discretionary money for textbooks and everyday expenses also adds to the total cost. To make ends meet, many Latino students work part time jobs in addition to taking out loans. Research shows that working more than twenty hours a week while enrolled in college lowers the chances of graduation (Orszag, Orszag, and Whitmore, 2001; Dundes and Marx, 2006), yet many students are in a situation where they must work to provide for their supplies. A part time job cuts down on the amount of available time for a student, as well as valuable opportunities such as professor office hours, spending time in the library, or stopping by a resource center to work on a skill such as writing. Working part time becomes a necessity, but it interferes with the ability to study. What makes ends meet in the short term harms the ability to graduate in the long term.

If cost is one barrier to success, another would be the type of schools that Latino students attend. If school choice is a buzzword for charter schools at the K–12 level, the equivalent term for Higher Education is merit based admissions. In theory, college acceptance is a meritocracy that measures academic success without considering financial need. In reality, college acceptance is a continuum of the poor quality schools the students came from. Recall that High Schools are rewarded for how many students they enroll into college, not how many complete college or the quality of schools in which their graduates enroll. Because Latinos attend low quality K–12 schools, the top students do not meet admissions requirements at selected universities such as Georgetown University. So, top students enroll at medium quality schools and average students, who are underprepared for college, are encouraged to enroll in any institution and wind up in poor quality colleges. The nation's most selective universities have become more ethnically diverse (still not matching demographic percentages) but less socioeconomically balanced over the past two decades and the majority of gains in enrollment for Latinos come from lower quality Higher Education institutions that graduate fewer students (Nichols, 2015).

According to U.S. News & World Report (2015), a college ranking, Georgetown University is a top tier school, ranked twenty-first overall in college quality but also in the bottom 5 percent of schools for low-income students and with a lower Latino percentage than the national average (Education Trust, 2015). It is the kind of college that few Latino or low-income students are accepted into or actually attend, which is unfortunate considering that the school has an excellent support systems for students. To examine the types of colleges Latino students most frequently attend, we can compare two public Higher Education institutions in the Washington, D.C., metropolitan area both accessible by public transportation—George Mason University (GMU), in Virginia, and the city's only public university, The University of District of Columbia (UDC). In doing so we will explore why GMU graduates 66 percent of students while UDC manages just 16 percent, whether selectivity and level of available financial support matters but also what types of internal programs exist that support Latino graduation rates.

Table 7.4. Graduation Rates, Enrollment Numbers and Average Price for Students

College	2013 6-Year Grad Rates	Under represented Minority	Pell Recipients Among Freshmen	Under represented Minority 6-Year Grad Rate	Average Net Price After Grants
GTU (a)	92.5%	13.7%	14.0%	89.0%	$10,197
GMU(b)	66.7%	19.6%	24.5%	68.4%	$13,249
UDC(a)	16.4%	62.3%	69.6%	17.4%	$14,830

Education Trust's College, 2015
Georgetown University, (b) George Mason University, (c) University of District of Columbia

George Mason University is ranked 135th overall by U.S. News and World Report's College ranking system and attracts an academically stronger applicant than UDC. This is the kind of school in which top Latino students from underperforming schools can gain acceptance, as acceptance rates at GMU are attainable at 67 percent. Higher quality applicants are more prepared and likely to finish but that does not guarantee success. GMU has resources to give more scholarships and on campus support, so students do not face the double burden of academic and financial pressure alone. GMU has higher quality academics, and in-house programs to help low-income and Latino students complete school. The Office of Diversity, Inclusion, and Multicultural Education program, for example, features thirty-eight on campus partners, as well as information on how to receive academic and financial support.[7] It is a holistic focus with a common goal — graduation for all students. This level of focus on ensuring students graduate helps ensure students feel supported during their experience at the school is reflected in their above average graduation rates for Latino and Pell Grant students (Nichols, 2015). At a school such as GMU, low-income and Latino students attend and achieve positive academic outcomes.

UDC, and other low quality academic institutions enroll the highest percentage of low-income and Latino students. A number of for-profit universities, notably Strayer University and University of Phoenix, also cater to underprepared students. Unlike GMU's end goal of graduation, this tier of Higher Education schools makes money off students without serving their academic or financial needs or advancing students towards graduation. Out of every ten students who enroll in UDC only two will graduate (Education Trust). Despite being ranked much lower than Mason, UDC still charges a comparable amount for tuition. The average net price for attendance is in fact higher than either GMU or Georgetown (Education Trust).

UDC has fewer resources for providing scholarships or on campus support. Therefore, the underprepared students have to work more in the classroom and outside the classroom to try to make ends meet. This double pressure helps to explain the low graduation rates. Much of the progress made in degree attainment and college enrollment numbers for minorities are clustered in low quality, for profit institutions. Though it appears to be a wiser option to begin earning credits at a community college before transferring to a state run school, many students lack an understanding of the college landscape to make these choices, and by default enroll in a school such as UDC. College admissions offices are incentivized to increase enrollment in order to maintain a school in operation, even if it seems unlikely that students will complete their studies, they are admitted and asked to take out loans.

A handful of schools have adopted a best practice solution for increasing graduation rates that is low cost and exportable, that of a peer networking system within the school of other students from similar backgrounds. The students who mentor are usually volunteers, and receive a benefit of portraying themselves as an expert, which provides motivation to finish school. Incoming students are offered a perspective from someone who looks and sounds like them, setting up the can-do-it mirror effect (if they can do it, I can do it). According to some students and administrators who I have interviewed, Salisbury College in Maryland but especially Georgetown University's Georgetown Scholars Program both follow this example.

Internal programs are important as scholarship funding has become an expensive way to affect graduation rates. Given the increase in college costs, which have risen over 400 percent since the 1980s, scholarship organizations are able to reach fewer students (Selingo, 2013). There is also the issue of front loading support. A scholarship is a costly way of betting on a student's success. If a student needs to take a medical leave of absence but is enrolled for more than one week in college, tuition money is nonrefundable. As previously discussed, tuition money is only part of the total financial burden. Students will receive a loan or grant but still need to work part time in order to make ends meet. Most traditional scholarship programs do not cover discretionary but necessary spending, and leave students on their own in this area. Perhaps the effect of a scholarship is not immediate and tangible for a student, as the money goes towards tuition and is not felt in a direct way by a student.

There is an underlying debate in the United States as to whether Higher Education is a public or a private good. A college degree adds over one million dollars to your lifetime earnings (private good) and therefore is the only part of debt that is not forgiven during bankruptcy. If you are earning a degree which allows you to earn more money over time, of course you should invest in it, part of the logic behind decreasing public spending and increasing the responsibility of taking personal loans goes. Yet the cost of college has increased over 400 percent since 1980, so the amount that a student is asked to borrow has risen exponentially. The days when you could wait tables over the summer to pay for your fall semester are over, with the current generation paying a higher proportion for college than any other generation prior. Colleges now employ more administrators than professors, driving up their own costs to operate, as do projects to build newer, more expensive dorms, academic buildings, and other buildings such as gyms which cater to student expectations but not student success (Selingo, 2013).

College graduates contribute to local taxes and businesses (public good) and are productive members of society. Regardless of whether you believe an individual or the state should invest in Higher Education, the worst outcome all together is when a student enrolls in college, accumulates debt, and does not complete a degree. Eight out of ten students who enroll in UDC will drop out and have debt (Education Trust). A large proportion Latino and low-income students follow this pattern, and Washington D.C., K–12 schools have not found a comprehensive way to address this issue. The college completion issue deserves greater attention and scrutiny as the United States becomes more diverse.

CONCLUSION

The issues surrounding Latino education require a community wide approach that requires first sharing best strategies and second a shared accountability around implementation of these ideas. The problem is bigger than any individual entity, so solving the problem requires new ways of thinking and collective problem solving. Nonprofits and other community leaders can facilitate the sharing of information, while policy leaders can adopt smarter ways to fund programs that work in achieving results. There are ways to improve the outcome, but these require different approaches and a renewed resolve that education, the route to equality and opportunity for Latino students, will be part of the solution for improving communities and the lives of Latino students. This problem is our problem, but recognizing a problem and working towards solving it is the first step in creating our solution.

NOTES

1. *K–12* is term used in the United States referring to school grades from pre-kindergarten (K) through High School grade twelve (hereby referred to as K–12). Students begin at age 3 or 4 and typically graduate at 17 or 18. The stages are elementary school, middle school, and high school.
Higher Education refers to public and private universities, colleges, community colleges, as well as for-profit colleges.
Nonprofits are organizations that use revenue to serve a purpose or mission, not make a profit. Well known international examples include Doctors Without Borders and International Red Cross.
2. The United States 2000 Census Data registered 35,305,818 Latinos in the United States, 12.5 percent of the total population and 2010 Census 50,477,594, 16.3 percent. In 2013, U.S. Census Bureau estimates 54,000,000 Latinas/os or 17.00 percent of the total population (U.S. Census Bureau, 2014), becoming the largest minority group in the United States.
3. Achievement gap refers to the difference in academic test results between ethnic or socioeconomic groups.
4. 2010 U.S. Census Bureau counted 601,723 residents in the District of Columbia: Black or African Americans (50.7 percent), Whites (38.5 percent), Hispanics or Latinos (9.1 percent), and Asians (3.5 percent). Latino population grew by 37.4 percent between 1990 and 2000 in the District of Columbia, and 7.9 percent, from 44,953 to 54,749 inhabitants between 2000 and 2010 (U.S. Census Bureau, 2010).
5. Tier One – There are three performance tiers for Washington, D.C. charter schools, Tier One is the top performing tier.
6. Students can earn college credits through Advanced Placement (AP) or International Bachelorette (IB) credits. These are more abundant in high performing schools, so many affluent students enter college with a handful of credits which allows them to take more classes. Alternatively, many Latino students are required to take remedial classes that do not count as credit but cost money and time. College admissions office use AP credits to compare students.
7. *See* the wage page Office of Diversity, Inclusion, and Multicultural Education at George Mason University: http://odime.gmu.edu/campus-partners/

REFERENCES

Brown, Emma and Scott Clement. (2014). "Middle schools present vexing problem for D.C. leaders as parents choose other options." In *The Washington Post*, February 14, 2014. www.washingtonpost.com/local/education/middle-schools-present-vexing-problem-for-dc-leaders-as-parents-choose-other-options/2014/02/17/29b95e24-93ef-11e3-83b9-1f024193bb84_print.html (October 13, 2015).

D.C. Public Charter School (2015) Capital City PCS-High School. Washington, D.C.:

D.C. Public Charter School Board www.dcpcsb.org/sites/default/files/48_Capital_City_PCS_High_School.pdf (October 13, 2015).

District of Columbia (2015) DCPS at a Glance: Performance. http://ich.dc.gov/page/dcps-glance-performance (November 27, 2015).

Diversity Data (2015) Share of Adults Without High School Diploma by Race/Ethnicity and Gender. http://diversitydata.org/Data/Rankings/Show.aspx?ind=235&ch=5&ch=1&ch=44&tf=3&sortby=Name&sort=LowToHigh&notes=True&rt=MetroArea&rgn=ShowLargest100 (October 17, 2015).

Dundes, Lauren and Jeff Marx. (2006). "Balancing Work and Academics in College: Why do Students Working 10-19 Hours Per Week Excel?" *Journal of College Student Retention*, 8 (1): 107-120.

Education Trust's College (2015) http://www.collegeresults.org(November 27, 2015)

FOCUS. (2014). http://focusdc.org/docs/brochure2014.pdf (October 17, 2015).

Institute of Education Sciences (2015) *The Condition of Education 2015*. Washington, D.C.: NCES, IES, U.S. Department of Education.

Nichols, Andrew H. (2015). The Pell Partnership: Ensuring a Shared Responsibility for Low-Income Student Success. Washington, D.C.: The Education Trust.

Orszag, Jonathan M., Peter R. Orszag and Diane M. Whitmore. (2001). Learning and Earning: Working in College. A report commissioned by Upromise Inc. Newton, MA: Upromise Inc.

Putnam, Robert D. (2015) *Our Kids. The American Dream in Crisis*. New York: Simon & Schuster.

Ripley, Amanda. (2008). " Rhee Tackles Classroom Challenge." In *Time*, November 26, 2008, pp. 36-44.

Ryu, Mykyung. (2010). Minorities in Higher Education: 24th Status Report. Washington, D.C.: American Council of Education.

Selingo, Jeffrey J. (2013). *College (Un)bound: The Future of Higher Education and What It Means for Students*. New York, NY: Houghton Mifflin Harcourt Publishing Company.

Thomas, Evan.(2008). "Can Michelle Rhee Save D.C.'s Schools?" In *Newsweek*, August 22, 2008.

U.S. Census Bureau. (2014). Annual Estimates of the Resident Population by Sex, Age, Race, and Hispanic Origin for the United States and States: April 1, 2010 to July 1, 2013. http://factfinder.census.gov/faces/tableservices/jsf/pages/productview.xhtml?pid=PEP_2013_PEPASR6H&prodType=table (October 14, 2015).

U.S. Census Bureau. (2012). 2010 Census of Population and Housing, *Summary Population and Housing Characteristics*. Washington, D.C.: U.S. Government Printing Office.

U.S. Department of Education, National Center for Education Statistics. (2015). Digest of Education Statistics, 2013 (NCES 2015-011) https://nces.ed.gov/programs/digest/d13/tables/dt13_330.10.asp (October 14, 2015).

US News and World Report. (2015). National Universities Rankings, http://colleges.usnews.rankingsandreviews.com/best-colleges/rankings/national-universities?int=9ff208 (October 14, 2015).

EIGHT

Where Do We Belong?

Latinas/os in Pursuit of Their Educational Dream

Viviana Cristian

On May 17, 2010, four undocumented students occupied the Arizona office of Senator John McCain. This action was followed by a flurry of high-profile public actions around the country. Undocumented youths poured into the streets, occupied the offices of other leading politicians, filled up blogs and editorial pages with eloquent arguments, lobbied senators and White House officials, and worked their networks to gain the backing of some of the most powerful unions and rights associations in the country. Their immediate goal was to pressure the Senate to support the DREAM Act... No longer would they accept their fate silently. They were asserting their 'right to have rights': the right to have a public existence in a country that had banished them to the shadows. (Nicholls, 2013, p. 1)

The Development, Relief, and Education for Alien Minors Act (otherwise known as the DREAM Act), would provide undocumented youths the legal right to stay in the United States and attend college.[1] Those who fall under this category and who have been fighting to be heard and have this act passed are known as the DREAMers (Nicholls, 2013; Truax, 2013, Beltrán, 2015; Olivas, 2013). For many years, these youths, as well as their parents kept a low profile in order for the U.S. government not to have a reason to deport them. Yet these parents left their home countries and worked hard to give their children a better life (Boehm, 2008). They have encouraged their children to learn English (at times to the detriment of their Spanish speaking abilities) and these children have become the interpreters for their family (Suarez-Orozco, 2000; Cristian, 2009). The children were able to attend primary and secondary education due to a ruling of the U.S. Supreme Court.[2] Many also worked while attending high school to be able to help the family. Still, they have been treated like unwanted guests.

The invisibility that their parents have maintained in order to help them has been adopted by these children. They have been forced to give up their "dreams" of going to college to get the same types of jobs as their parents due to fear and recrimination. The Minutemen,[3] the construction of the Border Wall (along the U.S.–Mexico border), the English-only movement,[4] the immigrant rights marches, the Great American Boycott,[5] and the organizations that have provided pro-bono legal counsel to unaccompanied minors are just some examples of how divided the United States has been about this segment of the population.

Based on ethnographic research that I conducted at George Mason University on Latino university students (Cristian, 2009) and my experience as an anthropologist and interpreter, this chapter studies how undocumented youth have gone from being an invisible and criminalized element to visible. An unapologetic group who demand to be heard and to have their rights, including the right to a higher education. I volunteer with an organization that provides free legal help to unaccompanied minors facing the immigration proceedings in the Washington, D.C., metropolitan area.

UNACCOMPANIED MINORS AND ASYLUM PROCEEDINGS

The number of minors immigrating illegally to the United States without the company of their parents has been steadily increasing in the last years (Passel, 2005; Uehling, 2008; Gonzales, 2009). This is not to say that it is a new phenomenon, it is one that has garnered the attention of the media and is a topic of hot debate. For those who are caught and taken into custody by ICE (Immigration and Customs Enforcement), they are then to face immigration proceedings to be granted asylum. There are those who do not have the money to hire a lawyer and, if necessary, an interpreter. Without legal representation, the children cannot understand the different aspects of the complicated proceedings and therefore are not able to present their case knowing all the options available to them. Those with viable claims are then at a greater risk of being sent back to an unpredictable, dangerous environment where they will be in peril of being killed.

For those who cannot afford either a lawyer or interpreter, there are organizations that offer the aid for free. For the last five years, I have been a volunteer Spanish language interpreter at one such organization— KIND (Kids in Need of Defense), which was created in 2009. According to their fact sheet, in 2014 nearly 68,000 children came to the United States alone (without a parent or legal guardian) and were placed in U.S. custo-dy. Many are escaping abuse or persecution; others are victims of traf-ficking. KIND finds pro-bono attorneys in highly regarded law firms and corporations who agree to represent KIND's child clients. The pro-bono coordinators in each of the KIND offices provide training on representing unaccompanied children in the U.S. immigration system and comprehen-sive mentorship until the case is completed. In all, this organization strives to ensure that no child who appears in immigration court is with-out legal representation.

KIND also recruits volunteer interpreters since the lawyers usually do not speak the same language that the child/client speaks, and the child has not yet mastered the English language to the level of being able to adequately express himself/herself. I was notified of my first case while at the SfAA (Society for Applied Anthropology) meetings in Merida, Mexico in 2010. The judge ruled in the clients' favor in 2015. Yes, it took five years for the case to reach its end. Due to the high volume of the cases, cases would be continued for two years, meaning it would be presented before a judge again in two years. During that time, the case would be sent to a different judge, the children/clients could have new lawyers, and their memories of the events dealing with the case would not be as crisp. Yet they must stay in a state of limbo, not knowing if they are to remain in their new home or be deported. *Please keep in mind* that I have interpreted for clients as young as eight years old and as old as seventeen years old.

As an anthropologist, I understand the concept of confidentiality as well as gaining the trust of the person you are interviewing. Gaining the clients' and their parents' trust proved to be harder than I had expected. I am a Latina, an anthropologist who has conducted studies on different aspects of the Latino population, and I speak Spanish fluently. I grew up being the interpreter for certain members of my family and then later on as a service for different organizations. I have translated documents for those seeking political asylum, and in other venues. I thought I was pre-pared and could handle any situation.

Yet I was not prepared for this new world that I had entered. The clients for whom I was now interpreting are minors going through the immigration proceedings process with a lot of trepidation. They have no idea whether they will be allowed to stay or be deported. They have been either abused by their guardians, or tortured and/or threatened with loss of life by a gang back in their home country, and then had gone through a harrowing journey on the way to the States. Some were helped and then abandoned by *coyotes*. One was kidnapped and held for ransom by a Mexican cartel until her parents were able to pay the money. Another was robbed twice while train hopping. They went at times without food. They had to evade any local police and try to blend in as well as they could with the locals so they could not be singled out. Their family had no idea where they were during this time until they were caught by immigration police and the police informed the family of the situation. These children were then held in a facility until they were reunited with relatives living in the United States. Their parents/legal guardians had not seen them for a long time, for some a number of years. These families clearly do not want to be separated again.

Meanwhile, the lawyer wants to present the best case possible in front of the judge so that the child can be granted asylum. She wants to know all that the client has gone through, as recorded in all the files; then discuss the options with the client and his/her guardian to see what is the best course of action. Since judges in immigration courts have gotten a bit jaded due to hearing cases that have turned out to have had false information, immigrant lawyers are now under more pressure to present cases with strong evidence and if possible strong documentation. I have interpreted in cases in which the lawyer had to tell the client and family that voluntary deportation was the best option since the client did not really have a case. In one such situation, the parents decided to go back with their child, even though they had another child who was born in the United States and they were in the process of attaining their residency. For them that was the only choice since they did not want to be separated from their child again.

One case was that of two cousins who had left their home in El Salvador without letting their guardians know and made their way crossing the U.S.–Mexico border before being caught by ICE agents. The female cousin was being represented by a KIND lawyer and I was notified to interpret for the young female. She was twelve years old at the time. Laura (not her real name) was living with her cousin and her grandmother in a town where gangs were the ones who were in control. The police either could not be trusted or could not be counted upon. One of Laura's friends had been raped on her way to school and she was afraid that she would come to the same fate. Her cousin Hector was being accosted by one of the gangs, giving him the ultimatum to join them or else. Laura was also feeling threatened at home. Her grandmother treated her like a slave keeping her inside when she was not in school, to do everything around the house which no one else was asked or expected to do. If it were not done to the grandmother's strict guidelines, the woman would be physically abusive, hitting her with any object she could find even if that object was the iron.

Both cousins, feeling that they had no one to turn to for help except each other, decided to leave. Laura's parents were living in the United States and she wanted to reunite with them. They took what they could fit in their backpacks, some money that Laura's parents had sent her, and left for the bus station. They went from bus to bus heading north. They also kept together and made sure to buy only food when absolutely necessary. They would sleep on the bus or at the bus station waiting for the next bus. Once in Mexico, Laura's cousin reminded her to speak as little as possible since their accents would give away that they were not Mexicans. They needed to stay away from any authorities.

Their luck ran out. They were low on funds. At a bus station, Laura was approached by a young man who held a knife to her and used her as leverage to get her cousin to do the young man's bidding. They were tied up and taken in a van. They were blindfolded and taken to a house where they were separated. Laura did not know it then, but they had been taken by the Zetas, a Mexican drug cartel that has been linked to murder of migrants, kidnappings, beheadings, and torture.[6] At the house she was asked a number of questions concerning her parents—most importantly their contact information and their names. Her parents were contacted and were threatened to send money or their daughter would be killed. It took some time since it was a substantial amount of money, but once the Zetas were satisfied, both cousins were taken with others across the border and released. Within fifteen minutes, Laura and her cousin were arrested by ICE agents.

Meeting Laura and talking to her, you would not have known that she had gone through this harrowing experience. She is a sweet, happy girl who would tell me about the soccer team that she is a part of and the good grades that she is getting in math and science. She is happy being with her family and hanging out with new friends. Every time I met with her and her lawyer, I kept hoping that the case was strong enough that the judge would grant her asylum. I did not want this to be another case of voluntary deportation. Laura has no support, safety, or future back in El Salvador.

THOSE WHO MADE IT TO COLLEGE

For the DREAMers who had not faced asylum proceedings and had been able to attend college, the journey has not been easy. They have had to navigate through state and federal laws, facing an uphill battle since only twenty states allow undocumented immigrants to attend public colleges and universities and pay in state tuition, but after meeting certain conditions (Olivas, 2013). One such state is Virginia (Collins, 2014). My dissertation topic centered around Latino university students at George Mason University, located in Northern Virginia. A report prepared by the Office of Equity and Diversity Services at George Mason in January 2004 emphasizes that the university is one of the most diverse institutions among four-year, publicly funded universities in Virginia. It has the highest proportion of Asian American students in the state (16 percent) and the highest proportion of Hispanic American students (7.1 percent). George Mason, in terms of its international population (3.8 percent), is second to Virginia Commonwealth University (8.3 percent). According to the report, since 1993 the student population has grown by 32.6 percent (6,946 students), which represents a 74 percent increase in minorities and a 22 percent increase in white students over a ten year period. For Hispanic students, the increase during the same ten year period has been a 98.6 percentage, from 857 to 1,702 students. In terms of undergraduate degree-seeking Hispanic students, the change has been from 575 to 1,265 students. It is a diverse university located in a metropolitan area that is unique in that it encompasses two states and the District of Columbia. George Mason fosters an environment where diversity is celebrated and encouraged (Cristian, 2009).

Since the students that I interviewed were either immigrants or the sons and daughters of immigrants, residency was frequently talked about during the interviews. Donna first came to the U.S. from Bolivia in 1992 with her mother and sister to get away from her father since he was physically abusive to her mother. They left without saying anything to anyone and crossed the border twice. The first time they were hiding from the border patrol, but her sister gave their location away by sneezing. Everyone there was taken in, questioned, detained in jail for the night, and let go the next day since the authorities thought the whole group consisted of Mexicans. Donna told me about the advice they received from the *coyotes* to be able to get through the process undetected,

> And they told us, whatever you do, say you're Mexican and if they tell you to, like, read, you know, some things, like the Himno de Mexico, just be like, I can't read that's why I haven't learned it, you know, that sort of thing. Uh, or I can't write, like, if they tell you to, like, sign stuff you're supposed to be, like, I can't write, or something like that. [*sic*]

The next day they tried to cross again by hiding in a car. She fell asleep during the trip and when she woke up they were in California. From there, they went on to Maryland where they had a couple of relatives and with whom they lived for six months. Later, they returned to Bolivia due to the death of Donna's paternal grandmother. Her father asked them to stay saying that he needed them. Her mother agreed on the condition that he enrolled the two girls in an American school located in their hometown. Not too long after coming back to Bolivia Donna's parents got divorced.

Donna's family decided to immigrate to the U.S. for a second time going from New Zealand to Bolivia to the U.S. Donna, her sister, and her mother flew to the Washington, D.C., area in 1998 to join Donna's stepfather who was living with Donna's maternal uncle in an apartment, while working in construction and cleaning offices at night. They not only left Bolivia without telling the biological father, they did not tell anyone they considered close to them. They simply announced that they were moving to another part of Bolivia. Donna could not tell anyone since her mother thought that just in case it did not work out and they got deported no one would have to know about it. She did reestablish contact with some of her friends from back home but for her the hardest contact to reestablish was with her biological father. It was a difficult and emotional call. She still keeps in contact with her father and has forged a relationship, though rocky one, with him.

Originally Donna, her sister, and mother went to live with Donna's maternal aunt in Maryland while her step-father was living with the uncle in Virginia. This household arrangement did not last long due to regulations concerning residential status for students in public schools in Maryland. They found out that they were able to go to public school in Virginia without too much fuss and so they all moved together into one apartment. Since she was the oldest, she was in charge of learning English first. With this competence, she became the family interpreter. Since her mom had some medical problems, Donna would miss school at times to accompany her mother to the doctor to interpret. She was in charge of paying the bills and when it came time to deal with the immigration lawyer she also filled out the paperwork to obtain residency. She confessed that she had been scared because she had heard about lawyers who disappeared with the money or who made false promises of completing the cases in six months. Here she was, a teenager trying to help her family to obtain their residency in the U.S. To cut down on costs she filled out as much of the paperwork as she could on her own. The whole process took two years. It included obtaining social security cards and work permits. They obtained their residency at the end of their period.

Unfortunately, Donna applied for college admission while trying to get her residency and that limited the colleges to which she could apply and afford to attend. She applied to different colleges but was not accepted since she did not have residency. The only place that accepted her was NOVA (Northern Virginia Community College),[7] but she had to pay out of state tuition. She applied to Virginia Tech and George Mason University during what ended up being the only year that she attended NOVA. They accepted her as an out of state student even though she informed them that she had received the letter that she would get her residency soon. Donna appealed their decisions with the help of a lawyer. She told them that her family has been paying taxes since they have arrived in 1998. Donna explained that there is a rule that you have to be paying taxes for at least five years to be considered an in-state student, so George Mason admissions personnel reversed their decision and accepted her as an in-state student while Virginia Tech still held firm to their decision. She started at George Mason in the fall of 2003. After the family members secured their residency, Donna's sister was able to attend Cornell University with the help of financial aid, while Donna stayed behind in Virginia struggling through the first year, balancing between taking care of the household and dealing with a different university environment. Her grades suffered in the process. Donna has been able to improve academically since then and she finds that she has an established an identity separate from her family on campus and by giving her parents more of the responsibility of taking care of the bills, etc. Even though George Mason was not her first choice for college, she is glad that she attended there, been part of its' diverse environment, and has tried to take advantage of the opportunities of being a Mason student. The last time I talked to her she had become the president of SHPE (Society for Hispanic Professional Engineers), a position she was very proud of attaining.

Eduardo was another student for whom not having residency played a part in going to college. He and his family came to the United States from Peru when he was sixteen years old. They settled in Virginia since they already had a relative living there. For him Virginia was a shock since in Peru everything was close by his place of residence. Since he entered the country without documents, he was afraid to get work and to apply for a driver's license because he did not want to be deported. Once he graduated from high school he still had not received his work permit so he thought that college was not an option until he found out from a friend that NOVA did accept those without papers as long as they presented their passport and other documents and pay out of state tuition. Moreover, since there was such a difference between in-state and out of state tuition, Eduardo had to get a job to cover expenses while he attended NOVA from 2002-2004. He worked with his father in a brick company. Eduardo got his driver's license and a car which his father bought for him. His job helped to pay for his car insurance. He obtained his work permit before he started attending George Mason University. Eduardo never did reveal how he was able to obtain a job or his driver's license. Eduardo did try to go to the dean after he had his work permit, but he was unable to change his status to in-state. The only other recourse left would have been to go to court. However, since he worked while he was undocumented, he was afraid of possible complications. Even though Eduardo has attained residency since then he continues to pay out of state tuition at George Mason. He told me that life would be easier for him if George Mason would let those with residency pay in-state tuition. Between working full-time and going to school full-time Eduardo does not have much of a social life. He was part of the International Student Association at NOVA and is a member of the Hispanic Student Association at George Mason but he just goes to an occasional meeting. He is proud to say that his job, where he is now an assistant manager, pays for eight thousand dollars a semester and his car insurance.

Eduardo told me towards the end of the interview that his experience at George Mason has been bittersweet. He would have liked to have had U.S. residence before going to college. He would have liked also to have had the college life of an American student in that not many live with their parents and they have the time to go to parties and activities both on and off campus as well as hang out with their friends. Eduardo told me that he has learned to organize his priorities and his time. He sees that for Americans, being independent means living on campus so they can get away from their home and do what they want while their parents pay for everything. If they do get a job, it is to pay for social activities and/or to go out with their girlfriends. For him he has the satisfaction that he has paid his own way for his education and has his parents' support both by living with them and through their encouragement.

Sandra was six years old when she came to the U.S. with her family from El Salvador. Her father had come to the U.S. when she was three years old and her mother when she was four. At six, she came with her brother, sister, and aunt through Mexico. At one point Sandra was separated from her siblings and aunt. She was in one taxi with an elderly man while the rest were in another taxi and unfortunately the driver of her taxi got lost. Since Sandra was six years old, she did not realize what was happening. Everyone was nice and in the end the driver was able to eventually find the rest of the group since he had driven the route before. Once they crossed the border, Sandra boarded a flight in Texas with her aunt to Virginia while her brother and sister were picked up by their dad's friend and were driven all the way to meet with the rest of the family. When she got off the plane, Sandra mistook her uncle for her father and went up to her uncle, hugging him calling him *papi*. All she knew was that one of two men would be her father, but she did not know what he looked like since she had no memories of him. Sandra was happy to be reunited with her parents, whoever they were.

It was hard at first to learn English. She remembers crying in class because she was so frustrated when she could not understand her second grade teacher. She did learn English eventually and became the interpreter in her family until they were able to cope for themselves. Unlike Donna, she did not feel pressure to stay at home because of her responsibilities. Sandra stayed at home to be close to her family and still be able to go to college. Since she and her family have been residents for a while now, she did not have to contend with the tuition issue. She knows that she should get her citizenship, but she is not motivated enough to go and start the process. This is different from Donna's view of getting her citizenship. For Donna, who is also an engineering major, being a citizen can bring more career opportunities especially for those looking for work or internships in any positions related to the government. Sandra knows that even after she becomes a citizen she will always be a Hispanic who was born in El Salvador and who one day wants to pass along her knowledge of the Spanish language to her children.

Teresa came to the United States from El Salvador when she was four years old with her family due to the civil war. I had assumed that her papers were all in order when I asked her about college and if George Mason was the only school to which she had applied. She told me that when she graduated from high school in 2001 that she would attend George Mason since it was her safety school. Also she had been in the EIP (Early Identification program), located on the GMU Fairfax campus, and financial aid would be offered for those attending George Mason. Because of her immigration status, anywhere else she would be considered an international student and would have to pay out of state tuition even if she went to a university in Virginia. George Mason has given her substantial financial assistance. She is not yet a resident though she has started the process by submitting the application. Her father obtained his residency three years ago though when he submitted his paperwork he did not submit it for the whole family. He now lives in Missouri with Teresa's youngest sibling. Teresa is waiting for her green card. She has sisters in El Salvador who, after coming to visit once on a tourist visa, have subsequently been denied visas to come to the U.S.. With a green card Teresa will be able to visit them. In the meantime she has found George Mason University challenging and rewarding. She has become more proud of her Salvadoran heritage and has taken the time to learn more about the recent civil war so that she can understand why her family had to make the decision to come to the United States.

Hernando's father was the first one to come to the United States to establish a home, get a job, and start sending remittances back to his family. His journey was unusual. From Bolivia he took a plane to Mexico. From there he crossed the border into Texas and continued his journey towards Virginia until he was caught by the Immigration and Naturalization Service (INS) and detained in jail. He called his brother who lived in Virginia and Hernando is not too sure about the details in this part of the story but basically his father was able to get out of jail and went to live with his brother. Hernando and his mother came over about a year later when he was almost three years old. They took a plane but he does not remember the trip at all due to his age. He did not know that it would be the last time that he would be in Bolivia. Hernando and his parents did get their residency about six years ago from the time that we had our interview, meaning in 2000. He does wonder why it took so long considering he has younger siblings who were born in the U.S. Now he is in the process of obtaining U.S. citizenship. He has filled out his application for citizenship. Since he got his residency in 2000 and he graduated from high school in 2002, he did not have to worry about tuition differences. He also went through the Early Identification Program (EIP) program and was awarded financial aid by attending George Mason. He has been grateful for that opportunity ever since. Hernando also stated that he hopes to go to Bolivia soon so he can finally meet some relatives for the first time and get to know a country that he has only known through books, his parents, and television. Even though he left Bolivia at a very young age and has not been there since, he is proud to be from Bolivia and when with other Latinos he identifies himself as a Bolivian.

When she was four years old, Vanessa literally crossed the border on the shoulders of a stranger while he navigated the currents of the Rio Grande. Born in Guatemala City, Vanessa's mother decided to emigrate to the U.S. to be with family in Virginia and have a better life than the one she could provide for her daughter in Guatemala. From Guatemala they crossed into Mexico going through jungles and covering themselves with plantain leaves when it rained and it was cold. They were shot at. As in Donna's case, Vanessa could not talk during the journey in Mexico so that their accent would not give them away. In one part of the journey they had to hide in the cargo section of the trains until they finally crossed into the United States. Once they crossed the border, they were picked up by some people in a truck and they had to pretend that they were part of the family in the truck. At a certain point they were dropped off and mother and daughter took a plane from Texas to Washington, D.C. Vanessa's mom is now a U.S. citizen. For Vanessa, the journey from Guatemala to Virginia demonstrated how much her mother sacrificed so that she could have the opportunity to get a good education and have a promising career. These memories have kept her motivated when she feels like "slacking off" in school.

Becoming a U.S. resident can make the difference on what college to apply to and what kind of job to get, which therefore made the trip to Virginia a motivational factor to work hard to get an education. They saw for themselves how hard it is to leave behind everything their parents knew, and in some cases everything they themselves knew, and come to a new country for better opportunities. They want to honor what their parents provided, yet residency has been a frustrating obstacle to attain their goals. Even with that obstacle they have managed to attain a means to attend and pay for college. Knowing what it has taken to reach that goal has gotten them to appreciate their ethno-national cultures more. Sandra was one who conveyed it best with knowing that even with becoming a U.S. citizen she will always know that she is a Hispanic who was born in El Salvador and one day wants to pass along her knowledge of the Spanish language to her future children.

DREAMERS IN THE LIMELIGHT

"Mi nombre es Fernanda Marroquín. Si estás viendo este video es porque fui arrestada en Alabama. Soy indocumentada, no me da vergüenza y no tengo miedo" (Truax, 2013, p. 14). (My name is Fernanda Marroquín. If you are seeing this video it is because I was arrested in Alabama. I am undocumented, I am not ashamed and I am not afraid.)

Fernanda's video was one of thirteen that went viral on the internet after they were arrested on November 15, 2011, in Montgomery, Alabama. In that video they explained why they participated in an act of civil disobedience which they knew would result in an arrest and possible deportation. They have been in this country since they were very young, yet they have been told to go back to a country they hardly know or have never visited. They felt ashamed of being undocumented and were afraid to even reveal that to their friends until they came to a realization. By revealing their status as undocumented immigrants and by having no fear, it gives them the power to help their community (Truax, 2013).

That is one act among many that DREAMers have done to bring national and international attention to what they feel and know should be their rights. They are much more vocal and use more ways of communication to get their message across than their parents. While their parents used immigrant organizations, Spanish language media, handing out of flyers, and mingled with citizens during protests to avoid detection by authorities (e.g., the immigrant marches of 2006); the children have used social media (e.g., Facebook, Twitter, YouTube), have committed acts of civil disobedience, have used both Spanish and English media, have openly said that they are undocumented, and have demanded to be granted their rights (Beltrán, 2015).

As mentioned before, the DREAM act first came into existence in 2001. This Act was a response to the Immigration Policy changes, the increased tensions between both sides of the illegal immigration debate, and the increased frustration of illegal immigrants who were tired of the unfulfilled promises made by the President Obama and the government (Beltran, 2015; Olivas, 2013; Truax, 2013). It unfortunately did not pass through Congress. Revised versions of the DREAM Act were brought forward for passage in 2007 and 2010, but both times there were not enough votes (Olivas, 2013). This legislation would permit undocumented immigrants to obtain conditional resident status if, after graduating from a U.S. high school, they continue higher education by attending university, vocational school, or an apprenticeship program and/or join the U.S. military. They must have entered the United States before turning sixteen years of age, be living in the country for at least five years, speaking English, educated in U.S. schools, and demonstrating "good moral character." If they satisfy these conditions, immigrants would then be able to get permanent status after graduating from a two-year college, within six years of the initial petition, or after serving at least two years in the U.S. armed forces (Culwell, 2010). The DREAM act could help 360,000 undocumented youth to continue on to higher education (Gonzales, 2009). It is an act that seeks to frame undocumented youth in nonthreatening innocence—as upstanding, academically successful, hardworking "citizens" (Beltrán, 2015).

Yet the Act has met with resistance, anti-immigrant sentiment continues, and since 2009 there have been more deportations than during the two full presidential terms of George W. Bush. That is why the DREAMers decided to take their cause to all possible methods of communication and have adopted strategies from other groups who have fought for their civil rights. One of those groups is the LGBTQ community (Beltrán, 2015).[8] They used the strategies of visibility developed during the gay rights movement. For example, the 2010 and 2011 "Coming out of the Shadows" campaigns included a series of speeches by youth who openly declared their undocumented status. DREAMers declared themselves as "undocumented and unafraid." This expanded in 2011 to "undocumented, unafraid, and unapologetic." Since then more and more undocumented youth have chosen to adopt this strategy through different types of protests—hunger strikes, sit-ins, rallies, etc. (Beltrán, 2015).

At the beginning of this section, there was a quote from Fernanda, a young lady who used the "coming out" strategy to bring attention to the DREAMers' cause. She did so by going down to the state capital in Montgomery, Alabama to protest and proclaim her status. Fernanda also took it viral, where others have as well. DREAMers have gone to YouTube and Facebook. They have created Web series such as "Undocumented and Awkward" and "UndocuCribs" (Beltrán, 2015). Fernanda's video was featured on a website called DreamActivist.org. The cyber-*testimonios* that the DREAMers post online reflect the journey they have gone through to come out and claim their rights and their status within the United States.

As Georgina Perez, a member of the Georgia DREAMers stated in her online video that was posted in April 2011:

> Through the last five years, as undocumented youth, we have done everything in order to get open dialogue with elected officials . . . and instead of our voices being heard, we're just not seeing any change... I will no longer wait for someone to come and dictate and tell me what to do while I'm being denied the access to higher education.[9]

There are DREAMers who have been praised by the First Lady of the United States, Michelle Obama, for their accomplishments. Each year the National Arts and Humanities Youth Program awards to outstanding out of school and after-school programs that are changing the lives of young people through the use of art and the humanities to increase not only academic achievement, but also graduation rates and college enrollment. On November 17, 2015 one of the twelve programs that was presented this award by Michelle Obama was the DREAM Program created by CityDance, Inc. located in Washington, D.C. It is an after school program that provides dance classes, performance opportunities, tutoring, and mentoring (Malet, 2015). One of the members of that program, who was there to receive the award (along with the Director of the program), is Valeria Cruz, a DREAMer from Honduras. A participant of the DREAM program for eight years, Valeria first came to the United States when she was two years old. Receiving this award has made her both a local and an international celebrity with news reaching all the way to Honduras (*El*

Heraldo, 2015). She told reporters that the program has taught her to be a leader not only in dance class, but to also be a role model to those younger than she was (Lugo, 2015). Currently a senior at Phelps Architecture, Construction and Engineering High School, located in Washington, D.C., Valeria is applying to colleges with a plan to study dance or communication (Ritzel, 2015).

Talking on the phone with her and with her mother, they both told me how being part of the program and getting the award has been so beneficial for Valeria and the whole family. Valeria's mother has raised her and her siblings on her own. For many years, Valeria's brothers were afraid of going for many jobs since they were undocumented and they did not want to run the risk of deportation. With Valeria's participation in the DREAM program, as a beneficiary of DACA (Deferred Action for Childhood Arrivals), and now receiving this award, her brothers are no longer afraid.[10] They have all officially come out of the shadows.

CONCLUSION: WHERE TO NEXT?

Through the DREAM act, undocumented youth want to fulfill their goal of attaining higher education. These DREAMers have taken up the torch from their parents to go to the government and demand change to the current immigration policy. Grateful for their parents' sacrifice, these DREAMers have gone public stating that they are unapologetic for being undocumented and for the decisions the parents made for them when they were young. They have already faced so many challenges. They have gone through a long, and at times, a dangerous journey to get to the United States to be reunited with their families. They have avoided being caught by ICE (Immigration and Customs Enforcement). They have been interpreters for their families, and adapted to a new culture. They have spent most of their lives in a country where they were been afraid to identify their status. Yet it has been the country they have known the most. They are proud to be a resident, a citizen of the United States.

NOTES

1. The DREAM Act is a bipartisan legislation pioneered by Sen. Orin Hatch [R-UT] and Sen. Richard Durbin [D-IL]. Under the provisions of the DREAM Act, qualifying undocumented youth would be eligible for a six- year long conditional path to citizenship that requires completion of a college degree or two years of military service. There have been revisions to the act and it has yet to be passed (Truax, 2013).

2. The Supreme Court ruling of Plyler v. Doe (1982) which held that a Texas statute which withholds from local school districts any state funds for the education of children who were not "legally admitted" into the United States, and which authorizes local school districts to deny enrollment to such children, violates the Equal Protection Clause of the Fourteenth Amendment (Varsanyi, 2008).

3. An activist organization started by individuals who patrol the U.S.-Mexico Border's flow of undocumented immigrants and who have been criticized for being xenophobic, violent, and vigilantes (Chavez, 2008,).

4. A movement whose goal is the establishment of English as the official language of the U.S. and the only language that should be used for official government documents (Chavez, 2008).

5. As a continuation of the 2006 U.S. immigration reform protests, the organizers called for supporters (immigrants) to—on May 1 2006—abstain from buying, selling, or working at any business as well as from working or attending school, in order to demonstrate the extent to which the labor of undocumented immigrants is needed. Supporters of the boycott rallied in major cities across the U.S. to demand legalization programs for undocumented aliens as well as general amnesty. For this reason, the day is referred to as A Day Without an Immigrant (Chavez, 2008).

6. Zeta started out as a paramilitary branch of the Gulf cartel and were recruited from the disaffected ranks of Mexico's elite special forces. By 2010, the Zetas, who are independent of the Gulf Cartel, were estimated to have more than 10,000 soldiers and had expanded beyond the borders of Mexico (Ryman, 2013).

7. NOVA (Northern Virginia Community College) is located near Washington, D.C. The College includes six campuses: Alexandria, Annandale, Loudoun, Manassas, MEC (Springfield) and Woodbridge. According to its website, NOVA is the second-largest community college in the United States, comprising of more than 75,000 students and 2,600 faculty and staff members. It also has a student body consisting of individuals from more than 180 countries.

8. LGBTQ stands for Lesbian, Gay, Bisexual, Transgender, and Queer.

9. *See* www.youtube.com/watch?v=mTeh1m0qiEU

10. DACA, which stands for Deferred Action for Childhood Arrivals, grants temporary status and work authorization to undocumented immigrants who had come to the country as children. Yet it is not a way to citizenship and could be revoked at any time by the sitting president. It also denies eligibility for many services including the Affordable Care Act (Nicholls, 2013).

REFERENCES

Beltrán, Cristina. (2015). "'Undocumented, Unafraid, and Unapologetic': DREAM Activists, Immigrant Politics, and the Queering of Democracy." In Danielle Allen and Jennifer S. Light (eds.) *From Voice to Influence: Understanding Citizenship in a Digital.* Chicago and London: The University of Chicago Press, pp. 80-104.
Boehm, Deborah A. (2008). "'For My Children': Constructing Family and Navigating the State in the U.S.-Mexico Transnation." *Anthropological Quarterly,* 81(4): 777–802.
Chavez, Leo .(2008). *The Latino Threat: Constructing Immigrants, Citizens, and the Nation.* Stanford, CA: Stanford University Press.
Collins, Eliza. (2014). "Undocumented immigrants in Va. can now qualify for in-state tuition." *USA Today.* May 5, 2014. http://college.usatoday.com/2014/05/05/undocumented-immigrants-in-va-can-now-qualify-for-in-state-tuition/ (November 25, 2015).
Cristian, Viviana. (2009). Who are We? : Cultural Identity among Latino College Students in Northern Virginia. Ph. D. Dissertation, The Catholic University of America.
Culwell, Alan. (2010). "The Dream Act - Immigration Law Reform in 2010?" http://ezinearticles.com/?The-Dream-Act---Immigration-Law-Reform-in-2010?&id=3361262 (November 25, 2015)
El Heraldo. (2015). "Hondureña será condecorada por primera dama de EEUU." *El Heraldo,* November 17, 2015. www.elheraldo.hn/minisitios/hondurenosenelmundo/suenoamericano2/902369-471/hondure%C3%B1a-ser%C3%A1-condecorada-por-primera-dama-de-ee-uu (November 18, 2015)

Gonzales, Roberto. (2009). *Young Lives on Hold: The College Dreams of Undocumented Students*. New York, NY: The College Board Advocacy.

Harin, Orin G. (2001). S.1291 Development, Relief, and Education for Alien Minors Act- DREAM Act. www.gpo.gov/fdsys/pkg/BILLS-107s1291is/pdf/BILLS-107s1291is.pdf (November 2, 2015).

Lugo, Luis Alonso (2015). "Michelle Obama premia 12 programas artísticos." *Vívelo Hoy*. November 17, 2015. www.vivelohoy.com/entretenimiento/8500928/michelle-obama-premia-12-programas-artisticos (November 19, 2015).

Malet, Jeff. (2015). "First Lady Michelle Obama Praises CityDance and Others at Awards Ceremony (photos)." *The Georgetowner*, November 19, 2015. www.georgetowner.com/articles/2015/nov/19/national-arts-and-humanities-youth-program-awards-ceremony-first-lady-michelle-obama-photos/ (November 23, 2015).

Nicholls, Walter. (2013) *The DREAMers: How the Undocumented Youth Movement Transformed the Immigrant Rights Debate*. Stanford, CA: Stanford University Press.

Northern Virginia Community College. About NOVA. http://www.nvcc.edu/about/index.html (October 27, 2015).

Office of Equity and Diversity Services. 2004 Diversity Facts in Brief. Fairfax, VA: George Mason University, 2004.

Olivas, Michael A. (2013). "Dreams Deferred: Deferred Action, Prosecutorial Discretion, and the Vexing Case(s) of DREAM Act Students." *William & Mary Bill of Rights Journal*, 21(2): 463-547.

Passel, Jeffrey S. (2005). Estimates of the Size and Characteristics of the Undocumented Population. Washington, D.C.: Pew Hispanic Center.

Ritzel, Rebecca. (2015). "Bethesda's CityDance receives Arts Program Award at the White House." *The Washington Post*. November 17, 2015. www.washingtonpost.com/entertainment/theater_dance/bethesdas-citydance-receives-arts-program-award-at-the-white-house/2015/11/17/2a3add66-8d6f-11e5-acff-673ae92ddd2b_story.html (November 19, 2015).

Ryman, Noah. (2013). Mexico's Feared Narco: A Brief History of the Zetas Drug Cartel. *Time*. July 16. http://world.time.com/2013/07/16/mexicos-feared-narcos-a-brief-history-of-the-zetas-drug-cartel/

Suarez-Orozco, Carola. (2000) "Identities Under Siege: Immigration Stress and Social Mirroring Among the Children of Immigrants." In Antonius C.G.M. Robben and Marcelo Suarez-Orozco (eds.) *Cultures Under Siege: Collective Violence and Trauma*. Cambridge, U.K.: Cambridge University Press, pp. 194-226.

Truax, Eileen. (2013). *Dreamers: La Lucha de una Generación por su sueño Americano*. Mexico, D.F: Editorial Océano.

Uehling, Greta Lynn. (2008). "The International Smuggling of Children: Coyotes, Snakeheads, and the Politics of Compassion." *Anthropological Quarterly*, 81(4): 833-871.

Varsanyi, Monica. (2008). "Rescaling the 'Alien,' Rescaling Personhood: Neoliberalism, Immigration, and the State." *Annals of the Association of American Geographers*, 98 (4): 877–89.

NINE

At The Crossroads of Racial, Ethnic, Sexual, Gender, and National Borders

María Amelia Viteri

This chapter, as well as the book on which it is based, continues to be made of *travesías* (journeys) and hope. *Desbordes: Translating Race, Ethnicity, Gender and Sexuality across the Americas* (Viteri, 2014) drew on multi-sited ethnographic data collected principally among the LGBT Latino communities in Washington D.C., El Salvador, and Ecuador.[1] I illustrate how sexuality and gender as a dimension of power shape and guide processes of migration and modes of incorporation. The fact that the conflations of race and ethnicity, gender and sexuality as inserted within a transnational framework and border continuum, have largely remained under-examined in the field of anthropology speaks to the importance of the themes this book highlights thanks to the editors to whom I thank deeply for this invitation. Within this larger ethnographic research study, I insert an analysis of Latina women organizing in the D.C. area in light of structural inequality. Together with the Latinas, particularly Central American, I combine and advocate for an intersectional approach to migrant and gender inequality. I build my analysis specifically on the Latina feminist grassroots organization known as *Madre Tierra* (Mother Earth, Pacha Mama).

Latina women account for approximately 4.5 percent of the population of Washington, D.C.: 2.1 percent born in the United States, 2.3 percent born outside the United States. The Washington, D.C., metropolitan area has one of the largest populations of Central Americans settled on the East Coast of the United States. More than 13 percent of the population in the D.C. metropolitan area is Hispanic (U.S. Census Bureau, 2010) and the population has been increasing. In 2007, Salvadorans represented 17 percent of the immigrant population in the area (Comey et al., 2009), many driven from their home country by wars in Central America fueled by U.S. support of anti-communist regimes.[2] The massive immigration of Central Americans to this area has created unexpected opportunities for Latinos to confront current migration discourses and Latino stereotyping. The estimated Hispanic population of the United States as of 2012 is 53.3 million, making people of Hispanic origin the nation's largest ethnic or 'race' minority, that is to say, 14 percent of the nation's total population — according to the U.S. Census Bureau (2012).

I use the word "immigrant" in reference to all the moments and spaces of the migrant chain (Castro, 2008, p. 246) including the effects of migration, and their role on the construction of daily life, as related to belonging beyond the legal marker of citizenship. Cultural translation and border crossing have been conceptualized in this chapter as nonlinear processes, and as such, in constant resignification.

DESBORDES OR UNDOING BORDERS

Following Cantú (2009, p. 26), sexuality as a dimension of power has shaped *all* migration in its practice, regulation, and study in profound yet 'invisible' ways. Both conceptually and methodologically, the queer standpoint reveals how 'homosexuality' as a marginal sexuality influences migration, and how heterosexuality, as a normative regime, shapes the social relations and processes of migration. As per Johnson and Jones's (2011) discussion, there has been a change in the 1990s trend of a "borderless world" towards Balibar's (1998) notion that "borders are everywhere." That is to say, the *loci* of bordering practices can no longer be isolated to the lines of a political map. "Where is the border in border studies?" Johnson and Jones asked the *Political Geography Journal* contributors in order to problematize both the idea of rigid borders as well as that of a borderless world. The concept of *desbordes* I present in my book with the same title captures this fluidity and mobility, and the way that immigrants and the borders encompassing them exceed any fixed definition. These are not (only) geographic borders in a territorial sense; instead, they bring in gender, racial, ethnic, national, and sexual markers as knitted in those geographical borders carrying their own markers.

Des- is a prefix in Spanish that implies undoing, a literal translation of *desbordes* would be "undoing borders." Moreover, *desbordes* implies not only undoing but also overflowing or exceeding all pre-discursive categories and analytical references around gender and sexuality. This is how I argue that Latinos — particularly LGBT Latinos — construct borders as they undo others, redefining new ways of belonging that confront the traditional conceptualization and idea of citizenship and as such, sexual citizenship. Confronting limiting and normative understandings around citizenship allows us a better understanding of the multiple ways in which Latino and Latina immigrants create community networks in the Washington, D.C., metropolitan area.

Along with the framework that enables the mapping of Latinos and Latinas social agency, the concept of *strategic distancing* enables us to conceptualize how race, ethnicity, class, gender, and sexuality are mutually constitutive with and through the way (normative and non-normative) citizenship and belonging mechanisms operate. For instance, it speaks to Halberstam's (1998) call to undo (a) category. Occupying gender in this particular usage refers to moving away from traditional ways of looking at gender, the body, and feminism (Viteri, 2014, p. xxiii).

The methodological implications of analyzing Latino identity categories through U.S. sex, gender, class, racial, and ethnic systems are considerable, as not only will the translation be flawed but people's daily negotiations will be erased. Deleuze and Guattari's (1987) rhizomatic analysis which is characterized by simultaneously going different ways and thereby inhibiting traditional categorizations and taxonomies as the emphasis is constantly changing, has also been useful to locate the impact of these categories in the lives of LGBT Latinos.

An indexicality of power—an analysis of the situational context and the lived experience as advanced by Butler (1990)—is a methodology I have used when examining identities as fluid and categories as unstable. Some of the questions that arose from the original ethnographic study as they relate to the current chapter are the following: What are the different intersections between sexuality, gender, race, ethnicity, and class that converge to produce specific 'subjects' in the Latino Diaspora the D.C. metropolitan area? How do LGBT Latino immigrants negotiate the contradictions and paradoxes of language, ancestry, homeland, and community involved in the deployment and displacement of identity?[3] For instance, the D.C. Latino population's migration journey and history, as inserted in the politics of the capital city, marks a stark difference with Latinos and Latinas in New York, California, or Texas as is made visible by this book.

MADRE TIERRA: A FEMINIST LATINA GRASSROOTS ORGANIZATION

The Latina women that founded Madre Tierra as well as every Latina that has been part of this organization in different ways, exemplify the multiplicity of struggles they have to go through, as their demands are unheard. Madre Tierra started in February 2004 with a small group of migrant women mostly from Central America, thanks to the persistence of a well-known and recognized Latina feminist and LGBT activist, Dilcia

Molina with whom my daughter Simone (six years old at the time) and I shared *vigilias* (eve/vigil) against gender violence and marched down 14th Street to the U.S. Capitol for immigrants' rights.

Dilcia Molina is originally from Honduras, and was granted political asylum in the United States in 2002. Dilcia Molina's story was featured in a 2003 documentary, "Dangerous Living: Coming Out in the Developing World," which highlights the struggles of LGBT people in the global south, that is to say, people in so-called developing countries mostly located in the Southern hemisphere. In November 2001, six military police officers raided her home in Honduras intending to rape her, due to her work with human rights, as Dilcia dismantled a girls' sex trafficking network and was a visible advocator for LGBT equality and rights. Unable to find her, the military police officers harmed her two sons. Right after she decided to leave to the United States with her two children.

Dilcia has been the manager of the "Entre Amigas" Project for women at La Clínica del Pueblo (LCDP) in Washington, D.C., for the past ten years. Madre Tierra and LCDP have joined efforts against violence, particularly migrants and vulnerable women. LCDP is the place where I happily spent most of my PhD years working closely with Dilcia on LGBT and Latinas' projects such as one addressing Latina sexual workers that consisted of both biological women and trans-women. This project looked at the impact of sexual work, working closely with the communities in order to map their housing situation, police violence rate, discrimination, and access to health-care services. We provided a safety net for Latina sexual workers while creating safe spaces at LCentro against police violence and guaranteeing access to health care services. Within the tradition of collaborative and participatory action research, Dilcia Molina served as a member of my dissertation committee, a rare occurrence in the academy. As I further analyze it in *Desbordes* (Viteri 2014), this speaks to Kondo's (1986, p. 76) call for a "more experiential and effective modes of knowing" in which the ethnographer's identity and location are made explicit and informants are given a greater role in texts (Narayan, 1993, p. 34).

Having said this, methodologies such as Participatory Action Research (PAR) enable informants and researchers to work together on common ground, considering the interests of informants first (Freire, 1972; Fals-Borda and Rahman, 1991). This methodology prompts researchers to work on social justice issues. By allowing my research to relate 'individual' narratives to 'community' narratives, engaged research becomes another tool for social justice.

According to Kemmis and McTaggart (1997), participatory research has been often associated with social transformation in the third world, having roots in Liberation Theology and neo-Marxist approaches to community development as in Latin America. It's based on an orientation towards community action as well as community-based analysis of social problems. Participatory action research aims to transform both theory and practice even confronting the limits of democracy in the United States and highlighting at the same time the need to contextualize race, class, and gender relations as it challenges the limits of multiculturalism (Naples, 1998). There have been numerous instances where strategic co-alitions and common struggles translated in specific actions. One of those spaces was the discussion "Creating Spaces, Construyendo Comunidad: the Latino LGBT Community in the D.C. Area, a Retrospective Look" that included a roundtable discussion, panel, film, and exhibit with prominent LGBT Latino leaders in the area, and with the active participation of the Latino LGBT History Project.[4] This event was part of the "Interrogating Diversity International Interdisciplinary Conference" at American University I founded and chaired in 2007 and 2008 together with my friend and anthropology colleague Aaron Tobler and a committee of committed social scientists, particularly anthropologists, thanks to the Department of Anthropology and the College of Arts and Sciences.[5]

Madre Tierra was born in Fredericksburg City, Virginia out of the realization of the need to fight for human rights, particularly those of Latino migrants as well as to provide services in Spanish for Latina women who were literally invisible in the town, hidden behind fear of deportation and/or by farm owners who kept them out of sight.[6] Maryland and Virginia have experienced among the largest increases in number of undocumented immigrants nationwide since 2009, with both populations rising by 15 percent during that time according to the Pew Research Center (2015).

Madre Tierra's innovative approach reminds us of the paradoxes and juxtapositions brought by migration flows that act in both micro—and macro–contexts (Lewellen 2002, p. 190). Sánchez Molina's (2006) analysis—based on ethnographic work in D.C. that places a Salvadoran woman's life story and her sociocultural, transnational configurations in the forefront—brings forward the inequality of migration processes. This global economic system driving women out of their countries and into forced labor creates precariousness for these women.

STRUCTURAL GENDER AND LGBT VIOLENCE

The Concilio Rappahannock Contra la Violencia Doméstica (Rappahannock Council against Domestic Violence - RCASA) opened up a physical space for Madre Tierra thanks to strategic lobbying by their founders. RCASA is a private, non-profit agency that started in 1986 as the Fredericksburg Area Rape Crisis Center. It provides a safe, healing environment for survivors of violence providing a range of supportive and therapeutic services. RCASA provides services for victims of sexual assault and their family, friends, and partners in the form of hospital and court accompaniment, hotline, counseling, and prevention services.

In the beginning, they doubted the scope of Madre Tierra as they had registered fewer than five Latino families per year requesting their services. However, through the partnership with Madre Tierra, they reached 250 people during the first year of their joint efforts. The issue was not that there were no Latinos and Latinas in the area, but the precariousness of their situation. The population was mostly composed of undocumented peasants, particularly women, working on Virginia farms, as well as many undocumented and documented working class men and women fearful of a very conservative "white" town and State, with little visibility of other ethnicities. Most of the Latino population spoke primarily Spanish with none or very little English, which made it even more difficult to access information and any type of services.[7]

During Madre Tierra's fourth year, the First Popular Education Center (Primer Centro de Educación Popular) was developed. It included workshops on migration rights, human rights, women and gender rights, among others. They also incorporated an interpreter service oriented towards social justice that could accompany those in need to the hospital, court or other important institutions.

Madre Tierra is now part of the *Coalición de Pueblos Inmigrantes de Virginia* (Immigrant Virginia Coalition) and the *Coalición Latina contra la Violencia de Género en D.C.* (Latina Coalition against Gender Violence in D.C.) The work, started primarily by two visionary and committed Latina women—Dilcia Molina and its co-founder María Cortez—has now extended not only to Maryland and Washington D.C., but to New Jersey, Texas, California, and Florida, to name a few of the states that have required their assistance. This assistance consists of expert witnesses on LGBT and domestic violence cases for political asylum as well as a referral system to aid Latina women in particular. Leslie Moncada, a Honduran therapist, has been another key actor in providing and securing psychological attention for many domestic violence victims.

Madre Tierra has positively affected the lives of at least 600 families, comprised of mostly Central American, working class and undocumented women. During their now eleven years of work in the D.C. area, Madre Tierra has supported and won political campaigns such as the Driver's License Campaign which granted driver's licenses to undocumented immigrants who have lived in the city for at least six months, it allowed increased mobility in terms of transportation, education, employment purposes, and identity.

Madre Tierra is unable to raise funds as a grassroots organization without non-profit status, which makes their work even more admirable given their ability to expand their important work. Nevertheless, it faces the constant challenge and precariousness of being primarily a Latina women's grassroots organization that depends on one or two people's commitment for its existence. That commitment is contingent on the staff holding other paid positions as their work for the organization is not remunerated and no one receives a salary for their work as Latina community organizers for social justice.

In the near future, Dilcia envisions an organization that can provide a political and feminist approach as it also provides a space for self-healing and self-care among Latina women. Her own experience as a lesbian, feminist, Central American mother who was granted political asylum triggered new forms of organization that they have incorporated in their organization. In addition, Madre Tierra has trained, educated and provided valued services to hundreds of Latina women.

Dilcia's agency as a Latina woman brings us face to face with the political question of how to not only create, but to be able to maintain social awareness that will contribute to reducing the social, gender, sexual, and economic gaps faced by a great majority of people around the world. It also makes visible how sexuality as a dimension of power shapes and guides processes of migration and modes of incorporation (Cantú, 2009). Our different subject positions, joined by mutual interests in social justice, enabled my research to come out of the community as well as to engage the community in unpredictable and enriching ways (Viteri, 2014).

MAKING FACES

Madre Tierra's Latina immigrant women have challenged normative definitions of gender including the stereotype of being submissive mothers and wives. The continuous negotiation around place, belonging, and ethnic/racial/sexual identities are articulated in those iterative moments that mark the possibility and impossibility of identity, and presence through absence (Butler, 1990). I will rely on Gloria Anzaldúa's (1990) metaphor of "making faces" for constructing one's identity, a creative, though draining, process. Rodríguez (2003, p. 9) defines Latinidad as the site where different discourses of history, geography, and language practices collide, whereas Dávila (2001, p. 2) uses Latinidad as a site where Spanish speaking is the basis for identification as is the case of Madre Tierra. The Latina women involved in Madre Tierra have confronted multiple disparities simultaneously. They are united by a shared language, in this case Spanish, while facing the lack of visibility and acknowledgement of the Latino presence in Fredericksburg—except for (negative) police attention. Their networks proved to be central in creating mutual respect as immigrant women pioneers.

The scope of Madre Tierra's outreach to vulnerable Latina women such as those in the precarious and invisible situations mentioned speaks to the strength of the connections with Latino migrants in the D.C. metropolitan area. Larger organizations with the capacity to raise funds as non-profits have not had the same ability to reach to the most vulnerable Latinos and Latinas in the area. The main reason is that the invisibility and the precariousness of certain groups of women are not easily access-ible to non-Latina women. Language definitely plays a key component as well as perceptions around race, ethnicity and country of origin.

As I discussed earlier, border crossing has entailed that Latinos and Latinas including mostly "non-white" ethnicities face an institutional ap-paratus that either denies them entrance or else deports them based on their undocumented condition. These conditions are aggravated by eth-nic/sexual/racial/gender identity status (Luibhéid and Cantú, 2005). Pass-port controls, border checks, interviews, interdiction, detainment, secon-dary inspection, profiling, and other tactics have served to establish or determine identities, to draw out 'confessions' of who one is (Epps, Val-ens, and Gonzalez 2005, p. 5). An illustrative example is Christina Madra-zo's case discussed by Solomon (2005). Madrazo is a trans-sexual woman from Mexico who was raped by a guard in an immigration detention facility in Miami (Florida) in 2000, as she sought asylum in the U.S. due to the gender discrimination in Mexico. The guard was granted a plea bar-gain with a lesser sentence. As the author illustrates, trans-sexualism has been constructed as a form of sexual deviance leading to the endorsement of violence that takes the form of rape.

Borders have served many purposes in defining citizenship, consider-ing that these borders are social spaces that are used to delimit sexual-identity positions, following Bell and Binnie's (2000, p. 110) discussion of sexuality and belonging. Nevertheless, this same space of the social opens up the possibility of reconfiguring sexual identities, usually driven by government-regulated agendas. As Dilcia undoes discriminatory and oppressive borders, she redoes other forms of understanding and respect through community action that comprises social justice based on a strong intersection of identities: Latina, Honduran, feminist, lesbian, migrant, and woman. Dilcia's resilience speaks to Cohen's (1980) analysis of pat-terns of conflict resolution used by Latino newcomers to cope with the newer environment.

There are still many short-term as well as long-term challenges and questions that remain. For example, how to develop both a sense of be-longing and an appreciation of cultural diversity that doesn't seek to homogenize all inhabitants to one national or language identity. In addi-tion, gender is an added vulnerability among immigrant women living in the D.C. area, because of the structural conditions of their lives that brought them there to begin with. On the other hand, the ability of Latina women from Madre Tierra to mobilize and create communities in a place where Latina women were rendered invisible in different ways and where discrimination against Latinos runs high—especially in certain ar-eas in Virginia and Maryland—makes us hopeful. An anti-immigrant sentiment has characterized some counties and localities in Virginia particularly against Latinos. Residences and anti-immigrant organizations have pressed for legislation demanding requirements for police to check the immigration status of those arrested and taken into custody, legal presence requirements for driver's licenses and state funded social services, among many others (Capps et al., 2011; Leitner and Stunk, 2014). Madre Tierra's perilous and dedicated work needs to be inserted within this harsh context as they simultaneously confront sexist, racist, classist and ethnocentric categories as those intersect national borders.

CONCLUSION

As I further problematize in *Desbordes* (Viteri, 2014), a methodology from the bottom up instead of from the top down speaks towards a decolonization of traditional forms of research and standard forms of knowledge and truth (Hall, 1997a, p. 184), following the tradition of feminist anthropologists (Behar and Gordon, 1995; Behar, 1993; Kondo, 1990; Ong, 1999).

Similar to *Madre Tierra* intertwining of personal development, political consciousness and the process of making connections between our lives and those of others (Hardy-Fanta, 1997), the practice of engaging in a reflexive process brings forward the political as the *cotidiano* (everyday) and the *cotidiano* as the political.

The importance of relating what could be understood as individual narratives to community narratives opens up the possibility of not only decentering researcher privilege (Slocum, 2001; Harding, 1987), but joining common struggles. Coming from a rather politicized Latin American scene, this background has helped me to strategically and politically combine the different subject positions I inhabit to build bridges between the grassroots/activist organizations and academia, as with Madre Tierra's case study. It enables, as I further discuss in *Desbordes* (Viteri, 2014), the invention of the place of the university and the Latino *barrios* so that one is not in juxtaposition with the other, but rather in constant dialogue.

The ethnographic significance of using a 'queer' perspective approach is relevant, as it confronts traditional concepts around race, ethnicity, class, gender, and sexuality among so many others defined in biological traits. Central Americans in the D.C. Metropolitan area have had a peripheral status in the academy as well as in the media. Research has mostly centered in Mexican communities located on the West Coast. By bringing these geographies (Washington D.C., and Central America) to the forefront, this book enables new perspectives on Latino immigrants, particularly Latinas.

For Boas and his students Margaret Mead, Ruth Benedict, and Edward Sapir, ethnography and ethnographic analysis had the potential to change the world, expand its scope to a broader audience, have ethnographers confront their own ideas and biases and, in the process, change society (Lassiter and Campbell in Viteri, Hill, and Williams, 2016). As a Latina, Ecuadorian, mother, U.S. citizen, and queer ethnographer, the important crossroads are those knitted with other Latina women and LGBT Latino communities in the D.C. area. This fabric is constantly defying any linear reading of national borders: by actively participating against discrimination and structural gender violence, Madre Tierra and the communities organized around it have extended (and expanded) their political struggles from Central America to D.C., beyond what is understood as the scope of legal citizenship.

NOTES

1. LGBT stands for Lesbian, Gay, Bisexual and Transgender people and communities.
2. *See* Zolberg, Suhrke, and Aguayo (1989), Gybney and Stohl (1988), Fagen (1988), Hamilton and Chinchilla (1991), and Coutin (1993).
3. Adapted from a question posed by Rodríguez (2003, p. 21).
4. As part of these and other similar efforts, Dilcia Molina nominated me for the Building Bridges Award, American University's Gay, Lesbian, Bisexual, Transgender and Ally Resource Center Achievement Awards, which I received in 2007.
5. An article that focuses on this experience appears in *LATISS Learning & Teaching: The International Journal of Higher Education in the Social Sciences*: "Students Educating Students In Understanding and Addressing Surveillance and Policing Policy: Insights from an International, Interdisciplinary Conference at American University." U.K., 2009.
6. U.S. Census Bureau (2015) estimates that Fredericksburg has in 2014 a population of 28,350: White (68.4 percent), African Americans (24.1 percent), and Latinas/os (10.9 percent). However, Latino population has increased very rapidly in the last decade; increasing 4.90 percent of its total population—according to 2000 Census data—to 10.9 percent.
7. 67 percent of Latinos living in the D.C. area speak languages other than English at home (Comey et al., 2009).

REFERENCES

Balibar, Étienne. (1999). "Class Racism." In Rodolfo D. Torres, Louis F. Mirón, and Jonathan Xavier Inda (eds.) *Race, Identity, and Citizenship: A Reader*. Oxford, U.K.: Blackwell, pp. 322-35.
Behar, Ruth, and Deborah A. Gordon. (1995). *Women Writing Culture*. Berkeley, CA: University of California Press.
Behar, Ruth. (1993). *Translated Woman: Crossing the Border with Esperanza's Story*. Boston: Beacon Press.
Bell, David, and Jon Binnie. (2000). *The Sexual Citizen: Queer Politics and Beyond*. Oxford, U.K.: Blackwell.
Butler, Judith. (1990). "Variaciones sobre sexo y género: Beauvoir, Wittig y Foucault." In *Teoría Feminista y Teoría Crítica: Ensayos sobre la Política de Género en las Sociedades de Capitalismo Tardío*. Translated by Ana Sánchez. Valencia: Ediciones Alfons el Magnanim.
Campbell, Elizabeth and Luke Lassiter (2010). "From Collaborative Ethnography to Collaborative Pedagogy: Reflections on the Other Side of the Middletown Project

and Community-University Research Partnerships." *Anthropology and Education Quarterly*, 41(4): 370-385.

Cantú, Jr., Lionel. (2009). *The Sexuality of Migration: Border Crossings and Mexican Immigrant Men*. Edited by Nancy A. Naples and Salvador Vidal-Ortiz. New York: New York University Press.

Capps, Randy, Marc R. Rosenblum, Christina Rodríguez, and Muzaffar Chishti. (2011). *Delegation and Divergence: A Study of 287(g) State and Local Immigration Enforcement*. Washington, D.C.: Migration Policy Institute.

Castro Domingo, Pablo. (2008). *Dilemas de la Migración en la Sociedad Posindustrial*. México: Miguel Angel Porrúa.

Chávez, Karma R. (2013). *Queer Migration Politics: Activists Rhetoric and Coalitional Possibilities*. Urbana, Chicago and Springfield: University of Illinois Press.

Cohen, Lucy M. (1980). "Stress and coping among Latin American women immigrants." In George V. Coelho and Paul I. Ahmed, Paul I. (eds.) *Uprooting and Development. Dilemmas of Coping with Modernization*. New York and London: Plenum Press, pp. 345-73.

Comey, Jennifer, Peter A. Tatian, Rosa Maria Castaneda, Michel Grosz, and Lesley Freiman. (2009). State of Latinos in the District of Columbia. Washington, D.C.: The Urban Institute.

Coutin, Susan Bibler. (1993). *The Culture of Protest. Religious Activism and the U.S. Sanctuary Movement*. Boulder, San Francisco, Oxford: Westview Press.

Dávila, Arlene. (2001). *Latinos, Inc.: The Marketing and Making of a People*. Berkeley, CA: University of California Press.

Deleuze, Gilles, and Félix Guattari. (1987). *A Thousand Plateaus: Capitalism and Schizophrenia*. Foreword and translated by Brian Massumi. Minneapolis, MN: University of Minnesota Press.

Epps, Brad, Keja Valens, and Bill Johnson González (eds.).(2005). *Passing Lines: Sexuality and Immigration*. Series of Latin American Studies. Cambridge, MA: Harvard University Press.

Fagen, Patricia Weiss. (1988). "Central American Refugees and U.S Policy." In Nora Hamilton, Jeffry A. Frieden, Linda Fuller, and Manuel Pastor (eds.) *Crisis in Central America: Regional Dynamics and U.S. Policy in the 1980s*. Boulder, CO: Westview Press, pp. 59-74.

Fals-Borda, Orlando, and Muhammad Anisur Rahman (eds.). (1991). *Action and Knowledge: Breaking the Monopoly with Participatory Action Research*. New York: Apex Press.

Freire, Paulo. (1972). *Cultural Action for Freedom*. Harmondsworth: Penguin.

Gybney, Mark and Michael Stohl. (1988). "Human Rights and U.S. Refugee Policy." In Mark Gybney (ed.) *Open Borders? Closed Societies?: The Ethical and Political Issues*. New York: Greenwood Press, pp. 151-183.

Halberstam, Judith. (1998). *Female Masculinity*. Durham, NC: Duke University Press.

Hamilton, Nora, and Norma Chinchilla. (1991). "Central American Migration: A Framework for Analysis." *Latin American Research Review*, 26(1): 75-110.

Hardy-Fanta, Carol (1997). "Latina Woman and Political Consciousness: La Chispa que Prende." In Cathy J. Cohen, Kathleen B. Jones and Joan C. Tronto eds. *Women Transforming Politics: Al Alternative Reader*. New York and London: New York University Press, pp. 223-37.

Johnson, Carey, Reece Jones, Anssi Paasi, Louise Amoore, Alison Mountz, Mark Salter and Christ Rumford. (2011). "Interventions on rethinking 'the border'in border studies." *Political Geography*, 30(2): 61-69.

Kemmis, Stephen and Robin McTaggart. (1997). "Participatory Action Research: Communicative Action and the Public Sphere." In Norman K. Denzin (ed.) *Interpretive Ethnography: Ethnographic Practices for the 21st Century*. Thousand Oaks, CA: SAGE, pp. 559-603.

Kondo, Dorinne K. (1990). *Crafting Selves: Power, Gender and Discourses of Identity in a Japanese Workplace*. Chicago: University of Chicago Press.

Lewellen, Ted C. (2002). *The Anthropology of Globalization: Cultural Anthropology Enters the 21st Century*. Westport, CT: Greenwood.

Leitner, Helga and Christopher Strunk. (2014). "Assembling Insurgent Citizenship: Immigrant Advocacy Struggles in the Washington, D.C. Metropolitan Area." *Urban Geography*, 35 (7): 943-964.

Luibhéid, Eithne and Lionel Cantú Jr. (eds.). (2005). *Queer Migrations: Sexuality, U.S. Citizenship and Border Crossing*. Minneapolis, MN: University of Minnesota Press.

Naples, Nancy (ed.). (1998). *Community Activism and Feminist Politics: Organizing Across Race, Class, and Gender*. New York and London: Routledge.

Narayan, Kirin. (1993). "How Native Is a 'Native' Anthropologist?" *American Anthropologist, New Series* 95(3): 671-86.

Ong, Aihwa. (1999). *Flexible Citizenship: The Cultural Logics of Transnationality*. Durham, NC: Duke University Press.

Pew Research Center (2015). Unauthorized Immigrants: Who they are and what the public thinks. www.pewresearch.org/key-data-points/immigration/ (November 21, 2015).

Rodríguez, Juana María. (2003). *Queer Latinidad: Identity Practices, Discursive Spaces*. New York: New York University Press.

Slocum, Karla. (2001). "Negotiating Identity and Black Feminist Politics in Caribbean Research." In *Black Feminist Anthropology: Theory, Politics, Praxis, and Poetics*. Foreword by Johnnetta B. Cole. Edited by Irma McClaurin. New Brunswick, NJ: Rutgers University Press, pp. 126-49.

Solomon, Alisa. (2005). "Trans/Migrant: Christina Madrazo's All-American Story". In Luibhéid, Eithne and Lionel Cantú Jr. (eds.) *Queer Migrations: Sexuality, U.S. Citizenship and Border Crossing*. Minneapolis, MN: University of Minnesota Press, pp. 3-29.

Viteri, María Amelia, Michael Hill, and Julie Williams. (eds.). (2016) *Espiritualidades en Quito: hacia una etnografía colaborativa*. Quito: USFQ and Fundación Museos de la Ciudad (Forthcoming).

Viteri, María Amelia. (2014). *Desbordes: Translating Racial, Ethnic, Sexual and Gender Identities Across the Americas*. New York: SUNY Press.

U.S. Census Bureau. (2015). State & County QuickFacts. Fredericksburg City, Virginia. http://quickfacts.census.gov/qfd/states/51/51630.html (November 21, 2015).

Zolberg, Aristide R., Astri Suhrke and Sergio Aguayo. (1989). *Escape from Violence: Conflict and the Refugee Crisis in the Developing World*. New York and Oxford: Oxford University Press.

Conclusions

Applying Anthropology in Multicultural Neighborhoods

Lucy M. Cohen

Evolving from an administrative capital to a political, economic, and communication center, the Washington, D.C., metropolitan area has emerged as a global metropolis, becoming one of the major new immigrant gateways into the United States and transforming the region into a multicultural society. As in other metropolitan areas in the United States, Latino populations—especially immigrants from Central America and Mexico—constitute by far the most important ethnic group in the region, followed by Asians from Korea, India, and Vietnam. One of the most important aspects of the growth of this Latino population in the region is the prominent role played by Central American women as immigrant pioneers who propelled the early development of migratory networks in the region.

After crossing several borders most Latino immigrants and their children have to meet the challenges of globalization in their processes of incorporation into the region. Facing different social and cultural barriers while adapting to this metropolis, most of them meet these challenges by building transnational bridges that connect societies and cultures. These circumstances have offered opportunities for anthropologists and members of related disciplines and professions to work together with community residents in activities that have contributed to knowledge and action. This volume shows how Latinas/os immigrants draw on a repertory of strategies to meet the challenges of adaptation in multicultural neighborhoods in the inner city as well as in outer and far metropolitan areas.

Drawing on ethnographic research and practices, the volume highlights processes through which Latinas and Latinos build communities while reshaping ethnic, gender, and generational identities. All contributors to this book have long experiences working as university professors, fieldworkers, anthropologists, and practitioners with Latino population in this metropolitan area. Theoretical and practical concerns have led them to study processes of settlement and adaptation of Latino immigrants in Washington, D.C., and its metropolitan suburbs. Chapters in this book focus on the processes of incorporation of Latino immigrants

and socio-cultural changes, as well as models of collaboration and interaction in community centers, non-profit agencies, health, labor markets,
and faith based communities. Special attention is given to ethnic and
gender identity.

MULTICULTURAL COMMUNITY CENTERS

Marcia Bernbaum examines the important role played by Latino-oriented
community centers established in Washington, D.C., since the 1960s, focusing on La Clínica del Pueblo. This agency was established in 1983 by
Salvadoran refugees and North American activists. While contextualizing its birth, evolution, and impact on its patients, she focuses on its
holistic approach to patients and culturally sensitive and relevant practices. The chapter charts the evolution of La Clínica del Pueblo by fram-
ing it within the contexts of the late Cold War and globalization. Bernbaum also identifies characteristics that have given the Clínica its special
identity or *essence*: "Health care as advocacy and social justice." While
analyzing its strengths and challenges over the years, she also explores
the impact that its services have had on patients, staff, volunteers, and on
Latinos communities in the Washington, D.C., metropolitan area.

According to Bernbaum, the period of 1995 through 2003 was one of
expansion, with support from the local community as well as the Federal
and local governments. Patients she interviewed reported that La Clínica
medical services had given them the opportunity to change their ways of
thinking, with emphasis on availability of medical services. La Clínica's
staff and volunteers highlighted its unique specialty programs, particularly HIV/AIDS and mental health programs. Dr. Juan Romagoza, a refugee from El Salvador who managed the health center from 1988 until
1995, contributed to the expansion of its services including mental health,
education, outreach, and prevention. Romagoza considers that La Clínica
del Pueblo's essence is based on the concept that health is care, prevention, orientation, promotion, and defence. In his words: "We motivated
the patients to take ownership of La Clínica, that this was their project."

NON-PROFIT AGENCIES

Patricia Maloof states that the "world is now witnessing the greatest
number of refugees since World War II along with large numbers of
migrant workers moving across borders." She distinguishes between
"crossing borders" and "settling" underscoring that immigrants' integration has to do with the immigrants' ability "to participate actively in a
host society through equality of opportunity and absence of discrimination on the grounds of ethnicity or national origin." She defines major
national models of immigrants' integration, such as assimilation, segre-

gation, and multiculturalism, and highlights how in the last decade its definition has changed in the United States. Melting pot, salad bowl, orchestra, and tapestry are some of its definitions. In the refugee resettlement program, Maloof states that in contrast to a "laissez-faire approach," a public private partnership with the federal government has existed in the United States. As an example, she describes programs implemented by the Catholic Legal Immigration Network, Inc. (CLINIC), the largest charitable immigration legal service network in the United States, around the country, and in the Washington, D.C., metropolitan area. In addition, she addresses its core approach, characterized by integration programs, and performance measures.

As a case example, Maloof presents "Hogar Immigrant Services" which is a program of Catholic Charities of the Diocese of Arlington (Va.). This program was established in 1981 to help immigrants and refugees to gain self-sufficiency and fully participate in the host society. Services in this program are largely family-based, helping to reunite families and eligible immigrants to apply for citizenship or residence. Volunteers collaborating in this program, who are "the backbone of the program," include pro-bono attorneys and teachers.

HEALTH AND CULTURE

The chapter "Pluralistic Universe in Multicultural Medicine: Latinas adapting Cultural Heritages in Medical Fields" focuses on ways in which Latino immigrants and their children settled in multicultural communities in the Washington, D.C., metropolitan area. The contributor discusses multiculturalism in health focusing on the circumstances of separation and reunification of parents and children. Implications for policy formulation and health and mental health programs are considered. Clara Chu's conceptualization of multiculturalism shows how coexistence of one cultural identity does not prevail over other identities in the national policies. The multicultural model is the opposite of the assimilationist model in which minorities are expected to abandon their traditions and values, replacing them with those of the majority.

Anthropologists and others who have studied Latino immigrants in Washington, D.C., a major metropolitan area in the United States, have found that Latinos bring together popular and biomedical traditions without conflict, to offer rational explanations for etiology and health practices to fit their new life situations. However, there is not a single integrated Latino theory of disease since Latin American popular medicine is multicultural in character.

Marta Barkell asked how participants viewed concepts of health and illness from their perspective. As women articulated a definition, it became clear that their definition does not coincide with the common definition of the World Health Organization (WHO, 2012). Their definition had a practical view of what health meant to them personally; centered on their ability to work, to take care oneself, or to be able to do the activities of their daily lives.

A growing body of research on cultural dimensions of health also addressed ways in which they managed their illness in new settings and aspects of culture, social relations, family, and work which interface with their symptoms. Since participants come from seven countries, there was considerable variation in their responses to how they took care of their health in their home country.

As these Latina immigrants have settled in their new environment, they draw on traditional and biomedical knowledge from their country of origin as well as from biomedical information obtained in the United States. They must negotiate different and often conflicting cultural expectations, and values and loyalties, regarding home and places of settlement. In the health domain they must learn to reconfigure cultural traditions and approaches to health care while learning to understand and negotiate the complex health care system of the United States.

LABOR MARKET

In the chapter "Waiting for a Job at 'New Corners': Honduran Immigrant Men Day laboring in Greater Washington," Sánchez Molina analyzes how men entered the day-labor market work which has expanded throughout the metropolitan Washington region. Based on ethnographic fieldwork carried out with these immigrants from 2007 to 2015, the author analyzes the workforce by gathering at "new corners" in different parts of the region. Data were collected through participant observation and informal and in-depth interviews in different social contexts.

As soon as they arrived in Greater Washington, most of these Honduran women and men settled in nearby and outer metropolitan suburban neighborhoods and entered the informal workforce that was unregulated by law and without labor benefits. Many of these Honduran immigrants had come to the United States hoping to fulfill the mythical "American dream," having imagined the United States as a country full of labor opportunities and economic success for all willing to work hard. It was a challenge for them to start work as day laborers in jobs they had not done before.

Nevertheless, their first labor experiences provided these new immigrants with a microcosm of the host society at large. Although these newcomers did not have many problems finding jobs during the early years of settlement, they had to face problems associated with legislation against undocumented migrants in some areas. Nonetheless, civil and religious organizations have supported these workers through newly established day labor centers. These organizations have been crucial for the development of local inclusionary policies, in view of the lack of a comprehensive federal migration reform. Sánchez Molina suggests that these circumstances have contributed to the growth of local policies which support local immigrant advocacy in multicultural communities and organizations.

FAITH-BASED COMMUNITIES

Tadeusz Mich emphasizes that although there are a significant number of studies of Latino immigrants in the United States, most of them have concentrated on the major urban centers of the United States. There are, however, a growing number of Latino immigrants, especially from Mexico, moving into a new "territory" in the far suburbs, such as Charles Town and Martinsburg in West Virginia. Based on his ethnographic data collected in these localities, he analyzes the role played by Latino immigrant women organizing and keeping alive Latino communities in American Catholic parishes.

Mich emphasizes the importance of studying models of faith-based communities in order to understand how cultural sensitivity and action work in growing Roman Catholic parishes. He underscores the approaches developed by Latino women organizers in West Virginia and Maryland faith-based communities where he conducted research. As an anthropologist and a Catholic pastor, he shows that while little attention has been given to the roles such immigrant women play in American Catholic churches, their work contributes to an understanding of the importance of women in the current transformation of the religious landscape of U.S. Catholicism.

EDUCATION

Shaun Loria draws on his experience in education, working in elementary, middle, and high school to discuss why Latinos in Washington, D.C., are not currently achieving educational success proportionate to their demographic representation. He draws on this knowledge to suggest how various institutions can work together to improve outcomes comparing charter and public schools in K–12 education. Loria notes that the achievement groups between socio-economic classes begin in elementary schools and grow each year so that by middle school and high school the gap between what wealthy students know and what low-income students know is seemingly insurmountable. He illustrates this issue noting that as Latino students are concentrated in low-income areas, in this region, they have lower quality schools and lower academic results. Public schools fit into larger gentrification patterns seen in the city, and reflect patterns in performance between ethnic and socioeconomic groups that result in disparity in education.

Loria suggests that many Latino parents do not make the wisest choice for their students' long term academic success. While the D.C. Public Charter School Board provides excellent online resources, there are few community forums hosted by bilingual representatives to provide information to parents who do not speak English and often do not have access to a home computer. Without this common language or access to technology, it is harder for Latino families, particularly immigrant families, to make informed choices for their children. Because Latinos attend low quality K–12 schools, the top students do not meet admission at selected universities. So, top students enroll at medium quality schools and overage students, who are underprepared for college, enroll in institutions of poor quality.

Viviana Cristian analyzed how minors who have immigrated to the United States without documentation to reunite with their families have to face many hurdles in order to attain the goal of higher education. In doing so, they try to navigate through state and federal laws, facing an uphill battle to attend public colleges and universities. Based on ethnographic research as a volunteer language interpreter with the organization KIND (Kids in Need of Defense), Cristian discussed her experiences in gaining the trust of students and their parents as clients who seek political asylum in the United States. She also discussed how under the Development, Relief, and Education for Alien Minors Act (the DREAM Act), undocumented youth would have the legal right to stay in the United States to attend college.

ETHNIC AND GENDER IDENTITY

Drawing on multi-sited ethnographic data collected in Washington D.C., among the Lesbian, Gay, Bisexual, and Transgender (LGBT) Latino community, María Amelia Viteri analyzes how sexuality is a dimension of power shaping and guiding processes of migration and modes of incorporation. She highlights how these Latino immigrants have to confront and re-signify experiences of heteronormativity as immigrants and Latinos. This important topic, which has received limited examination in Anthropology advances knowledge of intersectional approach of Latina feminist grassroots organizations drawn largely from Central American nations.

She presents the concept of *desbordes* to argue that Latinos construct borders as they undo others, redefining new ways of belonging that confront the traditional conceptualization and idea of citizenship, and as such, sexual citizenship. This approach contributes to an increased understanding of the creation of community networks in the Washington, D.C. metropolitan area.

CONCLUSION

This book shows ways in which anthropologists, members of related disciplines and professions, and Latina and Latino immigrants reconfigure life experiences, power relations, and problem solving in multicultural neighborhoods in the Washington, D.C., metropolitan area. Considering that immigrants settled in this metropolitan area come from diverse national and cultural backgrounds, contributors address questions related to social and cultural change and adaptation, Latinos agency, and applied anthropology in urban and suburban areas.

The essays of this book provide a range of theoretical and methodological frameworks of how anthropologists, social scientists, and practitioners approach both knowledge and its application. Authors bring together diverse knowledge and practice fields: Latino history in Washington, D.C., transnational migration, social services, health and culture, labor market information, faith-based communities, education, and ethnic and gender identity. In doing so, this research also addresses related questions: First, how do public and private institutions attempt to transform the lives of Latino immigrants through every day practices in a multicultural urban and suburban milieu? Second, how do Latino immigrants respond to their practices within local communities, non-profit agencies, health arenas, worksites, religious communities, and educational institutions? And third, this book offers models of ways in which anthropologists can work together with practitioners and community residents in activities contributing to both knowledge and action.

In summary, the volume advances knowledge about Latino community building introducing models of collaboration in community organization and advocacy. While acting as advocates and cultural brokers bridging Latino immigrant cultures and organizations, authors also assess and evaluate issues of public policy as new immigrants adapt in a major global society.

Index

About the Contributors

EDITORS

Lucy M. Cohen (PhD) is a pioneer of Latino studies in the United States, having worked with Latinos in the area since the 1960s. Among early publications on Latinos in Washington, D.C. and applied anthropology, she wrote an ethnography on Latino immigrants and health in the United States, *Culture, Disease, and Stress among Latino Immigrants* (1979). She has received many institutional and research awards such as the "Sol Tax Distinguished Service Award" in Santa Fe (New Mexico, 2008).

Raúl Sánchez Molina (PhD), who has worked with Latino populations in the Washington, D.C. metropolitan region since the 1990s, has written several books and articles based on his ethnographic research in the area such as *"Mandar a trae" Antropología, Migraciones y Transnacionalismo* (2005) and *Proceso migratorio de una mujer salvadoreña. El viaje de María Reyes a Washington, D.C.* (2006). In addition, he has edited the book *La etnografía y sus aplicaciones* (2009) focused on applied anthropology.

CONTRIBUTORS

Marta Barkell (PhD) has conducted pioneering ethnographic research on health and culture among Latinas/os in Northern Virginia. She is a medical anthropologist and a nurse who taught Medical Anthropology at Marymount University in Arlington (Virginia). She also volunteers at a public Multicultural elementary school in Falls Church (Virginia), working with the parent liaison office to help Latino mothers cope with the educational system and myriad life problems. She also volunteers at an Arlington medical clinic which provides health care to immigrants from several world regions.

Marcia Bernbaum (PhD) has spent most of her career in International Development living and working in Central America (Panama, Nicaragua, Honduras); she travelled extensively to El Salvador and Guatemala at the height of their civil wars. She has conducted in-depth case studies of grassroots programs that promote leadership and empowerment among members of the Latino community in Washington D.C. and has focused

187

on programs that promote human rights. She currently serves as an advocate for homeless in Washington, D.C.

Viviana Cristian (PhD) has conducted ethnographic research with Latino university students as well as immigrants and refugees in the Washington, D.C. metropolitan area. She works also as an interpreter for both lawyers and clients-unaccompanied children facing the immigration system. For the last four years, she has served at a contractor in the Department of Labor's Team concerned with Child Labor. As a Red Cross volunteer she has helped both English and Spanish speaking clients affected by disasters in the Washington D.C. metropolitan area, and other regions.

Shaun Loria (MA) is an educator and nonprofit director with a Master's Degree in Education from Arizona State University. He has relevant experience working with multicultural education in Washington, D.C. and abroad as well as experience with elementary, middle, and high schools in both public and charter school environments.

Patricia Maloof (PhD) is a medical anthropologist who has worked with refugees and immigrants in the Washington, D.C. metropolitan area for several decades. She is currently the Program Director of Migration and Refugee Services, Catholic Charities of the Diocese of Arlington (VA) and part-time instructor at the Catholic University of America. Dr. Maloof was formerly the Director of Refugee Programs with the United States Conference of Catholic Bishops and the Director of Development for the Catholic Legal Immigration Network, Inc. (CLINIC).

Tadeusz Mich (PhD) has long experiences working with immigrants from diverse cultures in the Washington, D.C. metropolitan area. He is a social scientist with World Vision International, which works to alleviate poverty and injustice, particularly for children, through community development. He has done fieldwork in Poland about agrarian beliefs, in the Amazon (Colombia) on Yucuna mythology and cosmology, and more recently on the experiences of the Latino immigrants in the United States. Mich published and conducted training on cultural sensitivity as it relates to development projects operated by NGOs in more than thirty countries.

María Amelia Viteri (PhD) is a specialist in the interplay of gender and ethnic identities, particularly of Latino immigrants in Washington, D.C. and New York. She teaches university courses in both Ecuador and the United States. She has written many articles on her ethnographic research in Washington, D.C. and recently the book *Desbordes : Translating Racial, Ethnic, Sexual, and Gender Identities across the Americas* (2014).